M. Mercier

Fragments of Politics and History

Vol. II

M. Mercier

Fragments of Politics and History
Vol. II

ISBN/EAN: 9783337071318

Printed in Europe, USA, Canada, Australia, Japan

Cover: Foto ©Suzi / pixelio.de

More available books at **www.hansebooks.com**

FRAGMENTS

OF

POLITICS AND HISTORY.

BY M. MERCIER.

TRANSLATED FROM THE FRENCH.

IN TWO VOLUMES.

VOL. II.

LONDON:

PRINTED FOR H. MURRAY, NO. 32, FLEET-STREET.

1795.

CONTENTS

OF

THE SECOND VOLUME.

Of

Wise

FRAGMENTS

OF

POLITICS AND HISTORY.

OF LUXURY.

WHERE is the boundary, the line of ſeparation between laudable and pernicious luxury? I am unable to mark it. I grieve to ſee ſo many hands employed on frivolous pieces of furniture, on uſeleſs jewels, on ſuperfluous articles of decoration, and on tranſitory and puerile forms; yet I love to behold the ſame luxury ſupply us with wines, with compound drinks, and with the fruits of the earth, which, in the wild ſtate, are poor and auſtere, but, by high cultivation, are brought to our tables independently of the ſeaſons, and acquire a plumpneſs and an exquiſite flavour. I condemn the luxury which engroſſes vaſt encloſures for the bloody territory of the chace; but I cheriſh that luxury which creates amuſements, Ælean games, and theatrical entertainments; thoſe entertainments which, by ſoftening the manners of the people, enlarge their underſtanding, and which would be the moſt perfect ſchool, if a wiſe police were to check the licentiouſneſs of authors, and to admit into the profeſſion of actors men only of regular deportment.

I love the luxury which corrects the bitters inſeparable from life; but I deteſt that which drains the ſubſtance of men to form tranſient enjoyments. How ſhall we ſeparate theſe two kinds of luxury, how ſhall we diſtinguiſh them even in our language? I would not chooſe to be a ſtupid or ferocious ſavage, with the bow as the only pledge of my ſuſtenance, differing little from a brute, and almoſt as miſerable; yet ſtill leſs would I be one of thoſe young men of faſhion who, to indulge their cruel and fanciful caprices, torment horſes, dogs, valets, and whatever they encounter with.

There is a luxury which, by quickening nature, opens the ſtores of her fecundity; which, if I may uſe the expreſſion, perfects the deſigns of the Creator; and which makes man a ſocial and enlightened being, kindling the torch of genius, and beſtowing on all that ſurrounds him a cheerful exiſtence, by the pliancy and variety of arts and talents. There is another luxury

which

which intoxicates man, which renders him obdurate, and which ſervilely attaches him to wretchedneſs, to puerility, and to purſuits which pride gloſſes, but which deſtroy inſtead of animating the human ſpecies. Still it bears the name of luxury, a word vague and undefinable, and which ought to be expunged, as breeding falſe notions. But without luxury there would be no arts. This reflection reconciles us ſomewhat to the term; for muſic, poetry, and dancing, are delicious arts which touch the ſoul.

Finally, when luxury, in times conſidered as barbarous, maintained many domeſtics, and ſometimes four or five hundred gentlemen in the ſervice of a baron, though reprehenſible, it was much preferable to that which heaps diamonds upon an ugly or dull courtezan.

I ſhould at preſent be almoſt equally afraid either to aboliſh luxury or to give it a ſtill greater extenſion. This word ſeems fated to embarraſs philoſophers, who know not where to ſtop, or to draw the line of demarcation; for the ages without luxury are remarkable in hiſtory for dreadful famines, witneſs the chronicles and ſtatutes of Charlemagne. But if reproduction depend on luxury; if, without this attraction, the hands of the cultivator would grow languid; if enchafed watches be intimately connected with the procuring of food; let us tolerate trinkets, that we may have cattle. This chain of connexion, though incomprehenſible, may really exiſt; and it belongs not to moral theory to combat what ſeems to ſatisfy all the world. Every one dreads abſtinence; and Diogenes alone could fancy that, if well borne, it might equal fruition.

The words moſt uſed are almoſt invariably the worſt underſtood. What is termed *luxury* is the perpetual ſpur which incites man to labour, which whets his induſtry, which animates him to lofty deeds, and which creates all the fruits and the varied bleſſings of the earth: it is a ſpring ever in action, that quickens nature; for nothing is produced but by the love of pleaſure and the humour of the conſumer.

Thus, there are no bounds to this taſte for luxury, which diſplays all the views of the creation. Aſſuredly the human race is happieſt in countries where luxury is known: whatever is for the uſe of man, all arts, and all inventions, flow inceſſantly from one hand into another. But in climates where the induſtry of man is cramped, the moſt luxuriant ſoil bears only uſeleſs vegetables. Man is there weak, and traverſes only deſerts.

To the word *luxury* let us therefore ſubſtitute the explanatory terms *ſpur* of man, *ſpur* of his labour, *ferment* of reproduction.

Luxury confers upon the earth its fertility. Separate then, it will be ſaid, the pernicious from the luxury that is uſeful. I would attempt it; but the taſk is difficult, and I ſhall defer it until another time. Meanwhile, if you cannot control yourſelf, why ſhould you reſtrain the taſte of the conſumer? He always gives you a labour for yours: the ſign which he preſents to you is the repreſentative ſymbol of his own induſtry, or of that of his anceſtors. Why deprive a man of his enjoyment? Do you wiſh that he ſhould ſink into ſloth, that he ſhould ſtifle the chief faculties of his ſoul and body, that he ſhould clog the habitual activity with which he is endowed? Suffer him to give nature every poſſible form; ſuffer him to combine matter; for from this modification will ſpring abundance. Speak not of the mere neceſſaries of life; he will never acquire them without having the idea of ſuperfluities, without the pain of labour, without the fruit of attention. To the end that all may enjoy, all muſt labour. The whole conſiſts in this, that the hand of man never ſhall remain idle, that his brain ſhall never grow torpid.

Luxury is a perpetual ſtimulant; leave to this ſtimulant the taſk of creating many different ſubſtances. What corrects the inequality of riches, is only this varied deſire of enjoyments; and thus it is that each finds his ſupport in the caprices of another.

You who quarrel with luxury, aſcribe to it ills which it does not occaſion; they have other cauſes. Conſider that this luxury which you condemn is what invigorates man, what triples his life, what charms his exiſtence. Man is not rendered happy by your moral precepts, but by furniture, clothes, utenſils, commodious houſes, wholeſome and well-prepared food: and without the luxury of enamelled gold-boxes, diamonds, pictures, bronzes, and ſtatues, we ſhould not have a multitude of agreeable and uſeful articles which are reckoned eſſential to our comforts.

The political machine is of large dimenſions, and has a connexion between all its parts. Declaimer, ſtop. Know you what you are about to ſay? Have you reflected well? Would you wiſh to deprive man of whatever is uſeful, convenient, and agreeable? Take care; the firſt invention was a luxury; the rudeſt clothing is a modification of nature; it is the effect of labour. Luxury is likewiſe a work of man's

hands;

hands; it muſt pleaſe ſome one ſince it is accepted. The more labours, the more enjoyments; and the more enjoyments, the more reproductions. Stop no ſpecies of toil, whatever it may be; for man knows for what he toils.

Declaimer, you would eat very coarſe bread, if the other arts did not improve baking; for it is an art to make bread. The fineſt paſtry, the lighteſt biſcuit, is no more a luxury than the worſt bread ill made. A more attentive labour is all that diſtinguiſhes good from bad food.

Activity in the circulation, ardour for labour, fertile and varied productions, theſe are what ſpring from luxury, that great incentive which toils inceſſantly on nature, becauſe it puts all in motion: and if it brings diamonds from Golconda, the firſt and annual advances of ſpecie neceſſary to cultivation are, on that very account, the more conſiderable.

Let the word *luxury* be no longer cited, therefore, in a bad ſenſe; let it be conſidered as a ferment of emulation diffuſed among men, which animates their induſtry, and which, from their reciprocal efforts, combines different inventions of which human genius profits. It is by the concourſe of ſo many effects that ſociety is elaborated, and gains every day a multitude

 of

of little enjoyments which form the national proſperity.

As ſoon as primitive equality is interrupted, and the right of property admitted, it muſt be left to luxury to break down the large eſtates, and throw the fragments into the hands of the claſs worſt provided for. Such is the work of luxury, which will reſtore ſome degree of equality, by making the rich perpetual contributors to the poor; no man will flouriſh in indolence; and the beſt cultivated and moſt proſperous kingdoms are thoſe where luxury reproduces ſubſiſtence. There are unqueſtionably ſome luxuries that are leſs uſeful than others: it is better to ſpend money on the fields than in the ſhop of a lapidary or a jeweller; it is better to plant three thouſand fruit-trees, than to condemn a piece of ground to ſupply a ſervile ſhade, which may afford a cool retreat for an hour or two in a year; or to cover the fingers with rings. But a falſe computation, or an erroneous whim, hinders not luxury, under another name, from being the ſpur of labour, the animator of empires, and the comforter of the human race; ſince by means of induſtry, kept perpetually in action, it gives birth to reproduction, and affords a multitude of enjoyments to all thoſe who love pleaſure, that is, to the whole race of men.

The evils which are aſcribed to luxury originate from the bad adminiſtration of governments. Beſides, luxury exiſts in infinite ſhades; republics and monarchies are at this time nearly upon a level, and do not reſiſt luxury. Man has too decided a taſte for pleaſures to baniſh it. If it be an evil, it is an evil which at preſent pervades all Europe. London, Paris, Naples, Amſterdam, Vienna, Peterſburg, Berne, and Venice, are in this reſpect nearly on a par. Luxury has found its way even into republics; they have diſcovered that this word is merely a bugbear; for the luxury of individuals can never exceed the general abilities of a nation.

All the clamours againſt luxury will not produce a reform of it. Civiliſation neceſſarily brought along with it the progreſs of luxury, and the love of ſenſual pleaſures. But if an age, emaſculated by the indulgence of luxury, has loſt the chivalric virtues, it has acquired in return the knowledge proper to form a good legiſlation. It frames laws which are truly calculated for men, and which ſecure the deſtiny of future generations. Poor and virtuous nations cannot trace the plan of public felicity; their hearts are upright, but their ideas are confined. Good education is the lot of nations which have many enjoyments; man reaſons

moſt

moſt profoundly in thoſe times which the rigid condemn. Thus every thing is compenſated, and a nation which poſſeſſes no longer the warlike virtues in the ſame vigour, has, at leaſt for its ſupport, maxims of polity which the adminiſtrators of nations will not dare to infringe.

VICIOUS LEGISLATIONS.

VICIOUS legiſlations form bad governments, which were never ſo in their origin. Under an arbitrary monarch theſe legiſlations ſleep: he perceives confuſedly that they are uſeful to his power, provided he wants that elevated genius which could lead him to reform the laws that oppreſs in detail, while he himſelf oppreſſes in the aggregate. It is an inſtinct of *arbitrary ſovereignty* to permit the continuance of whatever can haraſs the inhabitants of this earth.

A good legiſlation reſtores to each citizen a degree of liberty; and it is eaſy to perceive whether the government tends to deſpotiſm, by appreciating the repugnance of the ſovereign or his miniſters to a reform of the civil laws: it is impoſſible that theſe laws, when improved, ſhould not favour that *natural right* the very

name

name of which terrifies the adminiſtrators of a deſpotic ſtate.

There can be no liberty where knowledge and ſcience do not flouriſh: the more theſe are diffuſed, the more does the haughtineſs of power loſe its oppreſſing force.

Whatever belongs to deſpotiſm is vain: it places all its grandeur in a faſtidious pomp; and careſſes vices, becauſe it finds its account in particular ones. Thoſe who are tenacious of futile, and, moſt frequently, unjuſt privileges, bring about the deſtruction of ſtates: the nobles, who in ſeveral kingdoms have too great an aſcendency, are a *wedge* which ſeparates the ſovereign from his ſubjects, which diſunites them by acting equally on both. Replete with vanity, and infected by egotiſm, the public good occupies but little of their attention.

It has been remarked, that the beſt of the civil laws have been eſtabliſhed either during civil wars, or immediately after. This ought not to ſurpriſe us; the principles of government, whether good or bad, being in ſimilar conjunctures ſhaken, every one recurs to the natural rights of ſociety.

During civil wars the deſtruction of the ſtate is not to be dreaded. Notwithſtanding the people may be divided into factions, it is far

from

from being annihilated: it has, on the other hand, a ſuperabundance of vital action. If the father contends againſt the ſon, brother againſt brother, and citizen againſt citizen, the country is diſtracted, but not deſtroyed. The love of the public weal, predominating in the breaſt of each individual, is only deceived as to the means; and in all theſe *reparative* wars (which evinces the neceſſity ſometimes, and even the goodneſs of them) the triumphant party has invariably juſtice on its ſide.

What is a ſtate? is it not an aſſemblage of all the individuals of whom a nation is formed? Ought we to be ſurpriſed that theſe individuals have paſſions? can they be exempt from feeling, like the corpſes ranged in a line in a cemetery?

The inſurrection of a nation conſtantly criminates the adminiſtration: it at the leaſt wards off a greater danger; for citizens bear with patience ſupportable ills, and when they proceed to a formal diſobedience, it is becauſe there has been an infringement of certain privileges, of certain cuſtoms to which nations are ſometimes more attached than to the fundamental laws.

Theſe violent commotions are rarely without a real motive: the people find themſelves aggrieved, either becauſe an attempt has been made to deprive them of the uſages to which cuſtom has attached them, or becauſe their confidence has been ſhaken by an attack on their religious principles, or on the body of magiſtracy.

The tie which binds ſeveral thouſands of men to a ſingle individual has always appeared to me inexplicable: as it is drawn tighter, ſo it relaxes and elongates by a multitude of little unperceived cauſes. Men feel the neceſſity of a government: they applaud the acts of the ſovereign, when theſe acts are worthy the majeſty of the throne and that of the nation; but they deteſt the caprices of the man, more eſpecially when, by haſty edicts, he appears to entertain a high contempt for popular opinion.

The people bear more patiently great attacks, than little ones made repeatedly and at intervals, becauſe in the former they either ſee or ſuſpect the work of neceſſity, or of the general good; while in the latter they can only perceive a deſign to thwart and juggle them in what regards their taſtes, pleaſures, or habits.

The ſureſt expedient to appeaſe ſedition is to ſatisfy the people. A prudent and wiſe prince will reap a full harveſt of glory by retracting in time: he ought to know that in every political body there is a reaction; and if he has not been

ſurpriſed

ſurpriſed at obedience, neither ought he to be aſtoniſhed at reſiſtance.

Whenever the horſe winces, it is becauſe he is ill at eaſe, and becauſe his rider is impatient or unſkilful. The prince will diſplay a true greatneſs of ſoul, by not founding his obſtinacy on a falſe policy. If he errs in this particular, genius takes advantage of his error, fully aware that every legiſlation, to have its full effect, ought to concur with the conſent of the people. If they are not ſufficiently enlightened to receive a beneficent law, the prince ſhould wait till their eyes are more clearly opened; and it behoves him to ſubdue in himſelf every human paſſion, to the end that he may preſerve the glorious title of legiſlator—a title to which he can have no legitimate claim, provided he does not diſcover, by an inſurrection of the people, that their grievances are urgent, and demand redreſs. As every thing in this world is compoſed of parts infinitely ſmall, he ought, in caſes of popular murmuring, to conſider whether theſe may not have a concealed reaſon at leaſt tantamount to his own. Whatever he may have done in haſte, he ought to reconſider and amend.

If the revolt of the citizens has not had a juſtifiable cauſe, the ſedition will fall of itſelf, and

and will never gain over the ſuperior claſſes. But if the citizens have grievances that call aloud for redreſs, how can the prince conceive that the political body will be deſtitute of action, ſentiment, and life? Would he be honoured by commanding a troop of ſlaves, always trembling and ſubmiſſive in the renunciation of their will? Would he, in ſuch a caſe, be placed over men, at the head of whom he could be proud of his ſtation? The reaction of the citizens is a proof of national liberty.

The prince ought never to neglect the means of appeaſing a revolt; and here it more eſpecially becomes him to ſubdue in himſelf every perſonal emotion of vanity: he would render himſelf little and contemptible by an endeavour to give to his own will a predominancy, when it is oppoſed by the general will; he would furniſh to the revolters thoſe moſt formidable weapons, the courage and fury of deſpair; and he would be reſponſible for all the miſchiefs which might enſue.

I know of nothing finer in a ſovereign than an honourable retreat, a majeſtic pacification, or a generous avowal of a political error, even though he himſelf ſhould not have been deceived. A monarch whoſe judgment is ſound and clear will wait for a more favourable ſeaſon to effect thofe great changes which are the refult of many caufes happily combined: the clemency of a prince ought to defcend from the throne like thofe pleafant and refrefhing fhowers which, on a tempeftuous day, fall on the earth amid the clatter of the thunder and the majefty of the ftorm.

In almoft all infurrections the people of the inferior claffes are principally concerned. The power of the fovereign being fuperior to that of the fubject, it may be expected, in the hiftory of nations, that the power of the people will, at certain intervals, be in its turn greater than that of the fovereign.

In China there is a very wife law. When a province revolts, and the murmurs of the people are loudly manifefted, the Mandarin is inftantly depofed. In politics, the firft general clamour ought to be obeyed; and it is not until the fecond or third that the popular movement can affume the character of fedition or revolt. The people in their earlieft effervefcence are often appeafed.

The public felicity is proportioned to the more or lefs lively fentiment of perfonal independence. When encroachments are made on liberty, the people act in every poffible manner, until they are quieted by a redrefs of their wrongs.

Anaxarchus

Anaxarchus obferved to Alexander, that every act or will of a prince was equally juft and legitimate. In 1771 another Anaxarchus made his appearance in France.

Oppofe to Anaxarchus, Theopompeius king of Sparta, who confidered that he gave a new ftrength and confiftency to his authority, by fetting limits to it. Theopompeius was right: royalty has its bounds.

The ocean has its limits: fo has the univerfe; and the fun, which animates all nature, cannot deviate from the track which has been affigned to it. God himfelf, concentrated in the immenfity of his attributes, does no evil: he punifhes, he ought to do fo; but he is a ftranger to revenge, becaufe it is beneath him, unworthy of him, and would degrade his divinity!

LOUVOIS.

ALL thofe great military bodies which at prefent harafs and overburden Europe; all thofe armed foldiers who act againft each other; thofe military conftitutions which copy reciprocally, and which ruin the ftate, by taking from population the fineft race of men; the fcience of tactics and its skill in murderous manœuvres; that horrid quantity of artillery; those forces which drag after them two or three hundred pieces of cannon; the frontiers of states stuck over with fortresses; these fortresses buried under fortifications; immense armies; the equipments of war, and its incumbrances still more immense; the mathematics lending their aid to this infernal art: such is the work of Louvois. It was this minister who gave a wide field to the apparatus and preparations of war, who multiplied its resources so extensively, that the details of subsistence are as difficult as the springs by which he contrived to move upwards of an hundred thousand automata clad in arms. The fatal imitation extended even to petty princes.

The science of the commissary of the army, or of the quarter-master-general, is now ranked with that of the general. What man is now capable of commanding armies, when it is necessary for him to possess such a variety and extent of knowledge?

Thus is the military art totally different from what it was an hundred and twenty years ago. Chance and lucky accidents are at present the gods of armies, subordinate to the blind prudence of cabinets. Louvois was the real former of those numerous military bodies which have

every

every where ſtruck alarm into civil and political liberty. But what is moſt deplorable, luxury has penetrated into the heart of armies, and the officer who braves death cannot ſupport the ſlighteſt privations. Theſe effeminate creatures will no longer, in the ſame degree, be ſuſceptible to honour, fortitude, and the love of their country; they will give way, not to fear, but to the indulgence of pleaſure; and Europe muſt at preſent maintain near two millions of men carrying a muſket on their ſhoulders. Fortunately they counterpoiſe each other; but were the number of theſe ſoldiers ſmaller, would the equilibrium no longer ſubſiſt?

It has been ſaid, that the god Mars ſided with great armies. But what means this expreſſion? Signifies it *numerous phalanxes*, *thick battalions*? We cannot be too much on our guard againſt the ſcience of profeſſional people; the event of battles has almoſt always deceived them.

Liſten to facts. The innumerable hoſts of Perſians were defeated and deſtroyed by a handful of Greeks: thirty-ſix thouſand Macedonians ſhook and overturned their immenſe empire: a few Roman legions conquered the world. Since the invention of gunpowder, a few thouſand Swiſs triumphed over Auſtrian haughtineſs and the potent houſe of Burgundy. With a few piquets Turenne routed whole armies. I every where behold genius and ſkill put to flight, in ſpite of numerous battalions. For the moſt part, it is a ſingle regiment that turns the tide of ſucceſs. Navarre, Normandy, La Marine, I appeal to you, how often has victory perched on your ſtandards? What obligations did Cæſar owe to his tenth legion? Was it not ſtrange that an overſight, a word miſconceived, ſhould have occaſioned, through the medium of Louvois, that deluge of ſoldiers which impoveriſh Europe?

It is ſince Louvois, therefore, that political wants have been overrated; that in one country volunteers are enticed, in another levies are compelled; inſomuch that all the citizens are transformed into ſoldiers. Hence that tyrannical diſcipline, which, perpetually changing according to caprice, has ranked the ſoldiers of the European princes among the moſt wretched ſlaves on the globe.

It is ſince Louvois, therefore, that the petty princes of Germany ſell men for war as they ſell cattle for the ſhambles. The exerciſe of arms, which in free ſtates poſſeſſes a mighty attraction, becomes degrading and humiliating when no longer the reſult of voluntary choice. In Pruſſia a grievous law impoſes military ſlavery

on

on every ſubject: every Pruſſian is obliged to ſerve in the army from the age of eighteen to that of ſeventy; and, as if this were not enough, levies are made in foreign countries. Thus are vaſt military bodies multiplied in our times, to the miſery of human kind; and ſtates, whether great or ſmall, overburdened with regiments and legions of every kind, are expoſed to the convulſions of prætorian anarchy; a dreadful calamity, which threatens us all, more or leſs, from Madrid to Peterſburg.

It is ſince Louvois, finally, that the officer and ſoldier are almoſt at open variance with the citizen; that the former of theſe is proud, overbearing, and diſdainful; and that theſe hirelings exact the higheſt reſpect, and would fain enjoy it excluſively. Since the miniſter Louvois it may be ſaid that the kingdom is comprehended in the army; for, by a fatal prejudice, the military functions have acquired the lead of the civil employments. The legionary faſhions are obtruded every where with a ſort of audacity that ſeems to deſpiſe all the other conditions of ſociety. Thoſe military bodies which are formed to brave the enemy, that fatal multiplication of ſoldiers diſperſed and every where introducing a corruption of manners and libertiniſm, ſeem to threaten on all ſides their fellow-citizens, their countrymen, and are much more dangerous in peace than they are uſeful in war. It is in their exceſſive number that the danger lies; and of this Louvois was unqueſtionably the author.

Powerful voice of philoſophy, advance to the foot of the throne, penetrate into the magiſtracy, and may the thinking claſs arm all that can counterbalance this terrible load which oppreſſes equally the monarch and the people!

IN POLITICS, MORAL INSTINCT IS TOO LITTLE SEEN AND APPRECIATED.

MORAL inſtinct divines what the real grievances of the people are: it appreciates their miſeries, and diſcloſes the means calculated to reſtore the tranquillity that has been diſturbed; becauſe it is a natural inſpiration, it is ſure to gain its end. The romance of politics falls into vague ſyſtems; and the intelligence with which the placeman fancies himſelf to be gifted is not ſo ſure as this prompt ſentiment he carries within himſelf. Political theories are all of them incomplete. Had Fenelon been ſeated on the throne he would undoubtedly have filled it better than the moſt decided politician, becauſe ſentiment is of univerſal acceptation, and leſs

bounded

bounded than human intelligencies. He would have possessed less sagacity than a Ximenes, or an Alberoni, but would have been subject to fewer errors, under the guidance of the instinct which swayed Louis XII. and Henry IV. In rising states, or in those which are absolutely on the verge of decay, more genius is required than in a state so constituted as to give to every part of the political machine its proper play.

In spite of a bad government, of extravagant laws, and the caprices and passions of men in a public capacity, there is in the human mind, thanks to the part which instructs, a practice which influences states. In all modern revolutions it is probable that the change has been but superficial: the fall of empires, as well as their rise, seems to depend on those insensible ideas which are formed and maintained among nations. When the part which governs is unskilfully opposed to the part which instructs, the discordance is sure to be detrimental to the former: it loses its real force, and the contempt which necessarily ensues deprives it of the ascendancy it had abused. A contention like this is always indiscreet, not to say extravagant. Alas! why should not statesmen keep up a good understanding with the men who dispense them from long and painful meditations, who abridge their labours, and, after having done a part of their work, beſtow on them a celebrity in addition?

Monarchs ought to regard the human race as a part of themſelves; and in this way every ſovereign ſhould reaſon. - Theſe men are my equals—I might have been in their place; and my neareſt relatives, if they are not ſo now, may perhaps one day be confounded among them. Theſe men, many of them mutilated in battles, and all of them expoſing a naked front to the rude tempeſts of life, belong to me, becauſe they think, act, and feel as I do.

OF GOOD LAWS.

WHEN laws are good and uſeful, they ſurvive the fall of empires: thus ſeveral of the Roman laws, on account of the ſagacity by which they were dictated, have been ſince adopted by various nations, notwithſtanding the difference of time and manners. Having been founded on reaſon and humanity, the maxims they contain are equitable in the extreme; and we ought not therefore to be ſurpriſed on ſeeing the eighteenth century obey edicts framed thirteen

thirteen hundred years ago. But what ought in reality to surprise us is, that these nations, inheriting as they have done the sage and profound ideas of the ancients, did not reject what neither the government nor policy could consistently or ought to have admitted. It would be absurd to disdain majestical laws on account of their antiquity; and a new code might be made perfectly to harmonize with the enlightened reason of our predecessors, by a modification, not a destruction, of the edifice of the laws. The chef-d'œuvre cf legislation would consist in framing a civil code exactly according with the political government of a state; for the interior government has such an affinity with the exterior, that the civil code ought to be founded on this double basis. The wished for reform of the civil code can only be effected by removing the incongruity of certain laws with our principles and manners.

At certain periods states ought therefore to change the aspect of a jurisprudence which has been long received. Old existing laws, rendered nugatory by human malice, cease to have their wonted efficacy; and seeing that at this time manners accomplish more than laws, the latter ought constantly to change with the former.

Indolence oppoſes a ſtronger reſiſtance to the reform of ſeveral abuſive laws than a ſuperſtitious reſpect for them. The ſcience of right has gradually been obſcured; and the more the darkneſs thickens, the more difficult is it to find a courageous genius with ſufficient talents or audacity to ſimplify the laws, that is to ſay, to reduce them to fundamental and inconteſtible points.

Whenever the juriſprudence has loſt its perſpicuity, its force and dignity vaniſh. Science, in its increaſe, multiplies errors and becomes oppreſſive. A multitude of men plunge into the obſcurity; and taking advantage of the ignorance of others, and their propenſity to litigation, form a nation devoted to chicanery and fond of law ſuits. Then does the idiom employed in the tribunals ceaſe to be heard: commentaries, diſperſing round them the ſhades of erudition, leave every queſtion indecided; and the civil juriſprudence becomes to all a dark cavern, in which deciſions are formed at the will and pleaſure of thoſe to whom the power of deciding has been entruſted.

DATA

DATA IN POLITICS.

IN politics there are ſo many *data*, that it is almoſt impoſſible to foreſee future events. The iſſue of the war between England and her American Colonies was altogether problematical, inſomuch that he who ſhould at the origin of that great quarrel have calculated without prejudice, and without enthuſiaſm, could never have been perſuaded but that the advantage would have been on the ſide of England. She had in her favour the unanimity of her commanders, the unmoleſted tranſport of warlike ſtores, the diſcipline of her troops, and gold. As a ſovereign nation, ſhe promulged a ſtrong, perſuaſive, and energetic manifeſto, recalling to the recollection of the rebels the titles by which ſhe poſſeſſed the territory they diſputed with her; the ſuccors with which ſhe had ſupplied them againſt their enemies and her own; her coſtly protection at all times; the conſtitution under which they had lived; and the ſovereignty of the mother country: notwithſtanding appearances were ſo much in her favour, North America ſlipped through her fingers. That dazzling and overawing proſperity which extended from the banks of the Ganges to thoſe of the Tagus,

Tagus, vaniſhed before a handful of what were called *revolters.*

And at this time, where is the event that impreſſes the mind of the attentive obſerver with greater aſtoniſhment than that mute agitation of the *thirteen United States*, in their ſearch after a fixed point! Who will hazard a conjecture at what the reſult will be? The neceſſity and the nature of things, which policy thwarts but does not deſtroy, will eſtabliſh forms that will unqueſtionably ſurpriſe us equally with the great revolution we have ſeen effected.

MANUFACTURES.

COMMERCE, ſays Monteſquieu, at one time deſtroyed by conquerors, at another cramped by monarchs, ſhifts over the globe and flies wherever it is oppreſſed.

The hiſtory of commerce is that of the intercourſe of nations. A happy and almoſt general revolution has been effected on the ſurface of the earth, which is due alone to commerce.

But foreign commerce often carries away uſeful articles, and even thoſe which are the moſt uſeful, in return for mere ſuperfluities.

Perhaps

Perhaps manufactures have been too much vaunted and multiplied. At Lyons, at Geneva, and in the neighbourhood of Neûchatel in Switzerland, I have ſeen workſhops filled with a degraded ſet of men. Manufactures merely tend to ſteal and waſte the time, the ſtrength, the youth, and the exiſtence of a multitude of active poor. Theſe workmen are perpetually contending with the indolent rapacity of their employer. The keenneſs of the diſpute for wages begets hatred. In the neighbourhood of Neûchatel in Switzerland eſpecially, I have lamented to ſee manufacturers entice men from the pure and ſimple life of the country, where they conſtantly dwelt with nature, to confine them within the walls of diſmal priſons.

Cultivation is neglected for theſe *manufactures*, which enrich only a few families where the league of rapacity is eſtabliſhed and maintained. Morals are ruined in theſe workſhops, where men forget their virtues, where they become unfeeling, harſh, and bad fathers, becauſe they have to ſtruggle with the daſtardly avarice of a ſuperior.

Thus are the fields inſenſibly deprived of the precious claſs of labourers, of that claſs virtuous by nature, becauſe it has no relation but with the earth; and the ſoul is always endued with a mild diſpoſition, when the body, employed in the cheerful toils of agriculture, breathes a wholeſome air, and knows not oppreſſion. What pure and innocent enjoyments are the lot of the plough-boy compared with thoſe of the lad engaged in manufacture? Behold the inhabitant of the country, he loves all around him, the grounds, the vineyards, the animals, the children; his little field is daily courted by his hands: the artificer has a contracted ſoul, he is an egotiſt, he does not marry, he hates his maſter, his *priſon*, his labour. The huſbandman is obliging, becauſe there neceſſarily ſubſiſts between cultivators a reciprocity of ſervices: the artificer ſtands unconnected; his diſpoſition is altered as much as his health. The forſaking of a rural life ſpreads vice in a diſtrict, and all the tract in the vicinity of manufactures is infected with bad ſubjects. I appeal to experience: the *principality of Neûchatel*, among others, has loſt its morals and the advantages of its ſituation by the manufactures of *Indian gauzes* and *watches:* there a few avaricious maſters have literally changed a free and worthy people into a ſlaviſh unprincipled race of men.

COLONIES.

IN proportion as the frontiers of a ſtate are more diſtant, the government, formed on the model of the domeſtic ſtate, degenerates: ſuch a model is alone calculated for a riſing monarchy confined within narrow limits.

During the minority of children, the paternal authority has its full ſcope: when once they are of age, they become in their turn heads of families, and the father ceaſes to have over them the ſame power.

Thus, when a ſtate has planted diſtant colonies, or by the junction of ſeveral foreign provinces has augmented its force and its riches, as ſoon as theſe colonies or provinces can ſupport themſelves, they are tempted by their diſtance to throw off the yoke of the ſovereign authority. It is more difficult to direct the courſe of a great river, and to ſtay its rapidity, at the part adjacent to its mouth, than at that which borders on its ſource. Thus the ſtruggles of colonies, and the inſurrections of diſtant provinces, are always extremely haraſſing to the ſovereign, who has need of all his art and all his vigilance to maintain tranquillity. In ſpite of the niceſt management, colonies ſometimes throw off their dependance on a monarch, as well by reaſon

reaſon of their diſtance, as becauſe it is in the nature of nations to attempt, whenever they find an opportunity, the recovery of whatever power they have granted.

Is it not a violent and extraordinary effort to exact obedience from a man ſeparated by the barrier of the ocean, and ſituated in another hemiſphere? Was America created for Europe? Placed beneath another ſky, America is not within our natural limits; in her climate the European degenerates; her fields are to us a grave, and her productions in a manner ſo many poiſons. How coſtly an enterpriſe to have equivocal ſubjects!

It would be curious and intereſting to conſider the exiſting but inviſible cauſes of all the political events which we aſſign to *chance*, as an abyſs which would ſtupify and deafen thoſe who ſhould attempt to ſound it is hidden.

The war the Engliſh waged againſt the Americans, the poſſeſſion of whoſe ſea coaſt they had gained, drove the citizens into the interior parts of the country; and by this forced tranſplantation, the population was rapidly and advantageouſly increaſed. The effect of the depredatory incurſions made at the mouths of the rivers, was that lands which would otherwiſe have remained uncultivated were turned up by the ſpade and the plough-ſhare: the enemy rendered more effectual ſervice to the colonies than the latter would have rendered to themſelves.

To ſubject the events which ſpring up to political computations is a taſk of extreme difficulty: the profoundeſt inveſtigation cannot ſucceed in eſtimating what will one day be the correſpondencies of the United States of America, either between themſelves, or with other nations. One thing is, however, certain, that the liberty of the new world will conſiderably influence the old.

As in eventual calculations the greateſt uncertainty prevails, it would be highly preſumptuous to aim at giving a ſtamp and phyſiognomy to the future. By conſidering the manners and habitudes of the people, and the character of the ſoil and climate of any country, we may be enabled to foreſee with ſome degree of preciſion that what will be will partake of what has been: but the political convulſions that are to take place cannot be appreciated. The more we attend to hiſtory, the more we follow the inexplicable interweavings of facts, the more are we convinced that polity is the ſcience of the moment, and that, inſtead of attempting to divine it, we muſt wait the firſt play of the machine. Polity is the art of judging of imperceptible as well as real movements: but if it ſtrikes the blow before the preciſe time, it loſes its force, and throws a conſiderable and laſting impediment in the way of its progreſs.

CENTRAL POINT.

THE government ought to be one, that is to ſay, the *ſovereign* ought to be acknowledged unequivocally and without partition. The principle of unity is rigorous, ſo much ſo indeed, that the monarch who has abdicated his throne in favour of his ſon, when he aims at repoſſeſſing himſelf of the ſovereign authority, is no other than a ſubject in revolt againſt his King; and the ſon has then a right to puniſh him as a traitor who has forfeited his oath of fealty and obedience. Thus Victor Amadeus, when he endeavoured to reaſcend the throne, was treated as a conſpirator, and was legitimately impriſoned by his ſon during the reſt of his life.

In theſe caſes the intereſt of the government prevails over the ties of blood and the laws of nature. The father is ſubjected to the legitimate monarch, because there can be but one ſovereign in a ſtate.

Upon

Upon the same principle, the sovereign is invincibly bound to the state he governs: he cannot at his pleasure and caprice break through the compact which obliges him to reign. This law is founded on the danger nations would incur, by that greatest of all political vices, the diffusion of authority.

It has not been for this that nations have necessarily attached themselves to one individual rather than to another: the general will is invariably the supreme law; and on an occasion so important the people ought not to be perplexed and harassed.

In high polity extreme laws are useful and expedient: the obligation of obeying supposes the obligation of reigning. On the other hand the punishment of Cesar and some other sovereigns was justifiable, because they unlawfully extended the prerogatives of royalty.

The cases in which a sovereign can abdicate his throne are extremely rare; he can have no other excuse than a frank avowal to the nation: "I am altogether without capacity, and have "not even the resource of a choice of ministers; "permit me, faithful subjects, to live as a pri-"vate man." Such an heroical avowal would make an abdication more honourable than any we meet with in history.

But to abandon a nation which has inveſted him with the ſupreme authority, to deprive the government of its beſt ſupport, is to betray the confidence his ſubjects have repoſed in him, and to expoſe them to national calamities. Can there be a ſpectacle more outrageouſly ſcandalous than the flight of Henry III. who ſtole away ſecretly from his capital, and abandoned his crown to take up a richer one? What an infraction of a ſolemn oath! Is it poſſible for a monarch to diſplay a higher mark of contempt? Had Henry III. been arreſted in his flight, the nation would certainly have been juſtified in bringing him to trial; for every engagement is reciprocal.

Chagrin, diſguſt, and a levity of humour have cauſed ſeveral abdications. The ſovereigns were afterwards preyed upon by a violent regret, as if in the human mind nothing could compenſate for the honour of being at the head of a great nation.

Thus ought the perſon of kings to be eminently reſpected, as the part of the government moſt eſſential to public repoſe and good order. The ſovereign is the individual who cruſhes all the practicable views of a lofty, blind, and unbridled ambition. It is for this reaſon, and on account of the high intereſt of the ſtate, that

fanatics

fanatics and madmen, when they make an attempt on the perſon of the ſovereign, are not excuſed. It may appear, at firſt ſight, inconſiſtent to puniſh a man who is without the guidance of reaſon; but in theſe caſes policy requires what equity would otherwiſe condemn.

Finally, that which in a ſtate conſtitutes the ſovereign ought to be determined by regular, invariable, and conſtant rules. This may explain why an infant of fourteen years has been permitted to reign over France: policy will have it ſo, to avert greater calamities.

An African prince is aſſaſſinated in the midſt of his army, without either the privity or concurrence of the ſoldiery. Three conſpirators are ſufficient to dethrone the ſovereign: the murderer places himſelf on the throne he has imbued in blood; and he is acknowledged by the army. Why is it ſo? Becauſe the ſoldiery have need of a chief. The head of the government is of little import to them, provided when it falls off or is cut off, it regenerates. The army knows by experience that a coward will not ſupply the place of a brave man; and that the man who is unworthy of the ſupreme rank will not hold it long. He may for the moment be deſpotical, but he himſelf is not ſecure from the blow of the poignard. Such a form of government is, it is true, very imperfect; but under such an one many nations have existed and still continue to exist.

OF QUEENS.

WHEN the immensity of a state requires a considerable propelling power, a central and weighty point, and when a despotic throne has erected itself in the midst of a vast empire, it is then to be desired that the despot may be *a woman*; because the pity so natural to the sex recoils at sanguinary and terrible executions, and because a woman is calculated to soften the ferocity of the government. The slave wil feel less repugnance at prostrating himself before her; obedience will blend itself with the ascendency heaven has bestowed on woman; and the male subjects, disguising their servile state, will act the part of admirers.

In a mixed form of government such as that of England the throne is by no means improperly filled by women: as the sovereign forms only one part of the political machine, the sex is of little importance. In an unlimited monarchy, on the other hand, a woman ſeated on the throne is out of her place.

In Ruſſia a woman governs; and the women enjoy no conſideration whatever. In France the women are excluded from the throne: they preſide over all domeſtic concerns, and not unfrequently govern domeſtic affairs. What is it that the miſtreſſes of our kings have not done? during the laſt two reigns there have been ſeveral of their regencies.

OF GREAT STATES.

GREAT States are ſupported by their own maſs, and this is the reaſon why they are more ſubject to abuſes than any others. Great States commit great faults with more impunity than follows the commiſſion of ſmall faults in little States. Large Empires neceſſarily produce a certain number of great men; and only one of theſe is required at any given epoch to render the kingdom illuſtrious. It ſometimes happens that great States can even diſpenſe with great men; for when the monarch does not ſupport the empire, the empire ſupports the monarch.

After the unfortunate iſſue of the battles of Hochtet, Ramillies, and Malplaquet, France ſeemed to be verging towards her ruin: in two years ſhe recovered herſelf. Empires of a vaſt extent will invariably have proportionate reſources; and nothing but a reiteration of continued abuſes and abſurdities can give them a deadly wound. The citizens may be for a long time wretched; they may ſtruggle under a variety of ſufferings; but as empires ſuch as theſe convert their enormous maſs into a rampart, they ſubſiſt notwithſtanding, and ſurvive their immediate population. This is the greateſt political calamity which can afflict the human race.

Like that of an individual, the ſtrength of a ſtate is merely relative: ſmall ſtates may therefore poſſeſs a conſiderable degree of force and power, according to their poſition, and their commerce more eſpecially.

A ſtate which ſhackles the induſtry of its citizens, which clogs the exerciſe of the arts and of the various branches of commerce by eternal prohibitions, and ſubjects its manufacturers to a variety of taxes, undergoes a diminution of its ſtrength and grandeur, provided the neighbouring ſtate forbears to impoſe any reſtraints by its legiſlative acts, and allows the number of ſellers of every deſcription to multiply freely; for the more ſellers there are, the

more

more purchaſers will there be. The abundance of every ſpecies of merchandize favours the conſumption; and the conſumption will invariably be the moſt certain pledge of the reproduction.

The ſtate which is deſirous to enjoy its full vigour ſhould allow the activity of men to exert itſelf freely: the country in which commerce meets with a houſe of cuſtoms and receipts at every turning can never enter into a rivalſhip with the neighbouring ſtates. Money ought to be allowed the leaſt poſſible reſt; and ſales ſhould be multiplied by a rapid and continual circulation. It is to the circulation that nations are indebted for peculiar advantages; for thoſe even which nature herſelf had refuſed.

OF A STATE TOO NARROW.

POLITY, being unable to eſtabliſh a real equality in the fortune of the citizens, ſeems inſtinctively to reject a popular government. In vain have little republics imagined that the people would never ceaſe to be free; there is an invincible progreſſion, above all in modern ſtates, where commerce ſo quickly modifies the members of the ſame ſociety. The more

limited

limited it is, the more does the alteration become inevitable. The poorer citizens neceſſarily come under the influence of the rich. And theſe little republics, after having raiſed ſome unſucceſsful ſtorms, fall into all the ſnares laid for them.

It is the height of folly, in a Lilliputian ſtate, to believe that it will recover by force what has before been refuſed to its remonſtrances. The people are blinded indeed when they imagine they either can or muſt poſſeſs the chief power, becauſe they are more numerous than the party of the rich.

A poor nation has no other weapons than the inceſſant complaints and lamentations it makes. It muſt teaſe and weary out its adverſaries like beggars.

If, in a late inſtance, the people of Geneva had maintained the war of the pen, if it had not ſtepped out of the circle of pamphlets, if it had continued to refine on politics with the ſame obſtinacy, it would have tired the adverſe party, and have carried all its points even by diſputing in an unintelligible manner. But inſtead of diſputing in circles until the extinction of its natural heat, that nation of watchmakers ſeized the muſket, and mounted its mouldered ramparts. This ridiculous attitude hurt it

more

more than all the metaphyſico-political arguments it could have employed would have benefited it. It was a child that took in its hand a lance with which to wound itſelf, that covered its head with a helmet which could not fail to ſtifle it. The powerful, that is, the rich, plundered its borrowed arſenal; and the whole terminated by this expreſſion full of juſtneſs and truth: *A tempeſt in a glaſs of water.*

Ariſtocracy, eſpecially when it is confined within the limits of a city, is more mercileſs and unjuſt than deſpotiſm. In the latter, there is only one maſter, and the equality of condition affords ſome conſolation; the name of ſubject is ſhared among fifteen or twenty millions of men, who belong to a magnificent monarch. But to depend on the grandees in a diſtrict, a circuit, or a town, without a hope that equality can ever be renewed; to ſee the proud independance of ſeveral extending itſelf; to feel yourſelves degraded by men perpetually intriguing, who barter away even your paternal abode; to witneſs an offenſive league of a very ſmall number who quietly divide all the riches, and bend the people under their yoke, granting them nevertheleſs bread, a favour which they are at ſufficient pains to extol—this is the utmoſt pitch of miſery and outrage.

DESTRUCTIVE VICES.

THE internal vices which prey on a great ſtate are the waſteful expenditure of the public money, immoderate gifts and gratuities, and a non-obſervance of the laws. If the military body exhauſts the treaſury, if the nobility are prodigal in their claims, if the great have the addreſs to obtain a peculiar juſtice for themſelves, then do theſe miſchiefs become ſo many incurable wounds, which impair the ſtrength a fine kingdom, and deſtroy the admirable effects of brilliant enthuſiaſm and heroical valour.

Auguſtus maintained forty legions for twelve millions of livres (half a million ſterling) a year: his ſecret has been loſt. The worſt kings are thoſe who have diſſipated the moſt, becauſe they have held in their hands the public money.

In monarchies the greateſt defect has conſiſted in not paying ſufficient attention to the interior of the kingdom to ſecure the triumph of the ſovereign without. The perfection of this form of government would therefore conſiſt in provincial aſſemblies, by which the moſt diſtant parts of the monarchy would be kindled to life, the burthen of the taxes alleviated, and the people encouraged to prefer their complaints and make their requiſitions.

When the adminiſtration is divided into ſeveral departments independant of each other, they encounter and claſh in their operations, for want of a principle of unity. The regulations are at every inſtant changed; from the office of each department peculiar laws are promulged; and the public are entirely at a loſs to know by whom they have been enacted. Under theſe circumſtances the authority is always prohibitive, becauſe ſuch an adminiſtration is perfectly well adapted to ſloth and ignorance. Laſtly, no one can tell where the government reſides, each of the departments ſeizing on the legiſlative authority, and extending its boundaries. Public debates which announce that men's minds are in a ſalutary agitation, that they are zealous to render the government proſperous, are no longer heard. The diſorder of to-day, and the uncertainty of to-morrow, baniſh confidence. The citizen trembles for his property, becauſe he perceives with pain that every contract is broken through: anarchy prevails; and the ſocial contract is ſecretly diſſolved. There is more danger in all this than if each of the citizens brandiſhed in his hand a ſword.

NEW

NEW DISCOVERIES.

THE diſcoveries which may be at this time attempted are:

1. The examination of the fifth continent which lies in what is called *terra auſtralis*, ſituated between Cape Horn and the Cape of Good Hope. The exiſtence of this continent, about which doubts were entertained, is at length acknowledged: it ought to extend from twenty, thirty, or forty degrees to the antarctic pole.

2. The land to the northward of Japan, the great Jeſſo, and that which ought to lie between the extremity of ſouthern Tartary, and the extremity of America.

3. A paſſage by Hudſon's bay to the Eaſt Indies; and a paſſage by the frozen ocean to China, leaving Japan. As theſe two paſſages, the latter particularly, would conſiderably abridge the voyage from Europe to Aſia, an immenſe advantage would be derived from them to the nation which ſhould make the diſcovery, as well by the convenience of the navigation, as by the new tribes which might be diſcovered on the way. We know that two ſkilful navigators have determined one of theſe paſſages to be abſolutely impracticable; but what one does not find, another, more fortunate, diſcovers.

4. In

4. In America itſelf we have ſtill to diſcover all the land which lies between the Cordillera mountains, the Straits of Magellan, and the river of the Amazons—an immenſe tract which ought to contain prodigious riches, and which is partly inhabited by the Arauco tribes and Patagonians, partly by a great number of other ſavage or unknown nations.

5. The great continent of Africa ſituated between the ſource of the Nile and the Cape of Good Hope.

6. The iſlands ſcattered over the Pacific Ocean, in the direction both of north and ſouth. In the different parts of the globe the tracts of land I have juſt pointed out are as extenſive as the whole of the known world.

The poſſibility of theſe great diſcoveries is a ſubject I ſhall again take up; for Europe is not the world.

THE LOANS OF A SOVEREIGN *.

THE conventions ſovereigns make with their ſubjects are ſacred in proportion to the facility

* It will readily be perceived that this fragment was compoſed before the revolution, when the queſtion was agitated whether *the king would not find his account in a* ſtate bankruptcy.

with

with which they can break them. The reigning king reprefents his predeceffor, fince he retains for him the revenues, the homages, and the fupreme authority. If, after a century or more, he conftrains his fubjects to pay to him what is his due, for a ftill ftronger reafon ought he to liquidate the recent debts of the throne, when the palace in which he refides, and the magnificence with which he is furrounded, are the product of public confidence. The force of his empire is founded on the fums advanced by his faithful and defunct fubjects; by the unfortunate men who have delivered into his hands their *little ftock*, the fruit of their labour, their favings, their privations, the confolation and prop of their old age: is he to be unjuft, inftead of being juft and even grateful?

Are not the fubjects culpable if they revolt? And does not the fovereign revolt againft his fubjects when he breaks a folemn contract, when he annuls it by oppofing his might to equity, fheltering himfelf under the rank which places him above all reftraint? He will fpeak of the public wants, as if the wants of individuals were not equally forcible. Since he can either retard or difpenfe with the payment, on that very account he ought to be more prompt and more faithful, to fhun the reproach

of

of not having executed a convention ſynonymous to public faith; for what can be more ſacred than the words of a ſovereign, when he addreſſes his ſubjects thus: *Lend to me, my children, for the good of the ſtate; the debt ſhall be diſcharged by the ſtate and myſelf.* Now, the inheritor of the throne of the deceaſed prince is politically conſidered as the ſame perſon; and every argument to the contrary is a ſophiſm which attacks the probity of the monarch, who ſhould be leſs conſidered as the proprietor, than as the depoſitary of an immenſe treaſure.

If a ſtate could for a long time ſupport the credit of a fictitious money, without the poſſibility of its being counterfeited, there would no longer be any need either of taxes or finances; but it would be neceſſary in ſuch a caſe that the ſtate ſhould be iſolated. This fictitious money then anſwering every purpoſe of metals, would be ſtill more advantageous to a ſtate than coined ſpecie, ſince it would be more portable and more convenient. But the incomparable advantage would conſiſt in this, that the articles eſſential to the ſupport of life would no longer be ſent out of the kingdom, at the ſame time that the fictitious money would fertilize the lands, by its ſuſceptibility of a prodigious increaſe. According to this wonderful hypothesis, the state would gain every thing without the individual sustaining any loss: but it would also be necessary to come at the secret of isolating a kingdom.

In every state, indeed, fictitious money is infinitely preferable to the augmentation of the value of specie, or to the slightest alteration it can undergo: therefore in any country in which paper money is circulated, especial care ought to be taken not on any pretext to change the value of the coined metals. A state in debt acquits itself of its obligations without any disbursement, in the course of time, provided it understands how to balance the paper money with the metallic money, in such a proportion as that the merchandizes rising progressively in their value, each debtor shall in a given time gain the amount of the half of his debt. This is the only remedy; and in no other way can a state in debt free itself from its burthens without destroying the equilibrium, either by circulating too great a mass of specie among the lenders and the borrowers, or by draining them by an impolitic depreciation of the metallic money, if the fictitious money is no longer in circulation.

But we will quit these hypotheses, which are at the bottom no better than palliatives, although

though preferable to thoſe that have been adopted: the period is at length arrived when we ſee *loans* under their true aſpect.

OF NATIONAL PRIDE.

IT is important to eſtabliſh and uphold a certain national pride; for this it is that prompts to great achievements. National cuſtoms, imbibed in infancy, contract the force of practicable principles, and influence the ordinary courſe of life. The peculiar uſages and turn of thought which prevail in an empire are its baſis, the ſpring of the government; and beget a reſpect for the national character. It would be a dangerous imprudence to attack them; it would plainly be to alter the conſtitution; and when the natural force of public principles ſubſiſts no longer, their only ſupport is the power of cuſtom.

Adminiſtrators, intereſt the national pride, and it will perform prodigies; humble it, you will deſtroy the animation of the people, and extinguiſh the patriotic ſpirit.

It would be ruin and deſolation to cover the walls of cities with mournful hangings, after the example of the Carthaginians, who thus expressed their despair in the sad days of their adversity, when a sovereign or his minister loses the reputation of a state, by one of those political blunders which involve the disgrace of a nation.

Those souls which feel an interest in the glory of their country, bear with the errors of kings; but pardon not in a minister the injuries he does to the citizens. We need not wonder therefore at the grief that seizes true patriots when they perceive the fatal consequence of those little passions which ought never to have entered the cabinet. No subject ought to be mortified; for if the national pride were totally extinct, the delicious feeling of a paternal land would be gone for ever.

The woman who, on being condemned by Philip, had the courage to exclaim, *I appeal to Philip fasting*, gave an example to subjects of appealing from all the passions of sovereigns which might have a seeming tendency to humble them.

Heroic actions become monarchs, because it is thus that they dazzle the people. The latter more readily give up their rights, when they behold brilliant achievements. The admiration entertained by the French for the conquests of Louis XIV. disposed them above every other consideration to an unlimited obedience. A monarch

narch ſhould be conſtantly attentive to attract towards himſelf the regard of the public, by a multitude of generous acts; becauſe the minds of his ſubjects ſhould be occupied, nor ought they ever to loſe ſight of their chief magiſtrate.

COUNCILS.

IF, to render himſelf the moſt powerful of mortals, and to apply this prodigious aſcendency to an extraordinary and generous purpoſe, a ſovereign were to aim at the poſſeſſion of a part of the liberty enjoyed by his ſubjects, there is one infallible mean by which he might accompliſh this end, namely, to govern them in ſuch a way as that they might themſelves be the gainers, when they ſhould, with a full confidence, have ſurrendered to him that portion of their freedom which would then be ſuperfluous to them. Adminiſtrators of ſtates, honour men, honour them in their reſpective profeſſions, degrade none of them, and you will hold in your hands a power that has not yet been dreamed of.

A French writer, with a view of deſtroying the eſſential characteriſtics of monarchy, thoſe intermediate powers which, according to Monteſquieu, conſtitute the nature of the monarchical government, has attempted to prove that the kings of France have, without any exception, enjoyed an abſolute authority. Since this writer's work made its appearance, the king of France has not poſſeſſed an authority greater than that of his predeceſſors. He might have demonſtrated that from the reign of Clovis to the preſent day our government has been a pure and abſolute monarchy, which it has never for a moment ceaſed to be; but that the ſprings and counterpoize which balance the power of the ſovereign, created and combined by the general will, do nevertheleſs exiſt. The various tribunals might have granted to the kings of France the exerciſe of the higheſt deſpotiſm; but the tyranny would not preſs with too great a weight on the people, become enlightened, and the ſovereign himſelf would retrench the power which urges obedience, to gain the confidence of his ſubjects. The primitive laws of the French might be deſtroyed; but the genius and manners would reſiſt every meaſure of extreme violence.

In vain would two hundred volumes iſſue from the preſſes of the royal printing office: they would not render the power of kings more abſolute, becauſe nations are ſenſible that they will only obey to a certain degree, and that it is

in

in vain to ſay to a monarch, *Nothing either can or ought to reſiſt you*; the conſcience of the monarch would whiſper to him that he was abuſed, and the people would not be alarmed at this momentary deciſion.

The French will never dread their chief, whatever may be the authority with which he is inveſted. The genius of the nation will counterbalance the moſt unforeſeen attacks. A reaſonable authority will be the only one that will exact obedience: every other mean will be hazardous *.

Let the inquiſition be preached in France; let ſeveral bodies of the ſtate unite their ſuffrages in favour of the eſtabliſhment of that tribunal, it will never be acknowledged, becauſe it is inconſiſtent with the genius of the French. The field of Mars, in which the legitimate power once reſided, no longer exiſts; but the nation ſtill contrives to make itſelf heard: it ſpeaks out as it did at the time when the king was merely a general, a captain.

Finally, ſay to princes, *You have the excluſive right of exacting obedience, nothing can nor ought to reſiſt you; the only reſtraint you have to dread is the public conſcience and your own.* All this

* Has not this prophecy of mine been fulfilled in the ſtricteſt ſenſe?

will not augment their power. Let the intermediate authority, which is one of the constituent elements of our government, be or not be combated: it will in either caſe exiſt. This is not a modern invention of our philoſophical writers; it is becauſe reaction is as certain as it is neceſſary. The Abbé Mably had no occaſion to combat M. Moreau; he had no need to cite the moſt ancient and moſt reſpectable monument of our hiſtory, the general aſſembly, convoked in the field of Mars, in which the acknowledged power reſided. Whatever may be ſaid of the fortune and manners of the French, even had national liberty never exiſted, nothing would have prevented them from eſtabliſhing at this epoch a rigorous diſtinction between the power of the laws and the ſovereign.

STRETCHES OF AUTHORITY.

AN ill guided authority undertakes more than it can execute. This is the rock on which governments ſplit, when, not knowing themſelves, or rather wilfully miſunderſtanding their boundaries, they aim at the extenſion of the latter by a natural but dangerous propenſity.

Governments

Governments are at this time too enlightened to recur to a violent authority: at leaſt we have every reaſon to preſume ſo much. But there is an imprudent authority which manifeſts itſelf when it ought to be buried in oblivion. Opinions are not to be reſtrained, neither are popular attachments nor hatreds to be commanded. A miniſtry is diſhonoured by the alarms of which it is itſelf the cauſe. There are acts which by their very nature do not come under the cognizance of any tribunal; and to have recourſe to violent meaſures in repreſſing ſlight abuſes is to make an inconſiderate application of the royal or miniſterial force. The ſovereign ſhould never allow himſelf to be governed by his paſſions; in his Majeſty there ſhould be a ſort of apathy, which, like the law, ſhould be mute, or at leaſt tranquil.

The right of nations is ſo deeply engraven in the heart of man, that he conſtantly applies, both with reaſon and juſtice, the natural law to the affairs and conduct of ſovereigns as well as of the nations themſelves. He does not diſpute about words; neither does he remark whether the right of nations has been often confounded with the right of nature: he condemns whatever according to his opinion tends to diſturb general ſociety, be the pretext

on

on which it has been done what it may. Hence arifes that abhorrence which is attached to certain names, while others are equally cherifhed and beloved.

And hence that ftrong curiofity with which the conduct of fovereigns is watched, to the end that they may be judged, and according as they offend or refpect the natural right, be either praifed or blamed. Surrounded by their foldiers, public reafon forbids them to be cruel, violent, and hafty: the loftieft authority is thus reftrained; and it is no difficult tafk to perceive, that from one end of the earth to the other the general felicity is dependant on individual felicity. He who outrages the latter incapacitates himfelf from founding the former.

Into fome conftitutions rarely to be met with, thofe of piratical ftates for inftance, the fpirit of injuftice finds its way. As the character of the inhabitants is fraudulent and iniquitous, honour and the love of glory are not to be expected in the profeffion they exercife; and their rapine and extortions readily decide that the laws of thefe buccaneering nations correfpond in a great degree with the purfuits they follow.

The earlieft laws of Dracon and Charondas, written in blood, were unqueftionably at that time

time rather reſtraining efforts than inſtitutes of police. Before any attempt could be made to direct the courſe of the reſtraining virtues, it became neceſſary to prevent a violent and rapidly increaſing evil, as well as to nip the vices in their bud.

In cruel and ſanguinary nations it was the aim of their firſt legiſlators, to intimidate the banditti they had to govern, and by the terror of puniſhments to baniſh crimes. As well as the bents and propenſities they were to reſtrain, the laws were then atrocious.

Repreſent to yourſelf Minos, a legiſlator at Algiers. Philoſophy will there beſtow on him the place the poets aſſign to Minos the inflexible judge of hell, ſeated in the depths of Tartarus.

What is moſt to be admired in the Engliſh government, is that all the ſovereign's officers are reſponſible for their bad adminiſtration, and in general for whatever is done in their reſpective departments. The ſovereign is accountable for no fault ; but his miniſters are made to account for whatever they have done. In this mixture of reſpect for majeſty, and firmneſs for the rights of the nation, we cannot fail to perce ive a wiſe temperament which enſures happineſs to the prince and the people. Arbitrary authority

authority is not terrible because it is placed in the hands of a single person, but because its exercise is delegated to several; it is a club which each wields in his turn.

The love of the country, recommended as a moral virtue, is a chimerical command, provided the citizen is not attached to that country by the security, ease, and prosperity, he finds in it. It is a romantic sentiment when it hinges solely on the transitory glory of a monarch. The love of the country, and that of the laws of the country, are two distinct objects. The love of the public weal is founded in the nice discrimination of such a political law over such another. The love of the country may be injurious to the love of humanity, in the same way that self love may be detrimental to generosity: but the interest of the country ought to prevail over every other interest; and to this consideration men are more or less impelled against their will.

How can a love for the country reside in a nation where the wretched inhabitants every where display poverty, tatters, and the hollow and sunken eye of misery?

OF MILITARY BODIES.

THE ſoldier has no morality, and deſpiſes life more than he braves death. As his function is directly oppoſite to that which frames the laws, he is of all men the moſt ready to ſubvert them. The ſoldier defends ſociety, but the ſame force likewiſe deſtroys it. The ſoldier arrogates to himſelf a right of property in whatever comes within the reach of his ſword. How neceſſary is it in all governments to bridle the military body, and to hold it in a ſtate of complete dependance! How formidable a depoſit! In whoſe hand ſhall it be entruſted? It is on the knowledge of the juſt and preciſe point that the liberty of the citizens depends.

We cannot help admiring the policy of the French government, which has controled the regular troops in ſuch a way as that they are formidable neither to the prince nor the ſubject; whereas at Rome, at Peterſburg, and at Conſtantinople, alternately the terror of monarchs and the firebrand of revolutions, they have ſo often convulſed the empire and diſpoſed of the crown.

In France, the military body has no aſcendency over the municipal. The ſoldier reſpects

ſpects the citizen; and civil forms reſtrain the regiments which have no communication with the tradeſmen, or the other peaceable inhabitants of the cities.

The French army, all compoſed of diſtinct bodies, cannot poſſibly coaleſce into one maſs; becauſe ſome parts of it have no communication with the reſt, ſo different are their functions, and ſo various the principles by which they are diſciplined.

Had the government introduced into the management of the revenue a part of thoſe ſtrict and ſenſible regulations which have been framed for the military, we ſhould not have ſeen the adminiſtration of the finances open gulf on gulf;—we ſhould not have ſeen one abyſs leading into another, and the wretched ſubjects, acquainted with theſe robberies, reduced to fruitleſs complaints, and compelled to make good the peculations of certain public characters in favour. The ſweat of a whole nation, inſtead of augmenting at leaſt the patrimony of the ſtate, would not have ſwelled private fortunes, ſhamefully acquired, and more ſhamefully ſquandered; horrid wounds which draw tears from whoever loves his country; diſgraceful calamities and perhaps irreparable, while all other ills may be repaired!

Whither is it gone, that river of gold, the life of the political body, and which was destined to nourish all its parts? It has disappeared in a way equally mean and criminal; and at its horrid deperdition every citizen is alarmed, since it threatens to burthen him with new and enormous imposts. The finances of the state, totally drained, leave not even, as in Egypt, immense edifices; like the pyramids, which though useless labours, attested at least the passage through which the golden stream had strayed.

He who has land just sufficient for his subsistence will be obliged to sell it, or to labour in repairing the unpunished crime of certain individuals. O! grief. O! my country.

The imposts in France affect us in three ways: the first of these is personal; the second assesses properties; and the third attaches itself to the articles of commerce and provisions: but there are so many other fiscal inventions that they might compose a dictionary.

The royal treasury is really immense, amounting annually to 900 millions of livres, 40 millions sterling.

How moderate ought the imposts to be, when the state possesses such a capital? What great abuses must prevail in the management of the

the public treasures, to make it necessary still to borrow, if such a mass of money be every year laid at the foot of the throne? But, like a wave of the ocean, it retires the instant it advances, and the state bears the shock of this terrible undulation. The depredations are not discovered till they almost exceed calculation.

These horrible abuses originate from great military establishments.

OF THE LABOURS OF A PLACEMAN.

THE skilful minister who, immediately on his becoming an administrator, assembles and unites all the parts of a shattered government, and who, without destroying any thing, frees the political body from a multitude of ancient vices, providing it more particularly with a central point, a point of unity, is a man very rare to be found. He knows that it is impossible to give an absolutely new regimen to a worn out body, because the civil government is altogether distinct from the political government, and because in every state this double government resides.

When the mind of man has strayed into sciences which give no satisfactory result, he concludes

concludes by looking around him, and by seeking order in the point he inhabits. How much ought we to venerate the qualities of a statesman directing millions of men, whose character he is obliged to study, to convert to his own advantage their passions, their virtues, and their vices even; and producing general order from some partial disorders, at the same time that he anticipates the mischiefs he cannot shun!

There are abuses which the statesman can attack with an almost infallible success. It is easy to perceive whether the public mind is prepared, and whether the blow which is ready to be struck is authorized before hand by the sound part of the nation. It is then that he puts the axe to the root of the tree, which he severs; and because its fall was expected, it is viewed with calmness: its trunk rotted, and its branches decayed, its destruction cannot fail to be acceptable.

Thus then ought the part of the nation which instructs, aware of its rights and its high destiny, never to despair of those who govern, whatever their fate and their prejudices may be.

The part which instructs, or, if you will, the thinking class, will make it its daily study to purify the laws, to render them more simple and better calculated for man, and more espe-

 cially

cially to deſtroy a ſhapeleſs aſſemblage of prohibitory laws which make culprits. Oh! ought not the ſtateſman himſelf to ſuſpend their terrible and formidable action? His own conſcience would reproach him, were he to follow the literal ſenſe and expreſſion of the code. It often happens that he dares not invoke the law; a ſecret power repels his effort, becauſe the law in queſtion has been inſenſibly undermined by public reaſon: it has been demonſtrated to be falſe and abſurd by the part which inſtructs, at whoſe voice it has fallen into diſuſe. The placeman who ſhould contend for its re-eſtabliſhment, would ſeem to aim at the ſudden renewal of the barbarous age which gave it birth, and in which it was unqueſtionably no more than one violence oppoſed to another ſtill more dangerous in its nature. The ſtorm has ſubſided; humane and eternal principles muſt be had recourſe to; and nothing but extraordinary and unforeſeen caſes can juſtify, not a different, but a particular courſe.

The part which inſtructs has therefore eſtabliſhed the ideas experience has in the ſequel confirmed. It has decided on the contentions between public and private intereſt; but it would in its turn have its moments of error, if it were deſpotically to require that its ideas ſhould be

ſuddenly

ſuddenly realized: it ſhould propoſe, and not command.

The writer, in his cabinet, can by a bold flight compaſs the moſt arduous and difficult reforms; nothing reſiſts him, but all yields to his accompliſhed and tranſcendant pen. He ſeems to act on a ſoft clay which he moulds at his will, and which in an inſtant undergoes a new modification. Animated by the audacity of his conceptions, and powerful in his virtues, he feels no obſtacle. He is penetrated by a love for the public weal, and dreams of the fine romance of univerſal felicity. He communicates around him the flame which is kindled in his breaſt; and he fancies that in the ſoul of his fellow citizens it will conſume each degrading and perſonal paſſion.

The patriotic views of this writer cannot but be applauded; but if he were to be obliged to combine practice with theory; if his enthuſiaſm were to encounter a reſiſtance, how aſtoniſhed would he be at the ſhock and force of the little paſſions that are inimical to order! Miſerable acceſſaries, a glimpſe even of which had not come acroſs his ſight.

It is not from the great paſſions that the danger is to be apprehended: theſe are combated by open force and in the face of the nation. It reſides in the obſcure paſſions which are working far from the public eye, and in their dark and ſecret receſſes undermining the patriotic virtues. It is by theſe concealed attacks that generous projects are rendered abortive, as little contemptible worms ſap and inſenſibly deſtroy the ſolid banks which are the ramparts and ſecurity of a nation ſurrounded by the formidable ocean.

How would the writer then find his book perpetually deranged! All thoſe threads which he fancied he held ſo nicely arranged in his hand would be entangled or perhaps totally eſcape from his graſp; and he would ſoon perceive that the operations of meditating genius are unfortunately incapable of calculating their poſſibilities, unleſs by the lapſe of ages and the united labours of ſeveral generations.

The felicity of a nation, the ſudden regeneration of which is impracticable (and theſe inſurrections are extremely rare in hiſtory) is but partial, and cannot be otherwiſe than ſo. The love of the public weal itſelf enjoins the placeman to reſiſt too ſtrong an enthuſiaſm, and to be fully perſuaded that the happieſt changes are thoſe which are the ſloweſt wrought. He ought to know that whatever is haſtened is in danger of being deſtroyed; that projects are confirmed by their maturity; and that without patience and a ſage caution, they can have neither ſolidity nor depth. On the banks of certain rivers in Africa, there is a beautiful and richly coloured fruit which invites the hand to pluck it, and the mouth to taſte it: as ſoon as it is touched it crumbles to duſt.

The world belongs to men of phlegmatic conſtitutions, ſay the Italians. Their meaning is that theſe men are the beſt calculated to poſſeſs themſelves of the reins of government, and to govern.

FREDERIC.

WHEN nature forms the head of a Frederic, the force of his genius becomes a new law to which the human race is obliged to ſubmit, and which in a manner conſtitutes a peculiar government. Frederic, at his acceſſion to the throne, found the baſis of his authority to conſiſt in a large, well conſtituted, and well commanded military power, the danger of which he well knew how to conceal from his ſubjects. He was ſkilful, and his genius was grand: he did not ſtretch the cords of his inſtrument too tight; for he was alſo a muſician. His ſuperior capacity was enlightened by philoſophy; and he introduced into polity a perfect knowledge of men: he knew with an admirable precision the degree of liberty that they ought to be allowed.

Frederic cherished the arts, because he was aware that they never fail to present to man an image of grandeur and liberty, and that, above every other consideration, they disguise his chains. The idea his subjects entertained that he daily exercised the functions of his kingly office, encouraged the weaker to hope that they should not be tyrannised over by the stronger: each peasant had free access to him either personally or by letter. By this expedient the cultivators were universally attached to him.

Of how many combinations, then, is not the organization of a state susceptible, since the despotism of Frederic was able to create a kind of liberty for his subjects, and since, while he cherished his army, he protected the peasants against the violence of the soldiery? The spade had nothing to dread from the sword. This great friend to soldiers would not suffer a recruit to be taken from the canton without the approbation of the provincial council; and the land proprietors and their immediate heirs were more particularly excused from service. Unceasingly tempering his power, Frederic knew how to augment

ment it: the Prussian peasant forgot that he was a slave, and fancied his destiny bettered by every victory his sovereign obtained. With what surprising address did this warlike prince contrive thus effectually to disguise the terrible scourge of enrolments, and the servitude of the highways, concealing the true stamp and form of these harsh and tyrannical institutions! But the philosophy of Frederic smoothed every difficulty: he had the art of consoling the oppressed; and, combining natural and artificial means, evinced that a despot at once dexterous and moderate can supply the place of civil liberty, which, surrounded even by his soldiery, he can create,—so much do constitutive principles, as capable of being ameliorated by a single man as by a nation, obey the principles of philosophy.

His subjects enjoyed the freedom of the press, an advantage which procured him the suffrages of the considerable number of men who instruct and direct the rest. Jests, which were one of his favourite weapons, and which he managed with dexterity, were useful in warding off the sarcastic attacks that might have been made against himself; and this freedom of the press kept in awe the swarm of theologians and lawyers who might otherwise have discredited his

 code,

code, and have interrupted the courſe of his new and novel laws.

As Frederic governed by himſelf, he inſpired a greater confidence, and obviated every pretext and ground of complaint againſt the ſubalterns: this is what conſtituted his force. No doubt could be entertained but that the ſovereign was the fountain from whence good order iſſued; and as a reſpect was entertained for him who had diſplayed both genius and talents, the obedience became the ſubmiſſion of him who knows but little to him whoſe knowledge is vaſt and extenſive, or is at leaſt conſidered to be ſo.

More may at all times be expected from a ſovereign who governs by himſelf, becauſe he has greater opportunities to ſtudy the characteriſtic features of his people, whom he teaches to know him; and becauſe his compaſſion, if he has any, is more frequently wrought upon by private diſaſters. Frederic reigned by himſelf; and this deſpot beſtowed on his people a partial ſum of liberty. He was in ſeveral circumſtances greater and more generous, than if he had confided to ſubordinates the exerciſe of his authority.

The latter, having no reſponſibility of their own, obſerve in all caſes a mode of conduct widely different from that of him who commands them. This has been too often experienced,

rienced, more eſpecially in monarchical ſtates, where the part which governs conſiſts of offices and clerks. Theſe are more ſtern and intractable than the miniſters, becauſe, wanting a name, they are inſenſible to glory, and direct their attacks without its being poſſible to recognize by whom they are aimed. In the diſcharge of their duties they are ſlovenly, becauſe they can be ſo with impunity: they make their ſuperiors anſwerable for all the faults they commit; and revenge themſelves for their ſervile ſituation on all thoſe who have either diſdained or not heeded them. By ſuch men are our monarchies ordinarily governed.

It often happens that a ſtateſman, ſatisfied with the title of miniſter, and anxious not to have his pleaſures interrupted, abandons his truſt to ſome one who will ſuit his purpoſe, and eaſe him of its weight: the other parcels it out, and divides it according to his caprice or his intereſt, converting it to his own account in the moſt advantageous way he can.

In monarchies, therefore, the misfortune which attends men in place is, that they confide in ſubordinates, who, perfectly forgetful of the glory attached to the faithful diſcharge of the truſt repoſed in them, ſeek their own individual intereſt, ſell whatever they can ſell, and

do

do capriciously whatever they can do, without even being sensible to the least remorse or the smallest shame.

The statesman placed at the helm of public affairs having received a false light, is forced to adopt it, however good his intentions may be, because he can perceive nothing else. He is guided without any will of his own, and it is impossible that he should not fall into the snare, As he needs a decision of some sort, he takes that which presents itself: on this he seizes in the multiplicity of affairs, fancying, because he has modified it a little, that he has imagined it. He offers it as boldly as he would offer a truth; and while he is deceived, he himself deceives.

JUSTIFICATION OF ALEXANDER.

I HAVE heard Voltaire eloquent when he joined his voice to that of the few apologists of this most renowned conqueror. I shall here give the substance of what Voltaire used to say with much fire and with a gesture no less animated: he was fond of the thesis, he returned to it, and maintained it during the space of nearly four-score years.

Alexander,

Alexander, ſaid he, followed up the plan of his father Philip, who had formed the project of turning againſt Perſia the forces which the Greeks had ſo long employed againſt themſelves. Alexander, educated under Ariſtotle, united abſolute power and knowledge, which had almoſt ever been disjoined; he was deſirous that his conqueſts ſhould produce on earth a revolution different from all thoſe ſeen before; his ſcheme ſurpaſſed in grandeur the ſchemes of all the preceding conquerors.

When once at the head of all the forces of Greece and ſhortly after of Perſia, he believed himſelf deſtined not only to conquer provinces and ſubdue ſtates, but to unite men under the ſame law, which ſhould enlighten and guide all, as the ſun alone illumines the univerſe; which ſhould remove from among men all the differences that render them enemies; and which ſhould inſtruct them to live and think differently without hating each other, and without diſturbing the world, to compel others to change their ſentiments.

It was, if the expreſſion can be allowed, the views of Socrates, of Plato, and of Zeno, ſo promiſing in theory, that he wiſhed to reduce into practice; but to accompliſh this great work, it was neceſſary to unite authority to knowledge,

and

and to be ſufficiently powerful on the earth to eſtabliſh in it this happy and wiſe government, which virtue held out to thoſe philoſophers. Alexander believed that he was able to ſubdue by force all thoſe whom reaſon could not perſuade. In a ſimilar character has Mahomet ſince appeared to the world, but with views infinitely leſs wiſe. The vaſt project which we aſcribe to the Macedonian hero is not the offspring of our own imagination. Plutarch poſitively aſſerts that *Alexander held himſelf to be ſent from heaven as a reformer, a governor, and a reconciler of the univerſe.* Finally, Alexander built more cities than he deſtroyed.

PRECIPITATE LAW.

IN one of the wars of Germany an officer was carried to the hoſpital with a leg ſhattered by a ball. As he was covered with blood, the ſurgeon, who was running from bed to bed, ordered amputation, and continued his round. A leg clotted over with blood was laid hold of: *what are you doing, my friends*, exclaimed the officer, *that is my good leg*. However, notwithſtanding his proteſtations and entreaties, as there was a great deal to do, the barber ſurgeons cut it off. The ſurgeon major arrived with the bandages, perceived the miſtake, and anxiouſly ſet about ſaving the wounded limb, which with much pains and difficulty he effected: but the poor officer paid dearly for the officious precipitation of the underſtrappers.

This is the true image of a precipitate law. And thus the fatal and too prompt decree enacted in *the unfortunate affair of Nancy*, authorized a ſanguinary man, whoſe character has ſince been well underſtood, to perform *an amputation*. Alas! we know now how grievous the error was!

OF CIVIL LIBERTY.

CIVIL liberty conſiſts in being dependant on no other power than the legiſlative.

The people, forming every where the major part of the ſociety, ſhould not only have a ſhare in the legiſlation, but their intereſts ought even to predominate. Accordingly, from the origin of the French republic, the people have always formed the baſis of the legiſlative aſſemblies.

Political ſociety can be lawfully derived from a primitive contract alone, either expreſs or tacit, which

which at the beginning mutually connected the members of that society.

That is a vile and superstitious system, which, making the will of God to interpose in the establishment of societies, invests the chiefs of nations with a celestial authority; this system must be considered as proceeding from no other than the most erroneous notions of the nature of man and of that of the divinity.

Between equal beings endowed with the same physical and moral powers, conventions alone can modify their primitive state; conventions are the basis of every state of institution, and consequently, of every civil state.

The preponderance of the general interest over all private interests is what constitutes political liberty.

Every power relative to intelligent beings is a power of direction; it exists, and ought to exist, only for the good of the being over whom it is exercised.

The sovereign power is indefeasibly annexed to the body of the nation, because in the sole will of this body dwells that necessary tendency towards the public interest absolutely essential to the directing will of the body politic. *The interest of a people*, says Harrington, *resides only in the whole body of the people.*

 The

The right of watching over his own preservation is inherent in the individual; the right of watching over the collective preservation of those associated is inherent in the body politic.

Wherever the people do not personally enjoy, by virtue of the constitution, the transcendant power of inspecting all parts of the *sovereignty*, there is neither political liberty nor individual security, and by consequence the social aim is totally missed.

Let not the people however attempt to part what is essentially indivisible.

If the will of the representative body, perpetually deranged, were to pass by turns into certain individual wills, under the pretext of uniting the *sum* of all the individual wills, this would be anarchy.

OF THE AGRARIAN LAW.

THE advantage of society requires property to be distinct and sacred; an equality of fortunes cannot subsist: make a new partition, and it will not last the space of a year. The enjoyment of the fruits of my industry belongs to me exclusively; I ought to have the full and entire disposal of them. If my savings and my

acquisitions

acquiſitions are not ſecured to me in the moſt inviolable manner, my emulation is extinguiſhed. Thoſe who have but little have ſtill a right of property, and if the indigent were to attempt to raviſh it, who would not exclaim at the injuſtice? The right of property was the firſt inſtitution of infant ſocieties; and without inequality, no labour, no reproduction, no abundance could exiſt. The political body, deprived of its incitement, would remain ſtagnate, and the earth would withhold her treaſures: an equal and daily repartition would effectually ſtifle induſtry.

The agrarian law propoſed at Rome by the elder Gracchus ſeemed to favour the poor merely by a ſudden augmentation of their number: it could have no general utility. The proſperity of a ſtate being eſſentially connected with the right of property, ought we, for the intereſt of the preſent generation, to ruin that of poſterity? ought we, for an apparent good, to deſtroy the *meum et tuum*, equally founded on nature, juſtice, and reaſon? Labour, induſtry, and perſeverance, make eſſential differences in the lot of thoſe who are placed under equal circumſtances. Men, who are never miſtaken in matters of practice becauſe their ſenſations quickly ſet them aright, have perceived that they would all ſoon be indigent, if each had a right to an equal portion of land: the indolence of ſome, the lethargy and heedleſſneſs of others, the want of talents or of genius, all the vices would ſpeedily confound this equality; and all theſe little proprietors, feeling no want, and ſleeping over their firſt crop, would neglect both their perſon and their property: ſoon would thoſe who ſhould fancy themſelves above want, and who would therefore indulge themſelves in a torpid inactivity, ſink into poverty, and ſhortly into indigence. Happily the good ſenſe which nature has granted to man, preſerves him from carrying into practice the errors of ſpeculation. Every one, ſenſible that he would have ſomething to loſe, has refuſed to give up what might augment the comforts of his exiſtence; he has not yielded to ſo limited a plan, to ſo cold a ſymmetry, to ſuch computed partitions; he has thought it better to take his chance whether proſperous or unfortunate, and to abandon to his perſonal faculties the right of ſatisfying his imperious appetites; he would not renounce even in idea all the enjoyments that fall to the rich; for pleaſure belongs to the moſt aſſiduous labourers, and it is the love of property that begets attention to the cultivation, preſervation, and increaſe of one's possessions. A man destitute of talents is not formed for enjoyment: abolish inequality, you will quickly leave half the lands uncultivated, you will plunge every individual into indolence and torpor. The nerve of public prosperity would be so materially injured, that it would require ages to heal the wound of this delusive equality. But the people themselves have instinctively perceived the error, and have withstood the seduction of a captivating but most false doctrine: none except mad enthusiasts would now venture to preach it up. The people see wealth, foolishly squándered by the prodigal, pass into the hands of the frugal, who better understand how to husband it; they are conscious that the mutual interests of men require opulent families, and such as are otherwise; they are aware that the poor who are industrious, active, and laborious, can alone grow rich, and that, in the meanwhile, they may eat without humiliation the bread which they acquire by their honest occupation; lastly, they feel that the public derives more advantage from a general emulation than it could from the equal division which must annihilate the productive motion of the society.

The rich and poor living together, supply the bustle, the splendour, and the enlivening in-

dustry

dustry which embellish an empire; and as the unequal distribution of wealth is unavoidable, that want which rouses ingenuity and urges to labour, restores to the society all its force, and gives birth to an infinite multitude of arts, which, without inequality, would leave the human mind in its original state of ignorance.

FENELON.

LOUIS XIV. was jealous of Fenelon. The writings of this virtuous man lessened the glory of his victories, of his buildings, and of his sumptuous entertainments. Yet it was not Fenelon that censured his haughty government; it was that cool body which reads in silence, which weighs the actions of kings, and judges them, not by their palaces and their architects, but by the tranquillity and happiness of the country at large. The English who are just estimators, have always honoured Fenelon. Why? Because his Telemachus breathes a sentiment of peace, a wish for the good of mankind, which touches the soul. He directs all the powers of the state to patriotic objects; if his ideas are not profound, they are at least useful. This preceptor of the Duke of Burgundy has divined the ſcience of politics by his own heart; for the heart, as much as the moſt refined underſtanding, is deeply impreſſed with that knowledge, when it is truly animated with the pure flame of humanity.

Fenelon appears throughout an enemy of luxury; he regards every artificial multiplication of our wants as a beginning of depravation which perpetually increaſes. Such is the danger of luxury; it never ſtops, and becomes by little and little an excluſive and diſproportioned taſte. Our natural wants are limited; as ſoon as we paſs theſe limits, the imagination, kindled up, becomes depraved: ſoon do all the vices germinate in us; and Fenelon teaches us that every exceſs of enjoyment, every ſoft and delicate mode of life, corrupts the mind of man.

His opinion is exactly conſonant to mine when he indignantly cenſures all thoſe numberleſs artiſts, wholly occupied on the ſurface of things, on preparing ſuperfluities. The earth would quickly aſſume a different aſpect, he ſays, if we could dry up the ſource of all thoſe artificial operations which are generally ruinous to the people, ſuch as ſtatues, pictures, decorations, proud monuments, &c.; if we could renounce thoſe factitious arts which coſt ſo much time, care, and pains, to the injury of the uſe-

ful

ful and productive arts. We ought to distinguish the simple arts from those complicated ones which, for the few, create, with infinite labour, pleasures that fall not to the share of the general mass. Perhaps the time will come, so ardently desired by Fenelon, when, enlightened by a sound philosophy, every one will gladly exclaim, *How many things can I dispense with!* in such a self-denial consists a real opulence.

It is luxury that destroys all proportion in the distribution of the labours and productions of the earth: this Fenelon has asserted in all his writings; but he mistook the cause, for the word luxury has never been accurately defined. He saw everywhere the many obliged to feed and to amuse the few; his sensibility revolted because he perceived that the most burdensome charges, the severest employments, constantly fell to the lot of the poorest and most laborious men. On whom could he lay the blame of these calamities, when the true fundamental principles of every society ought to consist in the maintenance of moral equality and the security of the natural independence of men? Fenelon felt that the dignity of the human species ought to reside in the perfection of the political laws; he on this basis formed

 his

his famous *novel*. But there is no interval in reaſon between the philoſopher and the true friend of men: either he muſt fully and openly take the part of oppreſſed and degraded humanity against tyrants, or he muſt ſink into an ordinary man, the puſillanimous and unconcerned ſpectator of the calamities of his fellows, and muſt feel not that ſacred fire, that conſoling energy, which dares bid defiance to arrogant and perfidious falſehood, to deſpotic and powerful pride.

Mighty truths are tremendous thunders which overwhelm tyrants. Louis XIV. amidſt all his grandeur, felt the bolt of truth. Happy then was Fenelon, who, inſpired by the genius of reaſon, dared to pay a profound homage to nature and truth; to preach the rights of man, his liberty, and his repoſe; to thunder againſt political ſuperſtitions; to predict the progreſs of reaſon; to announce to poſterity, in the tranſports of a tender philoſophy, calmer days, virtues firmer and more vigorous, men more enlightened, more feeling, and more juſt! Happy age! the great family of men will one day be united, and will thenceforth form but one and the ſame ſociety; then will the code of natural laws be the only authority required to guide the multitude; moral equality will no longer be a problem; relative liberty and individual ſecurity

will

will be eſſentially ſacred to all; and univerſal order will one day be eſtabliſhed, becauſe the ſyſtem of reaſon muſt finally prevail.

Such was the novel of Fenelon, and ſuch, with but a ſhade of difference, was mine *. If the firſt right of man is that of exiſting, the ſecond is that of thinking: the latter is unqueſtionably the moſt grateful; but he who dares to attack the one or the other offends equally againſt nature and reaſon.

I have met in the works of Fenelon, with this curious paſſage of moſt difficult ſolution; "If certain nations could not be brought to a ſort of civilization but by giving them ſome ſuperſtitious ideas, ought we to heſitate? I think not."

All the excellent writings which at preſent reflect honour on France have been anathematized by the prieſts, or condemned to be burnt by the hands of the hangman, as if deſpotiſm had hoped in their flames (to uſe the expreſſion of Tacitus) to ſtifle the cry of ages, and to extinguiſh the conſciouſneſs of the human race. The author of Telemachus was perſecuted, and his book long underwent the ſevereſt prohibitions.

* See my year 2440.

CATO OF UTICA.

HE was a perſonage much more accompliſhed than Cato the cenſor, his grand-uncle; his manner of life was ſimple, his occupation the ſervice of his country; juſtice is not purer in its ſanctuary than it was in his heart; his virtue was neither cynical, nor invidious, nor arrogant; never led away by friendſhip or by enmity, he loved above all truth and the republic, and bore no hatred to men, but only to the diſorders which ſapped the conſtitution of the ſtate.

Cato, at the age of fourteen, was frequently carried by his governor to the houſe of Sylla: he there witneſſed the tyranny exerciſed over the citizens. Why, ſaid he to Sarpedon, don't they kill this tyrant? Becauſe, rejoined his governor, they fear him ſtill more than they hate him. Then give me a ſword, replied he; I do not fear him.

The ſun is not more conſtant in his courſe than was Cato in that line of conduct which he had embraced from reflection. Little anxious about what is commonly ſtyled glory, he was captivated with that particular fame alone which accompanies the ſtrict diſcharge of duty; he ſought

ſought to render to his country ſolid rather than brilliant ſervices. He entered on the ſcene of war to become acquainted with it, and after having, in a diſtinguiſhed manner, commanded a legion, he forſook the trade of arms, perhaps to the misfortune of the republic. From his youth, he acted up to the principles ſuited to the force and vigour of his mind; he went always with his head bare, early inured to the heat of ſummer and the cold of winter; he travelled only on foot, beſide his friends on horſeback, while his domeſtics followed him mounted; he had no deſire for riches, and was generous and liberal to ſuch a degree, that having ſucceeded to a valuable inheritance, he converted it into money, which he lent to thoſe of his friends who needed it.

The purity of his morals was the more remarkable, ſince he lived in an age when corruption was general, and in a manner faſhionable.

After he had attained the years required to be quæſtor, he ſolicited that office, but not until he had carefully ſtudied the laws and ordinances of the poſt he was to fill. The young Romans, who ſubmitted to that charge only as a ſtep to ſubſequent advancement, ignorant of the preſcribed

ſcribed regulations of finance, left the diſcharge of their function to regiſters or commiſſaries. Malverſation was there enthroned. Cato reformed abuſes, puniſhed frauds and falſehoods, and rendered the charge of the treaſury as reſpectable as was that of the ſenate; he was ſaid to have transferred the dignity of the conſulate to the office of quæſtor.

As quæſtor, he brought to juſtice the aſſaſſins yet remaining whom Sylla had employed in his laſt proſcription; and confining himſelf to the object of his charge, he required them to reſtore to the treaſury what had been paid to them by orders from that treaſury as the reward of their murders. Some of them had touched to the amount of two thouſand crowns for their bloody ſervices. Of theſe ſums he commanded the reſtitution, and the ruffians, impeached immediately after for murder, and convicted by the firſt ſentence, received the puniſhment due to their crimes. The profoundneſs of this ſtroke of policy is ſufficient to immortalize him.

Having been admitted into the order of ſenators, he pleaded againſt Claudius, who had calumniated the veſtal virgins, and had, by his accuſation, endangered the life of Terentia, the ſiſter-in-law of Cicero; he covered the accuſer

with

with confuſion, and obtained an order to baniſh him a while from the city. Cicero thanked the patriot: you miſtake me, replied Cato, thank the city, I had it only in view.

REFRACTORY CLERGY.

WHAT then is this fictitious being whoſe exiſtence, reaſon, philoſophy, and time even, ſeemed to have undermined. Nay! it rears an audacious and rebellious head!

Deſpotiſm, diſguiſed for fourteen centuries under the name of monarchy, has fallen into non-exiſtence by the voice of the nation; the privileged order which embraced a rank of noxious feudality, and which pretended to be interwoven with the national eſſence, has vaniſhed like a ſhadow; and when the law has declared the general will not to annihilate the prieſthood but to modify it, the clergy have with united force ſummoned up a reſiſtance which neither the king, nor the nobility, nor the ancient bodies of judicature have ever dared to plan: and the love of ſo much uſurped riches has ſtruggled more obſtinately than the delirium of pride.

What

What then is this phantom, which with one hand pointing to heaven and the other to hell, rules the earth with a look or a word? The clergy entwine their own cauſe with that of religion, which they pretend is wounded by the blows directed againſt its miniſters; hence the ardour of that body to promote ſedition, to profit by the fear natural to the heart of man, and to corrupt in him the awe inſpired by the preſence of divine majeſty; that religious awe, which begets adoration, and which is a virtue in an intelligent being conſcious of his unworthineſs. The prieſts have marred human nature, and ſubſtituting themſelves to God, the only worthy object of our homage, they have depreſſed the mind of man, inſtead of raiſing it on the wings of love and of confidence. Theſe prieſts, theſe unnatural men, who have no country, no ſocial laws, no ties of blood, no humanity, nothing, in ſhort, but their intereſt, ſacrifice to a papal idol only to ſhow the *nec plus ultra* of inſolent impoſture and audacious madneſs: they abuſe the moſt ſacred names only to diſguiſe the vile convulſions of avarice. Thus the centaur who raviſhed the comely Dejanira, pierced by an avenging arrow, bellowed with pain, and ſtaining with his impure blood the innocent beauty whom he embraced, roared in agony

that

that ſhe was ſlain. No, monſtrous impoſtor! Dejanira is always beautiful, always alive; religion ſtill remains untouched in ſpite of the rude graſps of prieſts. The centaur may expiate his crimes, the clergy loſe their mitres, but the adoration of the ſupreme Being ſtill lives unabated in the heart of man, and the tie which binds him to the divinity is equally ſtrong, equally cloſe.

The refractory clergy will, if they can, kindle up the flames of civil war to recover their exceſſive opulence; let our country periſh, they will ſay, it will be better than that we ſhould return to the rule of the apoſtles, to the morality which they have taught. Here, by perfidious and ſacrilegious inſinuations, they will ſeparate the wife from the huſband, the ſon from the father; there, they will diſturb the laſt moments of the dying man; they will cloſe the grave over the corpſe, and will wiſh to light up in the other world the fires they have been ſo eager to kindle in this. Such is the genius of the wicked prieſts who deplore the revenue of the altars, thoſe ancient offerings of ignorance and fear, and the immenſe treaſures extorted from families by a thouſand fraudulent means, or which have at leaſt been ſhamefully ſtyled ſacred property. Baneful prieſts! alas, you have corrupted what was moſt holy in the world, Chriſtian morality. *Corruptio optimi peſſima.*

How can prieſts preſumptuouſly ſeek to form an *order* in the *aſſemblies of our ſtates*; they, whoſe kingdom, by their own confeſſion, is not of this world!

ON THE TRANSACTIONS OF THE TWENTIETH OF JUNE, THE FOURTH YEAR OF LIBERTY.

IT has always been eaſy for the enemies of liberty and equality to calumniate the people, more eſpecially when the latter had not even dreamt of meriting the calumnies of the next day. The malignity of the court is known; it ſmiles, then reſumes its natural ferocity. What has not been ſaid againſt the people! Yes! on the 20th of June they were calm and well intentioned. Why is the houſe of the prince not always open to the people? Why, if he refuſes to communicate with them, ſhould the people not go to preſent their requeſts?

Let us ſuffer the *Calot* * of hiſtory to paint Louis XVI. with the *red cap* on his head,

* Calot was a celebrated French painter and engraver.

tippling prettily *to the health of the nation,* and on the morrow causing a *prosecution* to be commenced for a few panes of glass broken and *a silver chamber-pot stolen,* the whole to excite the pity of foreign powers; and commanding the promulgation of that false and unconstitutional proclamation which was a real declaration of war against the people. Ah! if, in the *name of the king,* the musketry could have been discharged against the citizens carrying *pikes!* What a happy day for the palace of the Tuileries! But the magistrate chose not to display the *red flag* for a *red cap,* because he saw that the plot went to assassinate the people, and recollected perhaps the joy of the bailiff in the comedy who called out: *Do give me a blow or two, I beseech you, for I have four children to maintain.*

Impartial history will give this procession to the palace the appellation of a civic *festival,* and will repeat this *bon mot* of Peter Manuel: *Never were there fewer thieves in the Tuileries; for all the courtiers had betaken themselves to flight.*

Let us suffer the calumniators of the people to gain a few crowns from the *civil list;* the language of slavery is familiar to them. The people, generous in the extreme, despise, forget, and pardon them.

I shall

I ſhall make a few reflections on *that day.* The policy which conſiſts in ſhedding blood is a very ſhort ſighted policy indeed: it was that of Breteuil, of Calonne, of Conde, and of d'Artois; but ſhould we not alſo have in our view a juſtifiable reſiſtance? And did not the ſage Petion plainly ſave, on that day, the palace of the Tuileries? For the gentleſt people on earth would have wreaked their juſt vengeance for a maſſacre *in the name of the king*.

It may be held a general rule, that when the majority of the people aſſemble, it is very rare indeed that they are not influenced by the moſt excuſable of motives. It is the preponderating ſum of all the perſonal intereſts united that neceſſarily impels every man to an enterpriſe which is executed as ſoon as conceived: and as the general good is and muſt be compoſed of the greateſt number of private benefits, ſuch a criſis requires the material poſſeſſion of certain rights, effaced or forgotten, but which muſt always be renewed when claimed by the majority. During ſuch a criſis, plain good ſenſe needs only to be conſulted for the ſpirit of the ſocial regulations. As the legiſlator could never foreſee all, he ought never to give to this ſpirit a *cruel* interpretation. All exceſs of juſtice becomes injuſtice, and circumſtances ſhould rec-

tify

tify the law, when there is a poſitive evidence of equity or of public utility.

When the principles of equity and benevolence are applied to the laws, when attention is paid to the relations of ſocial life, the art of governing men is attained. The vulgar know the laws only by their immediate effect, and the people are ſeldom miſtaken with regard to their utility. The practice of conſulting the public voice will become one of the great ſprings of government; the people redouble their patriotiſm and zeal when they are honoured, and conſequently when they are honourable in their own eyes.

A way to make good laws in extreme unforeſeen caſes, is to aſk in one's own mind; *if the public had its choice, would it confirm ſuch a ſtatute or ſuch a law?* This queſtion would reſolve in a ſimple manner a multitude of political and civil problems apparently very difficult.

It is expedient to eſtabliſh an invariable principle to which all the others ſhould refer, and this is the principle which we never ceaſe to repeat, *public utility.*

The laſt appeal of the laws ought to be to common ſenſe. Liberty conſiſts in the enjoyment of individual independence as far as its reſtriction is not indiſpenſibly neceſſary to the ſupport of the ſociety in general. If this definition be a good one, as I believe it to be, admitting that the individual liberty of the king was for *a moment* violated, ought he to have attacked the independence of every individual, and the fate of the empire, merely to interrupt *a civic feſtival?* The mayor of Paris therefore acted in obedience to true principles, for the *law* muſt not *ſlay* us. Let thoſe who adore an idol of fleſh be the ſlaves of their baſe thoughts; let them be the conſtant enemies of humanity: the Petions and the Manuels, and all thoſe who will tread in their ſteps, will be its reſpectable defenders. Hiſtory will blaſt their unreaſonable and cruel adverſaries.

LAWYERS.

DOES it appear credible, and yet the fact is true, that certain lawyers, with heads on their ſhoulders like other men, have puſhed fanaticiſm ſo far as to ſtart a queſtion whether the Emperor of Germany is not the natural ſovereign of the world? Bartholus, by way of adding to this abſurdity, conſiders as heretics all thoſe who dare to doubt that ſuch is the

caſe.

caſe. In *books*, and more eſpecially in thoſe of lawyers, we meet with *every thing*.

BLINDNESS.

IT is impoſſible to account for that blind attachment of people to their ſovereigns, who often wrong them, or ſeem very little diſpoſed to benefit them, unleſs it be from the confuſed idea of the riches and power which encircle thrones. To this involuntary reſpect for the ſplendour of monarchy, is added the antiquity of poſſeſſion, which nouriſhes a ſort of ſuperſtitious adherence in ſubjects, in ſpite of the neglect or injuſtice which they experience. Nations always preſume that their heads cannot be their enemies; they behold theſe chiefs drowned in ſenſual delights, and cannot imagine them to be cruel. It is only the moſt outrageous tyranny that can undeceive them, and ſhow theſe crowned men to be unfeeling or ungrateful beings who abuſe their tenderneſs and docility.

The king of the French conſtitution has conſtantly appeared its moſt unreaſonable enemy. Yet his numerous *political faults*, not to ſay more, have been all pardoned. Why? Merely becauſe he bears the name of *king*; it is a magical name which works like enchantment upon the brain of mortals. It is needleſs to trace the obſcure moral cauſes of this kind of ſuperſtition, when the facts are ſo clear in point. Words have governed, and ſtill will long govern men. Poor humanity!

A nation will not complain without having the moſt ſerious grievances. Naturally patient and forgiving, the people love kings, and never proceed to violence but in the laſt extremities. Force is then the only remedy againſt force, and every citizen is obliged to aid his country in reſiſting deſpotiſm, elſe he is guilty of treaſon.

We ſtand in need of our own thoughts, and not of thoſe of others; but thought is the work of God, why then ſhould I ſtop its courſe? Since the unalterable and indeſtructible principle which conſtitutes us, is the ſame with that of the divinity, all men are by nature *prophets*, and their vices alone hinder them from diſplaying their privileges.

Political ſcience is a ſimple matter, it conſiſts in diſtinguiſhing what is pure from what is impure. The ambitious and the wicked have an intereſt in involving it in intricacy, and in preventing things from being ſeen in a ſimple manner.

manner. Yes, the ſcience of politics is ſo ſimple, that in this age men can hardly venture to ſuſpect it.

DOUBTS.

MAN is made to govern and to be governed: and over the various combinations of governments chance preſides. The variety of theſe plans cannot but be infinite; and accordingly we find that each country has its government, differing from that of every other country, at the ſame time that it does not preſerve the ſame conſtitutional form for thirty years together. Here, the ſupreme authority is concentrated in the hands of a ſingle perſon, who, with the help of time, has uſurped the abſolute right of preſcribing laws and of cauſing them to be executed. There, this right is reſtricted, and belongs to a legiſlative ſenate, the conduct of which is ſubject to the inveſtigation of a few men who, under the denomination of the executive power, act as a counterpoiſe to its power. Elſewhere, the legiſlative authority is entirely confided to a few; while in other ſtates it is in a greater or leſs degree partaken by the many.

In a multitude of circumſtances all theſe governments have a ſurpriſing conformity: for example, there is no one in which this is not a principle,—*that the ſafety of the ruling power is the ſupreme law.* If we conſult the great book of hiſtory and the experience of ages, we ſhall perceive that the difference of governments is far more apparent than real, a circumſtance which does not, however, prevent very different effects reſulting from them, both with reſpect to external ſecurity and the internal happineſs of the ſocieties. It is, notwithſtanding, equally true that the ſafety of the people being every where the ſupreme law, and that for the moſt ſimple reaſon in the world, namely, that in the people the ſupreme power reſides, and is employed by them in the natural way which human reaſon dictates, deſpotiſm itſelf has ſeldom been able to eſtabliſh any other beſides laws equally favourable to the ſafety of all. This is ſo true, that there are ſtates where in reality the weight of the deſpotiſm falls on certain grandees alone, leaving the people tranquil and unmoleſted: if governments were to be appreciated rather by their *effects* than their *principles*, the theory would unqueſtionably be altogether changed.

Without public knowledge no government can

can make any progreſs: it very frequently happens that the government ſtill remains imperfect, becauſe the people either ſleep or are accuſtomed to the yoke; and this is the reaſon why the freedom of the preſs will invariably be the true thermometer of political liberty. It founds the ſecurity of the nation by which it is eſtabliſhed; and affords to each citizen the means of carrying before the tribunal of the public each erroneous deciſion, enabling him to fix the ſcandal of an iniquitous action on its real author or authors: no nation that is zealous to preſerve the freedom of the preſs can ever be ſubjugated.

The French government, utterly deſtroyed in 1789, bore no ſmall reſemblance to that of Morocco; and this I prove thus. In Morocco, the legiſlative and executive authorities entirely belong to the prince: accordingly he either makes laws or aboliſhes them, extends them or reſtricts them, ſuſpends them or enforces them, as it ſeems meet to his pride, his caprice, or his paſſions. In his royal head alone all the laws are written: the royal underſtanding is the author of them, their commentator, and their depoſitory; and ſometimes the prince, with his royal ſcimetar, amuſes himſelf by executing them himſelf, which is what the king of France certainly did not do, but he had janiſſaries and baſtiles for that purpoſe.

The king of France required armed guards and unarmed ſubjects.

It is, however, at the ſame time not to be doubted but that the worſt of adminiſtrations is preferable to no adminiſtration at all. Any government whatever has an advantage over anarchy; and it is better to have a murderer on the throne, as at Morocco, than to riſk the meeting of a deſpot at the corner of every ſtreet.

ROMULUS.

WE cannot enough admire the policy of Romulus. Happily that barbarian knew not the Greeks, nor the ancients in general, and perceived how dangerous it was to ſuffer the independance of the prieſthood on the ſtate, and to detach it from the political and ſecular power. He ſucceeded in his firſt attempt. Romulus alone, of all the profane legiſlators, diſcovered the true mixture of military and religious duties. He ſeparated royalty and prieſthood, and deſtroyed that immenſe fund of attributes and credit, as well as thoſe political, civil, and ſacred

qualities

qualities which the priefts of antiquity united in their perfons. Romulus created himfelf high-prieft in a growing ftate, which the divifion of the hierarchy and empire would have too much weakened. By this expedient he prevented the Roman mythology from multiplying without end, like the Grecian.

The office of high-prieft, the privileges of the altar, the auguries, the aufpices, and all the ceremonies of religion, were directed by a philofophical fpirit, being entrufted to grave perfonages, fincerely attached to the republic, to men of experience. Thus was religion liable to no interpretations contrary to the intereft of the ftate.

The Romans having confounded the hierarchy with the empire, the ftate was freed from that perpetual difcord between the two powers which has fo much haraffed other nations: fubtle and dangerous queftions were banifhed; the confuls, occupied with their civil functions and with war, were not apt to lofe themfelves in the ftudy of theological controverfies. The interefts of the confuls and of the heads of religion were the fame; and the people knew neither fanaticifm nor irreligion, but followed implicitly the cuftoms of their anceftors. The Romans were never feen to make the porticos and baths reſound with a multitude of vain diſcuſſions, as did the Greeks when they diſputed on the immortality of the ſoul. And moral controverſies were a diſtemper unheard of at Rome. Cicero, in diſcuſſing as a philoſopher the advantages of his nation, commends the Romans on the article of religion, which contributed much to their victories, by baniſhing all frivolous diſputes, the firſt ſeeds of incredulity: for we may infer the felicity of a nation from the rank which its prieſts occupy; every thing flows from this. Religious polity rigidly circumſcribed is the firſt token of public tranquillity.

INDIVIDUAL LIBERTY.

BY the laws of equilibrium we are enabled to ſupport a weight of about thirty-one thouſand pounds, well diſtributed over the whole ſurface of our body; and we cannot ſtir without raiſing this enormous weight. Thus, environed by a multitude of laws, that which ſecures to us *individual liberty* is the counterpoiſe of all the others; and without it we ſhould be every inſtant cruſhed.

PORTRAIT

PORTRAIT OF CHOISEUL.

RICHELIEU depreſſed the grandees to elevate the throne on which he himſelf was in reality ſeated, while the people were kept amuſed by the ſight of a royal phantom. His vigorous and conſiſtent policy curbed each haraſſing pretenſion of the nobility: the blood-ſtained hatchet of the executioners warned the *titled lords* and factious judges, that they were ſoon to expect an abſolute maſter who would ſilence both the importunate laws and the puerile declamations of the parliamentary magiſtracy. Richelieu made the intereſts of the kingdom his own: her enemies were his; and the glory of France was the conſtant object of all his toils. Throughout Europe the nation was reſpected, even by the monarchs who bowed to her yoke.

The dangerous Choiſeul did preciſely the contrary of all this. He made himſelf the king of the grandees, flattered them to be flattered by them, and allowed each of them to exerciſe the moſt abſolute deſpotiſm, which ſoon found its way into each department, and from thence into every part of the adminiſtration. Choiſeul tolerated, I ſay, all theſe concealed and ſubordi-

nate

nate tyrannies, provided they finally met and concentrated in his own.

This may be confidered as the language he held out to the grandees. I have made the king, who dreads me, fubordinate to you; to preferve your power you muft in your turn fubmit to me. I fhall exercife a co-partnerfhip of authority, which you may be affured you fhall inherit under me. We will all of us govern together; we will be fo many kings, and I will be the chief.

Each courtier relifhed the treaty, and co-operated effectually towards the nullity of the monarch, who had fimply the power of nominating to the ranks, pofts, and employments, which the grandees enjoyed to the exclufion of all who were not noble. Thus did Choifeul mufter around him all the paffions that corrupt; and in this way did he form that fyftem of a haughty and devouring ariftocracy, which, after having collected in one centre every vice and every encroachment that avarice and pride could fuggeft, was to make an immenfe fpace between itfelf and the people.

From that moment Choifeul ordered the courtiers, thofe political giants rotten with corruption, to feize on the four or five departments of the miniftry, and all the employments of the empire,

empire, undermining by every possible expedient the glory and the power of the monarch. While Richelieu was careful to humble all those among the haughty chiefs of the aristocracy who entered into a competition with the throne, Choiseul elevated them, not without a view of his own, and taught them to laugh at the idol, while, like the priests of old, they were eating the largest and best part of what was offered to it. Perhaps in France no man ever did so much mischief as Choiseul: he certainly of all others entertained the highest contempt for the people; and he considered as a strong evidence of genius the facility with which he took advantage of their torpor and passiveness.

It may easily be conceived that the grandees consented without difficulty to reign under him, because, when an employment fell to the disposal of any one of them, he exercised the same authority in his own particular district. An anecdote is recorded that the courtiers deserted the king's card parties, to rendezvous at the house of Choiseul, or at that of the duchess, sister to the minister, who, not having been able to subjugate Louis XV. subdued the master of the monarch. From that time the courtiers formed a determination to remain inviolably attached to the royal treasury, to help to fill it for themselves,

themſelves, and to accompany the king in his hunting parties merely to hunt for themſelves whatever ſhould fall vacant.

This character, by turns vile and audacious, governed by a woman who had entrapped the miniſter, juſt as the latter had *harpooned* his maſter, found his ruin accompliſhed by a little girl, by the king's new miſtreſs, to whom he refuſed the homage he had laviſhed on others. By this inadvertency he was loſt. It would appear that one meanneſs more would not have been ſo great a ſacrifice to him: he had attached himſelf to Madame Pompadour to betray her intereſt; but towards Madame du Barry he was lofty and diſdainful. As it frequently happens, this ambitious miniſter then made the falſeſt of all calculations.

To Choiſeul we are indebted for Marie Antoinette; and it is to be obſerved here that he deſtined for the father the princeſs he beſtowed on the ſon.

The nobles beheld with a ſecret ſatisfaction one of themſelves exerciſing this all-puiſſance, from which they drew immenſe advantages. Choiſeul connected himſelf with the peerage by inclination, with the magiſtracy by dread: but he employed the parliaments juſt as we make uſe of the pawns at a game of cheſs.

The

The gentlemen of the long robe were far from ſuſpecting this artifice; their pride and their pedantry made them view the matter in a ſerious light. After much diſſimulation, Choiſeul cauſed a declaration to be made, that *the parliament of Paris was eſſentially and primitively the court of the king and peers.* His motive for this was founded on his being himſelf a peer of the realm: he thus depreſſed and humbled the other parliaments, which were ſomewhat inconvenient to him, and with the ſame blow formed for himſelf a rampart againſt the authority of the maſter, provided the latter ſhould one day open his eyes. In making uſe of the expreſſion the *maſter*, in this place, I employ the language of courtiers. In this new court, *the court of the peers*, Conty, a prince of the blood, was heard to exclaim from iron lungs, that *the people were from their very nature taxable and corvéable* *. This exclamation, at which humanity was outraged, was merely an echo of the iniquitous and favourite maxim of Choiſeul: ah! could the arch-fiend himſelf have employed more infernal terms in the pandemonium of Milton.

* The *corvées* were perſonal ſervices *required* of the peaſants, &c. for the making and repairing of the highways.

Finding

Finding himſelf the real king of France, Choiſeul did not manifeſt ſuch a loftineſs of ideas as might have been expected: he conceived the deſign of becoming the miniſter of a foreign power, and for that purpoſe connected himſelf with, or rather entirely ſubmitted to, Auſtria, rendering himſelf the paſſive executor of her will. Vienna was deſtitute of finances; he remitted thither thoſe of France, and was alſo at the ſame time deſirous of becoming the miniſter of the court of Ruſſia. He was guilty, however, of the very fault there which loſt him with Madame du Barry: he took offence at an idle ceremonial, and alienated the affections of that court. Our political intereſts long felt the effects of this accident; and ſince that time the cabinet of St. Peterſbourg nouriſhed a ſecret deſire of revenge and repriſals on ours. This renunciation on the part of Choiſeul to the houſe of Auſtria utterly prevented him from appreciating the extent of the ſacrifices he made to his idol.

He unqueſtionably did not perceive how burthenſome the perfidious alliance of this houſe of Auſtria was to the nation: but the ruin of France was of little import to him; he was fearful of loſing his place, and therefore made the cabinet of Verſailles ſubject to the cabinet of

 Vienna,

Vienna, which would no longer allow in the miniſtry any other beſides men perfectly devoted to its intereſts. Then it was that Choiſeul gave his approbation to the treaty of Cardinal de Bernis, which treaty he rendered ſtill more burthenſome to France: he was in reality the author of that unfortunate *family compact*, which ſunk in Europe the political credit, and more eſpecially the conſideration annexed to the power of France. Alas! why were her intereſts ſacrificed to ſuch a degree? Becauſe this Miniſter was deſirous ſo to connect himſelf with the throne, as that no earthly power ſhould ſever him from it. It was with the ſame view that he protected the *crown of Spain*, which through an intereſted weakneſs he put on a footing with that of France. Thus was he the miniſter of Louis XV. merely to ſerve the other powers.

At the ſame time that he humbled himſelf before Spain, he was able to comprehend neither the genius nor the aſcendency of the King of Pruſſia: he was utterly averſe to England, becauſe a free government; and it may be ſaid with juſtice that he was the enemy of whatever was great.

It is known that he refuſed the propoſitions of Mr. Pitt, in 1761, relative to peace. His idle vanity led him to think that it would be derogatory to treat with a government in the ſtructure of which the *republican* form was blended: all his gaſconadings, however, did not prevent the Engliſh from ſhortly impoſing on us conditions more galling and ſevere than the preceding ones. His menaces were vain; and in the iſſue he gave up the part of Louiſiana which ſtill remained ours. All this was done to ſatisfy the caprice of a king of Spain; and he thus ſacrificed, in a moſt daſtardly way, the fineſt territory in North America.

What an enterprize was the eſtabliſhment of Cayenne! This trivial occurrence will in the page of hiſtory blend all the horrors of guilt and robbery with all the ridicule attached to ignorance and preſumptuous incapacity.

If it is Choiſeul who planted in the American colonies the germe which has ſince developed itſelf, we almoſt owe him thanks; ſince the example of theſe ſtates has ſerved to awaken our courage: but Choiſeul, who ſaw nothing in the world except a *league of kings*, provided theſe kings were to be the *mannakins* of their miniſters, favoured the liberty of France without knowing that he did ſo, and certainly without foreſeeing ſuch a reſult.

It was invariably the caſe that with immenſe

means he encompaſſed very ſmall ends, and all theſe means were ſubordinate to Vienna : provided Vienna was content, every other object was to him a matter of indifference. But the Engliſh muſt needs be combated, becauſe he could neither ſway them to his will, nor make them ſubſervient to his perſonal ambition : the numerous affronts we then received originated in him, and in that criminal coalition with the foreign powers, which, while Choiſeul affected to be apprehenſive of their menaces, exhauſted our treaſury of its gold and ſilver. How did he uſurp the title of ſtateſman, ſeeing that he did nothing that was great nor even rational ? It was by having creatures whom he enriched ; and as he laviſhed on them the public treaſures, they repaid him by unceaſing eulogies in the ſaloons of the capital.

He ſubdued Corſica ! it will require a long time to find out what this conqueſt could ever return for all it had coſt. He at the ſame time entertained a hankering after Switzerland ; but a ſmall inconſiderable Canton reſiſted ſucceſsfully all his efforts, and he was as much foiled there as he was by the Genoeſe populace.

Let me again aſk what he did ? He made himſelf *king of the nobility* ; and ſheltered himſelf under the protecting wing of Auſtria againſt

 the

the monarch himſelf: for an endeavour to lead him into a maritime war, which his blind hatred of the Engliſh ſuggeſted to him, he was diſgraced and exiled. During his exile however, as he had long been maſter of the *poſts* and *police*, in the latter of which departments, and at its head, he had ſtationed his valets, *Sartine* and *Le Noir*, two names to be for ever execrated, theſe ſlaves ſupplied him with all the ſecrets of the ſtate, inſomuch that by the intrigues he ſet on foot he was very near being recalled. It is to be obſerved that this baniſhment of his wrought no change in his innate fondneſs for deſpotiſm, which he conſidered as the only ſpring a ſtateſman ought to employ.

Shortly after, Madame Pompadour died, the preſumptive heir of the throne died, his own wife died, the queen died, and thoſe he did not love died alſo. Throughout Europe the reputation of Choiſeul was tarniſhed, but he turned a deaf ear to every ſcandal, which he was at no pains whatever to wipe away. The writers who after his deceaſe made out an inventory of all his *goods* and *chattels*, paid no attention whatever to his ancient renown, notwithſtanding his bounties enabled ſeveral of them to amaſs princely fortunes: his laurels were blaſted; but it will require ſome time to develop the hiſtori-

cal

cal facts respecting him which are still hid in a great degree of obscurity.

Had Choiseul lived he would undoubtedly have been the greatest enemy to liberty: he would have bestowed whole provinces on foreigners, provided the royal mannekin should be all-puissant, and he should be allowed to direct in the sequel, as was both reasonable and just, the said mannekin.

When public utility is reckoned as *every thing* the government is good; when it is esteemed as *nothing*, the government is bad. Choiseul gave efficiency to the supreme power merely to favour a small number of individuals distinguished by their birth or by their riches.

It is a curious speculation at this time to observe how *all the powers* were united in *the same person.* The Minister considering his master as a dolt, put himself in his place without any ceremony: the king, obedient with no other view than that of having more leisure for his pleasures, was careful at the same time to have his share of *rich royalty.* For example, Louis XV. after having *leased out* the farms as king, reserved to himself certain rights in them as a private individual. Choiseul found no difficulty in consenting to this, because he studied by every possible means to degrade the sovereign.

He was desirous that the genealogists should prevail over the philosophers; and propagated the illusion of the greater part of the nobles, which consisted in a belief that nobility in them was a natural character. In the time of Choiseul, the nobles therefore were not the slaves, but on the other hand the masters of despotism; since by a few falsehoods, a few reverences, and a few humiliations, they obtained ranks, posts, and employments, the lucrative salaries annexed to which constantly formed their basis, and which required no other task than that of flattering the master somewhat more expressively.

It must be confessed that Choiseul scarcely ever, in *his own name*, unbarred the doors of the royal prisons, citadels, and bastiles, for the admission of state criminals: he, however, abandoned these subordinate functions to the lieutenants of police and other ministers. As the nobles of his own party escaped the vengeful blow, he did not consider the imprisonment of the others as a crime. With money this minister commanded every thing, and knew of no other besides pecuniary recompenses.

Voltaire, dreading at Ferney the assaults of royal and sacerdotal despotism, knew how to sooth the despotism of the minister. As Louis XV, however, read sometimes, he one day found himſelf abuſed in a *pamphlet:* in addreſſing Voltaire, Choiſeul confined himſelf to two words—*be ſilent, you old fool.* Voltaire only eſcaped the baſtile becauſe he was conſidered as a *nobleman.*

Our miniſter had an adverſary in the duke d'Aguillon, who certainly of the two had the greateſt ſhare of talents, and who was repeatedly on the point of accompliſhing his ruin. D'Aguillon, ſervilely attached to his ſovereign, would no more than the other have concurred towards the liberty of the nation; but he would have been ſomewhat more adroit in his deſpotiſm. La Chalotais, the unhappy victim of their contentions, was indebted for life merely to the averſion of the former to the latter.

Choiſeul's beds of juſtice, thoſe of Meaupou, and thoſe of Laménie —— d'Aguillon would as well as the others have had his beds of juſtice, for every miniſter under the old regimen held them to be indiſpenſable. Ah! was not an attempt made to introduce them even into the national aſſemblies?

But the greateſt reproach to Choiſeul's memory, is that he neglected to give efficiency to the national force. Ours was embarraſſed under his adminiſtration by a formidable number of paraſitical members under the denomination of

 officers;

officers; and hence arose the prostitution of command which gave rise to so many colonels and superfluous officers.

The officers have ever since imagined that the soldiers were their property; and this laid the foundation for a treatment both impolitic and bad. Each war minister was determined to have a *military ordonnance* promulged in his name.

To Choiseul we are indebted for that aristocracy which preyed on the kingdom. What could be more absurd than the swarm of young colonels of his creation, so cruel and imperious to the soldiery, such rigid partizans of blows inflicted with the sabre, and who have been since termed the *framers of ordonnances*.

A dexterous policy is a true mechanician: it removes heavy loads with slight machines, insomuch that a great effect is perceived without the cause being divined. Choiseul invariably made great efforts to accomplish little aims; he sold France to pacify her, and converted her into a granary for all Europe: among the surrounding nations he had therefore the name of a great minister. Thus had he a centre foreign to his own country; and from hence other views, other plans of ambition, and other interests besides the universality of the French. Choiseul considered the cabinet at the head of

which

which he was ſeated as all France, and he parcelled out that domain to pleaſe crowned heads: it never once occurred to him that the firſt duty of a monarch was to convert every thing to the advantage of his people. Let us be no longer aſtoniſhed if the nobles beſtow on Choiſeul their remembrance and their regret, diſcovering abſurdity in every plan contradictory to his;—if, when they are told that, rigorouſly ſpeaking, it is of no importance to the conſtitution that the authority ſhould be placed in the hands of a ſingle perſon, and that the whole conſiſts in its execution being inſeparable from the law, they refuſe to comprehend you: they were accuſtomed to have as a king one of their equals, and as a banker a monarch ſqueezing the people for their profit. Oh! the good time! could any government be better calculated for the nobles! and if they dare not all at once call for its reeſtabliſhment, they at leaſt make every effort to prevent there being either laws or people: the nobles with them are to be every thing; for how can we comprehend a government without nobility?

An adroit polity is diametrically oppoſite to that which allows inſincerity and ſcandalous fineſſes of every deſcription; degrading artifices that are within the reach of every man of a

common

common underſtanding. Poiſon, deception, and treachery, are falſe traits of a political character: the true ones are ſtamped by a genius able to conduct and combine, and whoſe enterpriſes are great and well-concerted, while he poſſeſſes the ſtrength and elevation of ſoul neceſſary to great deſigns. Can we by theſe traits recognize Choiſeul, he who knew alone how to intrigue, or to ſacrifice in its ſtead the deareſt intereſts of France; while a true policy conſiſts in coming at the means of giving to the ſurrounding ſtates an appropriate form and natural limits, thus rendering them, by the juſt relation which enſues, the ſupport of the ſtate with the direction of which the miniſter is charged?

A ſubtle, cloſe, and ambitious man is conſidered by the vulgar as well ſkilled in polity, at the ſame time that theſe traits denote a little genius. My politician has an almoſt inexhauſtible fund of great reſources, and is neither elevated by good, nor depreſſed by bad fortune: with a glance he calculates preciſely the degrees of obſtacle and poſſibility; he knows the ſeaſons when he ought either to conceal or publiſh his views, to act with precaution or to proceed with a bold and firm ſtep: he underſtands above all how to direct with a ſkilful hand the ſprings neceſſary to his operations, and is convinced that

the

the moſt ſublime political ſyſtems are nothing more than the execution of the ſimpleſt principles. Laſtly, the moſt eſſential object of policy is the general and particular knowledge of characters, by the help of which the miniſter converts men into his inſtruments. It is difficult to apply to Choiſeul any one of theſe rare attainments.

One of the maxims of policy is to maſk a deſign by contrary appearances: this is a ſtratagem which may be ſeen through; and therefore every plan in politics ought to be entirely concealed, ſince a quick, impetuous, and deciſive ſentiment is preciſely the contraſt of a phlegmatic policy. Now, there never was a miniſter more heedleſs than Choiſeul, at the ſame time that he never underſtood, ſudden as he was in his reſolutions, to ſtrike a great ſtroke. This proves that while many ſet up for politicians few are fitted for the taſk in which they engage.

If it were poſſible for me to reſtore Choiſeul to life, I would addreſs him thus: "Even although all thoſe you called ſubjects ſhould conſent to eſtabliſh and ſupport the moſt abſolute and moſt deſpotical authority, it would not on that account be the more lawful, ſeeing that men cannot renounce, either for themſelves or for their

their defcendants, the eternal laws which pro-fcribe tyranny."

Let nobles regret Choifeul, and endeavour to give him the ftamp of a great man; they have their reafons: but he will never be fuch in the eyes of the impartial judge. I confider the panegyrifts of Choifeul as the warm partizans of public depredations: the French nation has too grievous complaints againft the nobles to confider them otherwife than as the moft determined enemies of its rights and its liberty. They have armed their odious privileges againft the country; they exhaufted the ftate treafury, and the people were condemned to fill it; and while the cultivator bedewed the earth with the fweat of his brow, the chace of the nobles devoured his crops: if the peafant drove the game from his kitchen-garden, the galleys were his portion; if he had the audacity to repel the attacks of *Monfeigneur's* dogs, the prifon doors were unbarred to receive him.

The pofts of honour and emolument were beftowed on the nobles alone, while the trouble-fome and ill paid employments were conftantly the lot of one clafs. The nobles were at the head of our armies, but this was merely to ferve their private ambition: to obtain their confent to march, they were to be dearly paid; and the degraded ſoldier who gained the victories was to be ſhot at and expoſed to every danger for five ſous a day.

When the taſk of regeneration was effected, the nobles could not comprehend it: ignorance made them obſtinate; they were deſirous that what was called the third eſtate ſhould remain in its priſtine ſtate of degradation; and on the 29th day of June 1789 they marched troops againſt the National Aſſembly! Through the organ of the King they dared to demand the maintenance of their inſolent privileges.

It was a noble who, a few days after, took upon him, ſword in hand, to aſſail the people in the garden of the Thuilleries, and to murder a defenceleſs old man. On the preceding 12th of July, the nobles projected the maſſacre of the Pariſians, who were ſo generous as to pardon them, and to ſuffer them to make their eſcape.

In the month of September 1789 the nobles attempted to convey the King to Metz: on the February following they formed a plan to carry him off; and four months after they effected a ſimilar plan.

In the army the nobles took an oath to fight for the conſtitution, and they broke it the next day, betaking themſelves to flight, and plundering

ing the *military chests*: they unceasingly tormented and harassed the patriotic soldiers, tried to corrupt and disorganize the army of the line and the marine, and to light up the flames of civil war.

They dared to menace our frontiers, to combine with the deceased Leopold and Francis, to unsheath against their country their sacrilegious swords, to levy troops, to treat with foreign powers, to bestow on one of their accomplices the title of regent of the kingdom, and to provoke the coalition of monarchs against liberty and the rights of man. They thirst after our blood because they have lost a few ravenous privileges: and if they could come off victorious, the French would in their eyes be no other than so many negroes.

Lastly, the nobles formed the Austrian committee: conspirators at Paris as well as at Vienna and Coblentz, they insult human reason, the national dignity, and the majesty of the people. They bellow with rage at not having any longer a Choiseul for a *king*, one who should subjugate the monarch for them, and afterwards abandon to them the spoils of the country. Have not the officers of our armies been constantly found to be the greatest enemies

of

of public liberty? This again brings Choiſeul to my recollection.

If we recollect that no one in that day could do more good than the miniſter of the *king of France*; that the latter reigned over his people by affection, the people over Europe by the urbanity of their manners, and Europe over the reſt of the world by power, we ſhall find that Choiſeul, far from availing himſelf of this advantageous preponderancy, diminiſhed in every ſenſe both the royal and national authority; and that finally he has inflicted almoſt incurable wounds, in the contemplation of which Auſtria now prides herſelf with the arrogance that is ſo familiar to her.

CHAIR OF ST. PETER.

IT is natural enough that ſeveral nations ſhould have choſen the *Sun* as the object of their veneration and as the emblem of the divinity. Of all the objects which ſtrike the eye, no one is more reſplendent: as well as all nature, it animates and enlivens our exiſtence. Unqueſtionably the homage of antiquity was addreſſed to this luminary as the moſt diſtin-

gui-

guiſhed object in the univerſe, conveying the ſublimeſt idea of the divinity. It is very wrong ſurely to beſtow the name of idolaters on the Magi, and Guèbres *; by means of great viſible images theſe philoſophical prieſts raiſed the ideas of the people to the great inviſible being, concealed behind that ſun which each morning is ſent to manifeſt his glory. If, in proceſs of time, the religion of the Magi, diſguiſed by covetous miniſters under impenetrable myſteries, was clad beneath a thick and obſcure veil, it was the conſequence of an intereſted policy, totally independent of the firſt principle, which led to the adoration of the ſupreme being in the moſt beautiful of his works.

The religion of the Magi never produced the calamities which have encompaſſed and ſtained with blood *the chair of St. Peter*. Undoubtedly an emblem like this cannot be compared to that of the ſun. Around this *chair* we ſee biſhops and popes, holding a crucifix in one hand, and a poniard in the other; and, guided by their example, men who profaned the name of Chriſtians, and who ſacrificed twelve millions of their fellow creatures in the new world, who ſacri-

* The old inhabitants of Perſia who worſhipped the fire and the ſun, and whoſe deſcendants, refuſing to become Mahomedans, ſtill adhere to the ancient worſhip. Tranſlator.

ficed them, I ſay, to the croſs! Oh! moſt holy religion! thou haſt had moſt execrable chiefs. On the pretext of ſupporting your moſt ſacred doctrines, they have endeavoured to lay the eternal foundation of their inſatiable ambition, of their ſordid avarice. John XI, John XII, John XVIII, Gregory VII, Boniface VIII, and Alexander VI, have filled the vatican with ſacrilege, poiſoning, and inceſt. The voice of their ſucceſſors has lighted up inquiſitorial fires in every part of the world. Were ever maſſacres occaſioned by the Elements of Euclid, by the problems and theorems of Archimedes, or by the morality of Socrates or of Marcus Aurelius? No.

OF MOSES.

HIS altar yet ſtands. What a great man was Moſes, who at once diſcloſed the religion moſt adverſe to idolatry, and the religion that announced a juſt, an auſtere, and an only inviſible God.

Alas! if the ſuperſtitions to which a carnal and groſs people were prone, had not disfigured this important dogma, ſo powerful a truth would have been ſufficient to command the adoration

 of

of the univerſe through endleſs ages; and all the idolatrous kinds of worſhips, of which ſome engendered others, could not have obſcured that continual revelation which enabled man to live inceſſantly in fellowſhip with God.

A great idea obtrudes itſelf upon me while I contemplate Moſes. Perhaps incredulity would never have planted its dangerous ſtandards, if the theology of Moſes, ſo ſimple and ſo majeſtic, had conſtantly rejected the marvellous dogmas which were propagated on pretext of embelliſhing or reforming that great and primitive light, whence flowed morality and all its admirable precepts.

How powerful is the ſway of religion over man! Of all the influences on private morals, none has ſo much efficacy. Humble yourſelves, ye who ſpurn adoration; you can never admire nor exalt your frame; you will continue little, naked, and miſerable, ſince you are inſenſible to the affecting truths of the majeſtic harmony of the univerſe; your heart will remain cold, and you will perceive nothing in nature but your voluntary abjection.

With the idea of God, all is alive and animated. However ſuperſtitious a religion may be, it is always admirable in one view; for it enjoins the adoration of the ſupreme Being, which

which awakens in us the thoughts of a juſt, beneficent God, who governs the world and reads the bottom of our heart. While the earth is covered with an innumerable multitude of men condemned to the moſt painful toils, they cannot diſpenſe with a conſoling religion; for the unfortunate need a God the protector of the feeble, a God who counts their ſighs, and who will reward their ſubmiſſion.

The intention is what conſtitutes the ſincere adorer. Though he be ſurrounded with ſuperſtitious rites, it is always the ſupreme Being that he ſeeks through the darkneſs of his underſtanding; it is the confidence he repoſes in the aſſiſtance of the God who directs him in his prayers and in his ſacrifices. An able legiſlator ought to avail himſelf of this propenſity, to favour the cauſe of morality and complete the triumph of good order; but he can expect nothing beneficial to reſult from atheiſm. Whimſical ceremonies refine by degrees, and the moſt abſurd theology falls, and becomes the religion of Ariſtides, of Socrates, and of Plato.

Let religion then have its temples, its altars, and its worſhip. God needs not our homage, but it is of moment to us that we ſhould pay it. It is religion which teaches man that God loves us, and has created us to raiſe us to a level with himſelf. Atheiſm degrades man by depriving the univerſe of that luminary of ſplendor and juſtice which is indiſpenſable to him, and by denying him the comforts of ſociety: it ought therefore to be held in deteſtation. Religion informs men that there is above them an ever preſent judge, whoſe eye, continually open, obſerves their actions and thoughts: this reflection juſtly alarms the wicked, and encourages the good. All the religious ſentiments combined have in every nation given birth to public worſhip: if happy, men aſſemble inſtinctively to honour God in their gladneſs; if miſerable, they meet together to implore his aid.

Religion claims our veneration, becauſe it eſtabliſhes the moſt entire equality among the children of men. When they ſhall have ſtudied it carefully, they will be convinced that nature never formed the diſtinction of maſter and ſlave. As all created beings are equal in the ſight of God, ſo religious nations, convinced of the juſtneſs of many exalted maxims, will be leſs tempted to adopt a government in which every thing is caſt into the one ſcale to depreſs the other, to create, for example, an order of *patricians* and an order of *plebeians*.

ANARCHY.

CIVIL ſociety has two extremes to fear; human paſſions may either precipitate it into deſpotiſm or into anarchy. Courtiers eſtabliſh deſpotiſm by extending immoderately the royal prerogative, by perverting the laws to their private views, by impoſing ruinous taxes, and by converting the ſoldiers of the country into the executioners of the citizens. Courtiers, actuated by caprice or by a deſire to protect the invaders of the rights of men, have contrived to turn the military force againſt the ſocial body, and to tear out the bowels of the ſtate.

But anarchy, which is the other extreme, preſents images if poſſible ſtill more frightful. All the baſes of government are deranged; ancient regulations no longer exiſt; the laws ſleep; the functions of juſtice are interrupted; unity, ſo neceſſary in every government, gives place to multiplied powers, to diſcordant intereſts, to contradictory orders; the multiplicity of means ſerves only to render the ſprings of government more complicated; punctuality, celerity, and œconomy, become impoſſible in the exerciſe of adminiſtration; it injures itſelf, and, inceſſantly oppoſed, it attacks all the properties which were formerly ſupported by ſolid foundations. Thus mankind wiſhing to avoid one precipice, fall into another. A deſpot may be ſoftened, a tyrant may be enlightened; but nothing can inſtruct a furious multitude, which makes of its violent and blind paſſions as many laws, perpetually growing worſe and worſe. Anarchy is then moſt to be dreaded; it is the moſt grievous diſtemper that can afflict the political body. Let him therefore who poſſeſſes wiſdom, prudence, or force, become a magiſtrate in this criſis, let him recall every thing to unity of action, let him ſhow the madneſs of the little private paſſions and their baneful effects on general order. Nothing can be accompliſhed without an union of wills; but it is tranquillity alone that can reſtore their purity and their gravity.

The calumniators of our revolution have not failed to talk of the pretended anarchy that prevails in France. But he who can deliberately conſider the play of the political machine will ſet a far greater value on the judiciary laws and the laws of police, than on thoſe political laws of which the application is often uncertain and almoſt always of unfrequent occurrence. But it is a matter of fact that the deciſions of the courts have their full and due execution over the whole of the French territory; that the

ſentences

ſentences of the police have no where met with the leaſt obſtruction; that commercial articles of every deſcription are ſacred on all the roads; and that real property has never received the ſmalleſt attack. Now, when the laws of police poſſeſs energy, he who can form a right eſtimate regards them as infinitely more precious than the other laws: partial diſorders have never been communicated to the general maſs. The enemies of liberty have in vain contrived plots and uſhered in new crimes, but all theſe impious efforts have been unable to diſorganize the nation; it has ſurvived every cataſtrophe, becauſe, though divided on its political laws, it has been united on the laws of utility and daily application. The throne could not do the people all the miſchief it meditated, becauſe the people made an effectual reſiſtance, and becauſe by knowledge the effect of every baſe libel was defeated. If the cruel and cowardly enemies of this people, ſo patient and ſo generous, have ſometimes drawn on their heads a precipitate vengeance, clemency has inſtantly ſucceeded to theſe acts of rigour or of juſtice; the people, conſtitutionally mild, pardoned their executioners: they ſaw treaſon lurking under the diadem, and they expected and ſtill expect that time will change a ſyſtem of perfidy for the intereſt of him who dares to purſue it. Laſtly, taking the amount of the loſs of men, inſeparable from great events, we ſhall find it to be inferior to what Louis XIV. ſacrificed in a ſingle battle dictated by his pride.

Theſe dealers in human blood, who have empurpled the earth, and whoſe ferocious intentions have ever purſued the traces of liberty, theſe are the perſons, and it well becomes them, who would condemn us to ſlavery, by upbraiding us with what we have been obliged to do in order to ſecure our independence and the happineſs of our poſterity, with what we have done for the cauſe of France and that of the human race.

What would they not attempt againſt the ſtandards of liberty, if their ſoldiers were not ready to open their eyes; if theſe ſoldiers, compelled by force to ſerve againſt the cauſe of equality, againſt their own cauſe, and diſciplined by blows of the cane, began not already to reflect that all the violences, all the crimes impoſed on them, muſt neceſſarily recoil upon themſelves, and their children, in their turn, become ſlaves; and that the horrible obligation to ſhed the blood of men for the whim of a deſ-

pot

pot will be the greateſt of crimes if they ſhould heſitate longer to break through ſo unreaſonable an engagement.

HORATIUS WHO KILLED HIS SISTER.

THE love of the country, the love of liberty, begets men who do not reſemble thoſe of another age. When the famous Horatius, on his return from battle, killed his ſiſter, it was neceſſary to have been born and educated at Rome to form a competent judgment of the deed. Horatius returned from a combat terrible to him, but deciſive to the liberty, the glory, and the ſafety of the country: covered with the blood of his brothers, whoſe death he had witneſſed, and covered alſo with the ſpoils of the Curiatii, whom he had had the courage and good fortune to ſubdue, he diſplayed theſe to his fellow citizens with the tranſports of a Roman who had juſt ſaved Rome, had freed her from the yoke with which ſhe was menaced.

One of his ſiſters was betrothed to one of the Curiatii: ſhe ſaw in her brother's hand the ſcarf ſhe had given to her lover; and, neceſſary and inevitable as the combat was, ſhe reproached him with it, and aſſailed him with all

all the fury of deſpair. It was a lover who ſpoke, and it was to him who had been the murderer of her lover that her reproaches were addreſſed: the ties of blood loſt their force in that which attached her, and which had juſt been broken. On another hand, it was a brother who had juſt eſcaped from the utmoſt peril, the vanquiſher of the mortal enemies of Rome, and her deliverer: all theſe titles were abſorbed in grief; and this ſiſter could find in her brother no other than the murderer of Curiatius. A barbarous and unnatural monſter, a tiger thirſting after and glutted with blood, were the only names ſhe could find for a conqueror who had achieved an immortal deed uſeful to his country. Miſerable wretch! replied Horatius, threatening her, you reckon as nothing two brothers you have juſt loſt; you load with curſes the only one that remains; your heart is filled by the paſſion alone for your lover! Covered as I am by your own blood, nature, mute and betrayed in your heart, does not even allow you to perceive the loſſes you have ſuſtained: your love knows the loſs of him only; in my preſence you regret Curiatius; and you have not a tear to ſhed for your generous brothers! You are by birth a Roman, you

ſpeak

ſpeak in Rome, I have juſt ſaved Rome, and it is I whom you reproach.

His furious ſiſter made him this reply: " Rome, the ſole object of my hatred; Rome, to which you have juſt ſacrificed my lover; Rome, which gave you birth, and which you adore; Rome, finally, which I deteſt, becauſe ſhe honours you; may all her neighbours, conſpiring together, ſap her badly ſecured foundations; and if all Italy will not ſuffice, may the Eaſt unite againſt her with the Weſt. May an hundred nations collected together from the extremities of the univerſe paſs mountains and ſeas to deſtroy her; may ſhe overturn her own walls on herſelf and tear her entrails with her own hands; may the anger of heaven, kindled by my prayers, pour on her a deluge of fire, which, accompanied by Jove's thunders, may reduce her laurels to powder, and her houſes to aſhes; and may I, the ſole cauſe, hear the laſt Roman breathe his laſt ſigh, myſelf expiring with pleaſure!"

Horace, not yet recovered from the agitation he had been thrown into by a combat in which death had preſented itſelf to his view with more than common terrors; Horace, overwhelmed with grief at the loſs of his brothers; Horace ſtill furious, and with reaſon, at the mention of the

the name of Curiatius, was no longer maſter of his indignation :—he poignarded her.

THE VAUDOIS *.

IN the year 1685, the court of Verſailles, having revoked the edict of Nantes, preſſed that of Turin at the ſame time to expel all the proteſtants from the vallies of Piedmont. The orders which the Vaudois received in conſequence of this ſolicitation were ſo prompt and ſo rigorous that they had not leiſure to conſider what ſteps to take. Their goods, their houſes, and their flocks, were ſeized. No conſolation was left them, but to lead away their wives and their children, without knowing what country would receive them. The entrance of Dauphiné, where they had yet many brethren of the ſame communion, was ſhut againſt them ; Italy preſented no favourable aſylum, ſtill leſs did it afford the hope of ſuccour and of comfort. Diſtant more than fifty leagues from Switzerland, and igno-

* Theſe people received their name from Peter Waldo, a merchant in Lyons, who expoſed the ſuperſtition of the Romiſh church in 1160. Baniſhed out of France, he retired with his diſciples to Piedmont, where they ſettled and cheriſhed undiſturbed their religious principles. *Tranſlator.*

rant whether in that country they might ſettle, or at leaſt receive any aſſiſtance, they durſt not hazard the journey. In this ſtate of perplexity, what choice remained to people ſunk at once from eaſy circumſtances into the moſt frightful poverty? Deſpair drove them to take arms, with the firm reſolution of periſhing or of retaining their poſſeſſions.

Of about twenty thouſand men, fourteen thouſand ſtood on the defenſive, but without chiefs, without guides, and without ſkill in the military art. They were brave from conſtitution, and raſh from neceſſity, but timid from ignorance. Some regular troops were diſpatched againſt them with orders to engage. The officer who commanded this party having overtaken them, poured on them a volley of ſmall arms, which killed thirty, and then ſummoned the reſt to lay down their arms, with a promiſe that they ſhould depart unmoleſted. All of them were married men, and at this inſtant their wives and children, in the hope of ſaving the ſtay of their miſery, intreated them to yield. Theſe poor unfortunate men, too credulous and too fearful, urged by the ſentiment of a genuine tenderneſs, and unacquainted beſides with the talent of capitulating, ſurrendered at diſcretion. But Oh! perfidy! far from ſuffering them to depart, they

were

were conducted, to the number of fourteen thousand, into different prisons, where the bulk of them perished amidst all the evils which misery and captivity engender.

A very great number of women and children, who were incapable of prevailing on themselves to quit their country, were obliged to change their religion, to remain where they were. The rest passed into Switzerland, Germany, and Holland, having nothing for their support but the alms which pity distributes always in too scanty portions. These poor women with their children languished in foreign countries, while their husbands rotted alive in the dungeons of Piedmont. They were kept there till England and Holland solicited their enlargement. Of fourteen thousand, scarcely three thousand escaped from their cells: the rest, not so robust in point of constitution, sunk under the inhuman treatment of the slaves of fanaticism.—This recital would move the most obdurate heart.

IDEAS ON RELIGION.

I SHALL not examine whether the idea of the Divinity is innate, or the effect of the conviction of a supernatural power, the existence of which

which is demonſtrated by the contemplation of all nature. All the nations of the earth have entertained a notion of a more than human power, which they have made to reſide in one or ſeveral beings: with theſe the elements have been filled; and from hence myſteries have ariſen. Every perfected religion conſiſts in three things, the kind of idea it affords of the ſupernatural power, the worſhip, and the moral.

May we not reſort to the axiom of Paſchal, which I ſhall tranſlate in a clear and intelligible ſtile? It is dangerous not to believe enough, and it is not inconvenient to believe more than is neceſſary, when that only is believed which accords with the ideas of a ſupreme and veiled grandeur that environs man, and forbids him in his pride to comprehend every thing: it is certain that the laws of abſolute neceſſity, the laws of the human race, ſpring from religion, that is to ſay, from the idea of the Divinity. I do not think that civil laws have ever been known to ſubſiſt without a religious worſhip of ſome kind. The connection of public morals with religious forms appears to me to be demonſtrated in each page of the Hiſtory of Nations.

We are acquainted with thirteen hundred different faiths, and perhaps there are as many of theſe as there are men on the ſurface of the earth, ſeeing how probable it is that two men are not to be found who think in a manner exactly conformable on every point: but to reject that which all faiths, with an unanimous conſent, admit, appears to me to be a preſumption not leſs abſurd than it is daring.

The completeſt victory of the atheiſt is reduced to the eſtabliſhing of doubt; and a doubt ſuppoſes the poſſibility of the thing doubted.

To have a deep ſenſe of religion, that is to ſay, of the ſyſtem in which man adores and humbles himſelf, becomes a ſublime ſentiment: then it is that the ſoul of man is elevated, and his being ennobled, while he is borne above terreſtrial things, and made to embrace a future ſtate of grandeur and felicity. Hymns of gratitude are poured forth from the bottom of his heart; an elevation of thought follows each humble adoration he pays; and it is in proſtrating himſelf before God, that man diſcovers in himſelf his noble origin, and the end for which he was created.

GREAT IMPULSION OF THE HUMAN MIND.

THE epoch of revolutions is arrived. After ages of ſlavery and error, people have felt the neceſſity of acquiring knowledge; and reaſon, revolting againſt theſe tyrants, combats in defence of human dignity, and promiſes the earth triumphs as yet unknown. Perhaps Africa and India, witneſſing our activity, will quickly ſhare it, and reſolve at laſt to riſe from their humiliating ſloth. Nothing is beyond human ſagacity; if it has hitherto failed, we cannot infer from thence that it will always fail. I admit the ſuperb hopes of certain orators of the human race; and prefer them to thoſe contracted, diſcouraging ideas which dwell in cold minds: I therefore believe that ſtates may be founded on the ſolid baſes of juſtice and reaſon. I can conceive this. A few clear laws are ſufficient to heal every diſorder; but unfortunately that ſimplicity is not recurred to till after errors innumerable are exhauſted.

I delight to contemplate the progreſs of reaſon in the world. A true coſmopolite enjoys all the bleſſings that light upon his fellow-creatures; nothing is foreign to his heart, which dilates over the whole earth; he fancies himſelf

 aſſiſting

aſſiſting in all the triumphs of patriotiſm; he perceives the inquiſition expiring under its extinguiſhed piles; he views men of genius, the true friends of humanity, rivalling the ſun that illumines the deſerts of ſpace. Has the improvement of the human ſpecies attained its utmoſt limit? No. France, the depoſitary of the ſacred fire, will continue to cheriſh in its boſom the germes of talents and of genius. As Greece anciently gave laws to Italy, and Egypt to Greece; ſo our legiſlators, while they labour for the felicity of France, are the benefactors of all mankind; they will renew in our ſight, but with a livelier ſplendour, the proſperous days of Memphis, of Rome, and of Athens.

Yes, even the people yoked to the car of the Sultans, muſt ſoar above their preſent condition; they will fly from the miry paths of ignorance, and in ſpite of barbarous policy, in ſpite of habitual indolence, will ceaſe to merit contempt. The imperious cry of misfortune proclaims to them the neceſſity of the arts and the influence of cultivated genius; philoſophy, accompanied with the engraver and the printer, is about to deſcend from the Tanais to the Boſphorus; it will open the gates of the ſeraglio, and the porch of the Divan will reſound in half a century with the oracles recorded in the declaration of the rights of men.

On reading the hiſtory and annals of ancient nations, we perceive with pain that many held a retrograde courſe. Under thoſe famous porticos where Socrates and Plato enlightened the univerſe, the Califs, the Imans, the Derviſhes, and the Muphtis, thicken the ſhades of barbarity; the unfeeling Ottoman tramples under foot the aſhes of Ariſtides and of Solon; the trophies of human glory lie neglected in the midſt of deſerts; and the traveller, wandering among the ruins of Thebes, of Palmyra, and of Alexandria, can hardly diſcover the traces of their ancient ſplendour. But the invaluable art of printing will ſuffer men no longer to retrograde in their ſteps.

OF WOMEN AMONG THE ANCIENTS.

IN Greece the women ſeldom appeared in public, and never at the Olympic games: it was on this account that the ſpirit, the magnificence, the glory, and the liberty of the Greeks did not ſuffice to give to the mind the degree of heat which belonged to it; love was wanting.

A falſe philoſophy often ſeparates us from the ſociety of women; while a true and exalted one conſtantly urges us towards them.

In their treatment of the women the Romans were greater and more equitable than the Greeks: it was worthy of their good ſenſe. At Rome a great conſideration was paid to females, who had every where a diſtinguiſhed place aſſigned them, and whoſe funeral orations were pronounced.

The women, however, were alone ſeen at the ſhows, the threatres, and, during the latter periods, at the feſtivals given by the Emperors. There was none of that general ſociety which characterizes our manners, and conſequently the urbanity and ſuavity of our uſages were unknown there. It is not preciſely aſcertained whether at Rome the women were for any conſiderable length of time in the enjoyment of a kind of equality in the ſociety of the men.

The more we advance northward, the more we find the authority of the women augmented, and jealouſy proportionably diminiſhed: notwithſtanding their barbarity, neither the ſavages, Scythians, nor Goths, ever entertained a thought of depriving them of their liberty. In Europe their happineſs began as ſoon as theſe nations had formed any eſtabliſhments: however, when the

the northern nations were tranſplanted in Spain, they borrowed the jealous uſages natural to that country, and, if we may credit what travellers tell us of the incontinence of the women who are in any degree unreſtained at Guſco, Lima, and Goa, neceſſary to ſuch climates. By ſimilar uſages men cannot be bound or reſtrained, becauſe with them love is an ardent and excluſive paſſion.

VOLTAIRE.

I WISH to exculpate myſelf from the charge brought againſt me in ſeveral journals of having been unjuſt in my criticiſms on Voltaire, who was himſelf extremely unjuſt towards Rouſſeau. I have conſtantly allowed Voltaire to be a great poet, and have not denied the ſervices he has rendered humanity, whether by attacking fanaticiſm and impoſture, or by making theatrical poetry ſubſervient to a tolerancy of opinions, or, finally, by interſperſing, in the ſmalleſt of his works even, thoſe humane and amiable maxims, which, indeed, with an unpardonable levity, he forgot, when he took upon him to cenſure in his verſes the Abbé Desfontaines and Fréron.

But had Voltaire the ſtrong and thinking head of the author of the ſocial contract? Had he his temperament and philoſophical countenance? Did he conceive, embrace, and analyze the political principles by which nations are to be regenerated? Did he penetrate into that which conſtitutes ſociety, the equality of rights, the ſeparation of powers, and the national ſovereignty? Has he not produced a very weak criticiſm on the *ſpirit of laws?* Has he not called the *ſocial contract* a ſorry pamphlet? Monteſquieu characterized this poet very finely, when he made uſe of this expreſſion: Voltaire! Oh! he has too much wit to comprehend me.

It was certainly proper to pierce the *Centaur* who was carrying off the beautiful *Dejanira*; but alas! was it neceſſary to wound by the ſame blow the innocent beauty the raviſher held in his arms? Rouſſeau, equally vigorous, was more adroit; his arrow pierced the monſter without wounding the moral.

I have remarked that when nature produces a great man, ſhe immediately creates another who ſeems to be born to temper and correct the ideas of his rival. Rouſſeau is the corrective of Voltaire: by blending the writings of theſe two great men the accents of their genius become no longer discordant, and the great harmonies of universal morality are revealed to the intelligent reader. This is, if I mistake not, a most admirable *final cause*, which, unfortunately for him, the author of *Candide* did not perceive.

Even although I may have leaned rather too much to the side of Rousseau, was I so greatly in fault, when we owe to him the finest parts of our constitution? Could we have introduced into it *three lines* of Voltaire? I doubt the fact. The generation now springing up will view our books in a very different light from the one in which we see them; and we ourselves have revived many old books which had been contemned and misunderstood. Who will take upon him to affirm what will remain of Voltaire an hundred years hence? It is an argument of extreme rashness to weigh, in any particular case, the amount of the human capacity: to these intrepid judges time gives the most formal lie. But there are readers who will not allow themselves to be imposed on by the great celebrity of a name, who spend whole nights and days in the study of a *pamphlet*, and who can find nothing but four or five of the ideas of *Bayle*, repeated in sixty or seventy volumes: to them the sportive sallies of a luxuriant fancy, and the ſtile which faſcinates without convincing, are of no account.

NATIONAL ASSEMBLY.

A REPRESENTATIVE aſſembly alone can act with grandeur and amplitude. As it exhibits the general will of the nation, its power is univerſal, and its wide empire comprehends and regulates every object, without regard to local conſiderations: the great end which it propoſes is the good of the whole.

A ſingle houſe of legiſlation has ſimplified our government; for it needs no counterpoiſe. The right delegated to the king of refuſing his ſanction to the decrees of that body is ſurely only a right of ſalutary reviſion, *an appeal to the people*, and nothing more.

Never was the dignity of the monarch greater; he was advanced to reſpect by the legiſlative aſſembly; but, by an inconceivable blindneſs, he has miſtaken the exaltation of his glory and the luſtre of his throne. No one of his miniſters has followed the ſpirit of the revolution; they have never choſen to exerciſe an active authority; and the efficacious interpoſition of the monarchs has never come ſeaſonably.

ſonably. Nothing now remains but that the executive power ſhould influence by its action the aggregate of the political hierarchy; but this, however, it is unwilling to do. When force is really employed for the public good, it is always ſacred.

Every thing is now ſubject to the national authority; it holds a permanent ſway. The abſolute aſcendency of public opinion has eſtabliſhed theſe indeſtructible baſes. We were right when we formed the legiſlative body into one houſe, and ſpoke with ſome diſdain of Engliſh liberty. With us an impious, a deſtructive ſyſtem, obliged a general arming of the kingdom; yet it was at the ſame time requiſite that the miniſters, in circumſtances ſo urgent, ſhould no longer be ſubject to the ſupreme will of the king, but to that of events; for they were no longer the depoſitaries of the royal authority. The executive power is therefore become the enemy of the country, ſince it is no longer abſolute maſter of the finances. But this order of things cannot ſubſiſt; as the executive power refuſes to act, it will be compelled to act, and the majeſtic ſimplicity of the political machine will then unfold its ſublime play.

Invited to liberty, which puts it in our power to reform our government, to regulate the monarchy, to dictate laws, to set the springs of the state in motion, to dispose the physical and moral forces of the nation, to what a height are we arrived!

The most towering political systems merely consist in the simplest principles reduced to practice. Establish two houses, you will speedily have two orders, and no doubt the aristocracy will then preponderate; and aristocracy, composed of the great, whose lustre can be no other than an emanation from the throne, must by its very nature dread the power of the people, and favour that of the prince, the clear fountain of titles, of honours, of pensions, and of favours. Thus, the aristocratical interests are evidently confounded with those of the monarch, and can scarcely ever be separated.

Louis XVI. in *a resolve of the council of state*, dated the 8th of August 1788, had promised in the face of Europe to restore to the nation the full exercise of all the rights which belonged to it; but he wished only to deceive the national assembly, to make it subservient to the re-establishment of the finances, and the filling up of the deficiency; after which he would have opened a new account.

Agesilaus,

Agesilaus, finding that he had been deceived by Tissaphernes, who had perjured himself, conceived from thence great hopes of success in the war, and inspired his troops with a strong contempt of a prince, who, by his false oaths, and his contravention of the most solemn treaties, had provoked the indignation both of gods and of men.

Every chief is dependant, because nature admits neither despot nor slave: it is the perfection of the political state that the chief of the nation be only the preserver of its liberty, its protector, and not its master.

Our princes wished literally to make a different race of men among men; but the people are in their turn the kings of the earth.

A great state, resting on itself by its own weight, is the most proper for expelling ancient abuses, as the ocean casts upon its shores every substance foreign to it: nature there facilitates all the efforts, renders all the labours profitable, and favours the true principles of political œconomy, by affording the productions which industry can raise from an extensive territory: in this vast reservoir of individual faculties, the general interest prompts to great undertakings, by securing to each labourer, and that in the most

moſt ſacred manner, the full enjoyment of the fruit of his ideas and of his toil.

The criſis of revolutions diſcovers and brings forward the moſt concealed talents. Every one finds his ſtation; and we are aſtoniſhed at the ſudden appearance of extraordinary men of conſummate ſkill in affairs, and endued with all the public virtues, but whoſe name was even unknown.

Our conſtitution approximates thoſe of the Greeks, that is to ſay, it has a republican caſt. That theſe forms of government were favourable to the production of talents, has been demonſtrated. Every road was open, whether by the ſhort duration of the magiſtracies and of the command of the army, or by the authority of eloquence and the hope of attaining all the employments of the ſtate. The bar and the army formed two immenſe fields for different geniuſes. Accordingly, if we ſurvey all the nations which have figured on the globe, it ſeems impoſſible not to regard the Romans during the pureſt ages of their republic, as the people, obſerves Monteſquieu, who have the moſt honoured human nature.

The great queſtions on the rights of the people, on the theory of legiſlation, and on the influence

fluence of the freedom of thinking and writing, are become familiar to us; we are thoroughly acquainted with every thing that regards the public weal.

If politics be the morality of ſtates, was the vain and barbarous diſtinction of noble and plebeian calculated to ſubſiſt in a country where all the citizens muſt labour in concert to ſupport the rights of reaſon and of juſtice?

Our ſeigneurs, with their *immunities* and *privileges*, after having annihilated the rights of the people, have made every effort in the eighteenth century to prevent their renewal.

The title of *monarch* was never juſtly applied to the kings of France; there is the ſame difference as between *adminiſtration* and *deſpotiſm*, I *will* it, I *ordain* it, my *will*, my *good pleaſure*. Will nations long be ſatisfied with theſe terms?

The pope, as a judicious hiſtorian remarks, would have deſired to be conſtantly conſidered as the ſole magiſtrate and the only ſovereign in the world.

But philoſophers began happily to triumph over *prieſts* and *tyrants*, when it was impoſſible to ſilence the voice of thoſe men of every nation and of every age, who, connecting their own cauſe with the intereſt of all, have enlightened and aided humanity.

In

In proportion as the number of men who think increaſes, their propenſity to independance acts with more energy; they feel themſelves ſtronger; and they perceive, by a natural inſtinct, that their liberty augments, becauſe they afford each other mutual aſſiſtance. Thus, are large ſtates deſtined to great convulſions: in their wide extent the current of mighty revolutions cannot be ſtopped; the obſtacles only create a new energy, and the events correſpond to the boldneſs of the enterprize.

France is the firſt and the fineſt kingdom of the world, that which poſſeſſes moſt acquired riches, and where it is eaſier than elſewhere to augment and preſerve them, where men are more induſtrious, more laborious, and more ſober, and where the love which they naturally bear to glory has all the effects of patriotiſm: this kingdom will therefore ſoon be filled with freemen. The reſources of the French nation will ever prove ſuperior to all her poſſible wants.

Our ariſtocrates reſemble the old wolf in the fable, who having loſt his teeth offered to make peace with the ſhepherd; but the ſhepherd ſmiled at his propoſal, and inſtantly diſpatched him.

A free people, brave and virtuous, quickly enjoy

joy all the fruits of the arts and all the treasures of the earth.—Let us appeal to antiquity.

The league of Aratus displays the highest skill; it comprehended in idea all the Greek cities. The plan of Aratus was to expel the kings and tyrants, and give to Greece a liberty more solid than that which had hitherto been to it a source of perplexity. Aratus formed a single power out of many, which he connected together in a close confederacy. Here was really the image of the new *departments of France*; equality must have subsisted among the towns as among the citizens. No one gave its name to the republic, no one was disdained as unfit for the place of meeting of the general council: the jealousy of honours or pre-eminence could not disunite them: all at once subjects, and sovereigns, no domination was felt. This noble project, extremely laudable, and the greatest that could present itself to the mind of a Greek, has been renewed in our own days by the national assembly.

Add to this that Aratus preferred a foreign king, whom the Greeks styled a barbarian, to any Greek of eminence like himself.

Society may attain a degree of perfection that far exceeds our most sanguine imagination. No! man was not born to misery and servi-

tude;

tude; nor are there two modes of well being; truth is one and indivisible, and the spirit of liberty necessarily doubles the force of man.

How many writers are there who examine nothing but the bottom of their own heart, and, deciding from their own conscience, calumniate mankind by that mean disposition to detract which is the portion of narrow minds? But self-interest cannot be regarded as the sole motive of human actions. Man is naturally disposed to restrain his rights, that he may leave to others the free exercise of theirs. He keeps therefore in view the general interest of the human race; for the societies which men form with each other tend by their nature to maintain and secure the independence and equality of men. It often happens that we cannot labour for the public good without incurring a certain, inevitable loss. How often have men been seen courageously to sacrifice their life for the advantage of their country?

Every thing plainly shows, that upon the whole, man acts generally from natural impulse, and rather for the general benefit and preservation of the human race than with a view to his own.

Many violent, and sometimes indecent scenes, which disturb the deliberations of the national

assembly,

aſſembly, are ſeverely blamed: they evidently proceed from the inſolent minority, and from that cruel and baſe party which pretends to dictate laws to us, but which would not even enjoy, if unfortunately victorious, its hateful victory. Theſe ſtorms are perhaps neceſſary; the tempeſt which aſſails the veſſel alſo ſpeeds it on its way. When the people unanimouſly regard liberty as their patrimony, that character always creates a certain keenneſs of temper, and produces moſt violent contentions between thoſe who hold different opinions concerning ſtate affairs. The writings of Ariſtrophanes and Theophraſtus are full of nothing but raillery againſt the faults committed in the aſſemblies of the Greeks. Only recollect the mutual abuſe of Æſchinus and Demoſthenes: and in full ſenate, Cato and Cæſar attacked each other in the moſt opprobrious language. So that we muſt not ſeek in their public aſſemblies for what we are told of Athenian and Roman politeneſs. The greater the danger appears, the eaſier is the eloquence which takes fire juſtified, if not by its exceſs, at leaſt by its triumph. The executive power, ever rebellious and preparing behind covered entrenchments the ruin of the laws of the country, provoked the indignation and the voice of furious eloquence; for the latter, luckily for us, rose to the level of the monstrous and sanguinary audacity of the former. Eloquence has more than once thundered against criminal measures emboldened by indulgence, and has disposed the people to assume a stern and determined attitude.

Finally, the despots threaten us: all kings, it is said, style each other brothers. But are not all nations sisters, and can they behold with indifference the disasters which afflict them? Nations will be seen to unite and rally; for it is the interest of all to chain down despotism. But if the power of a state consists in the number of its subjects, in their means, in their capacity, and the accumulated product of their forces and resources, France has nothing to fear from its neighbours. Let all her citizens adhere to the legislative body: submission to the laws is the pledge of victory. Hobbes remarks very judiciously, that there can be no solid government without a centre of authority from which no recourse can be had to another power.

OF VIRTUOUS MEN OF LETTERS.

WHILE time brings revolutions over the whole face of the globe, and infinitely varies the picture of events, it causes new ideas to circulate which have also their force and their empire.

Emanated from a few thinking heads, they penetrate the minds of the great body, and make a permanent impression. This course of morality has its ascendency and its duration. Since the different parts of Europe have kept up a correspondence, and all knowledge tends to the same focus, the voice of philosophers produces a cry almost unanimous, that swells, resounds, and rules even the thrones, which seemed the last term of human power.

There is certainly something above *them*, opinion. The imprudent monarch who defies it, weakens and disjoins his authority: and such is the undoubted empire of new and luminous ideas, that, by their beauty, their evidence, their depth, and their utility, they give law to the part which governs. Knowledge is become useful in all governments: they seem now ready to submit (with more or less opposition) to those opinions which are destined to produce by degrees the most incredible changes.

This new action of *a few individuals* upon the universe, this moral empire which directs the physical force, is a thing truly new, and which never occurred in history till the invention of printing.

These opinions are mixed with good and evil, like every thing else; they have at once their utility and their danger. Sometimes the minds of men are not ripe enough to adopt them; and, on the other hand, they may too much inflame unprepared heads, and derange the political balance too suddenly. Enthusiasm might then assume the place of reason; and though enthusiasm be the worker of great achievements, it is never beneficial or desirable except in a serious, important, and arduous crisis.

Perhaps there exists an art of judging these new opinions, of elaborating them, and of rendering them thus more salutary. Amidst the progress of the human mind, evil, by an almost invincible destiny, places itself by the side of good. Often the virtuous man is forced to sigh, even while he is filled with admiration. Might not a more attentive choice separate what is baneful in the mixture of those real benefits lately poured upon society?

When the human mind has conceived a new idea, it can seldom preserve a just medium; for

man

man delights in extremes. The effort he makes in burſting from his old chains precipitates him into the oppoſite extreme, and, proud of having got rid of his weighty fetters, he does not perceive that he is only adopting new prejudices, and that he ſubmits to the moſt abſolute prepoſſeſſion, at the very moment he thinks he has eſcaped from it for ever. Thus man has confounded diſtinct notions, and has believed that he had improved all, becauſe he trampled with a haughty foot upon many wrecks.

Such is more eſpecially the diſpoſition of the preſent age. Elated with ſome undoubted conqueſts, it ſeems more impatient to deſtroy than to rear. It has brought the ancient opinions under its examination; but was it not too much elated when it gave them up to ridicule and contempt? This love of novelty may have its dangers and its exceſſes. Will the continual ſtruggle againſt error ſuffice to guard againſt it? And if genius were as cautious as it is impetuous, would it not reſt contented with having overturned cruel and pernicious prejudices alone? We ought to irrigate and fertilize, and not to overflow and lay waſte. Among the new and prevailing ideas, there are ſome which, judiciouſly choſen, may afford the greateſt advantage to ſociety, and complete the triumph of reaſon.

After genius has expanded fully in every direction, it would be deſirable, I think, that ſome one ſhould ſtart up endued with a calm and penetrating judgment, to ſeparate truth from error. It is he alone that can weigh without partiality, can decide without preſumption, can moderate the heat of enthuſiaſm, and yet not weaken truth: finally, it is he that can ſafely proceed between the exceſſive timidity which ſuperſtitiouſly reveres ancient cuſtoms, and the temerity which would break down every barrier.

The ſpirit of the age has diffuſed much light, partly by conducting reflection towards uſeful objects, and partly by generalizing principles which were loſt becauſe ſcattered and diffuſed. There is no ſcience at preſent, but muſt acknowledge that this ſpirit has enlarged the bounds of its circles. If it has erred, it was by the immenſity of the objects which it embraced; it was by attempting to apply too haſty a calculation to complicated operations: it was perhaps, if I dare declare it, by not repoſing ſufficient confidence in human virtue, and by not eſtimating the efficacy of that active force.

Such

Such is the firſt error, if I am not miſtaken, of the governing body: it has expected every thing from its material ſprings; it has reaſoned on objects which it ought rather to have felt, as if ſentiment were not likewiſe a ſtream of light, ſtill prompter and more active. Why not believe that enlightened virtue, in any man, as in a nation, is more knowing than the moſt quick-ſighted policy?

It is virtue that perceives rapidly, and by inſtinct what muſt turn out for the general advantage: with the eye conſtantly fixed upon ſuffering humanity, it has that generous emotion which dictates the beſt maxims. Reaſoning, with its inſidious language, may beſtow bewitching colours upon ambiguous enterpriſes. Never will the heart of the virtuous man of letters forget the intereſt of the meaneſt citizen; and if he be compelled to ſelect his ſacrifice, the numerous and unfortunate claſs will be preſent in his memory. He will chooſe the leaſt evil, and in ſuch a way as not to dread the pen of the hiſtorian who will deſcribe to poſterity his combats and his deciſions.

Thus, in their origin, growing nations have divined the ſtate beſt calculated for them; and remote from political light, or even deſpiſing it, they have had the advantage of improving a perception vaſtly ſuperior to the rage of ſyſtems, which aiming to control every event, give occaſion to numberleſs overſights.

Place, then, the virtuous man before the able politician, reſting aſſured that the former will diſcover by his love of the public good what the other will not perceive by the pride of his conceptions.

If he watches the ſpirit of the age it is not with an intention to cruſh it, or to ſtay its progreſs, but only to give it a more uſeful direction. The pilot obeys the ſea on which he is borne; he follows the inevitable currents; he varies his management according as the weather is calm or tempeſtuous. In like manner, the man in office yields to the national bent, and turns his thoughts to the general will; he chooſes to follow this movement rather than to oppoſe it. If he is attentive to catch the wind of this predominating ſpirit (a wind vehement and irreſiſtible), he will bring about great things without convulſion and without requiring an effort. He will hold a lever of vaſt power, calculated to overturn the moſt numerous obſtacles: he will bargain for the glory and felicity of the nation, and will find the minds of all diſpoſed to obey, becauſe they will be moved only by their own inclination. They will go greater lengths with

peaceful

peaceful legiſlators ſuch as theſe, than if they were impelled to obedience by force, and even by the empire of the laws.

Moſt writers agree to praiſe the paſt ages at the expence of the preſent; but the reading of hiſtory is ſufficient to controvert ſuch an opinion. The ſuperſtition and barbarity which darken remote times, extinguiſh every wiſh we might entertain that we had come into the world at thoſe fatal periods.

Unqueſtionably the art of living in ſociety is improved; and errors and prejudices, in paſſing from one age to another, are blunted by degrees. In reading ancient hiſtory, and reflecting on what has paſſed, it appears that the human race then enjoyed a very ſlender portion of happineſs. But taught by fatal experience the miſeries attending ſuperſtition, we have contrived to dam up the ſource of that ſcourge, to enjoy the light which ſurrounds us, and to improve the benefits of it for our own felicity, for that of our contemporaries, and for poſterity.

Europe, in general, is better cultivated, better inhabited, better defended: thoſe ſudden invaſions which formerly deſtroyed kingdoms, are no longer practicable; artillery has made war leſs ſlow in its operations and leſs dangerous; the invention of printing has rendered the com-

munication

munication of ideas prompt and eaſy between the different parts of the world; and amidſt the moſt bloody war, invincible and neceſſary ties maintain the right of property and avert great calamities.

However remote we may be from perfection, we conſtantly advance in improvement. We debate on the means of beſtowing felicity on our own country, on our ſociety; and theſe *dreams* lead invariably to ſome wiſe reſult. Excellent and ſound principles eſtabliſh order in *theory*, which announces an enſuing *practice*, not perfect, but bringing a greater ſum of tranquillity and happineſs.

Good books have diffuſed knowledge through all claſſes of the people; they adorn truth. Theſe writings already govern Europe; they inſtruct governments in their duties, they apprize them of their faults, their true intereſt, and the public opinion to which they muſt liſten and conform. Theſe books are patient maſters that wait till the adminiſtrators of ſtates are awake and their paſſions calm.

Policy is founded, like geometry, on the moſt ſimple principles; the whole conſiſts in knowing how to deduce conſequences. The character of a people changes from age to age, and that change ought to be ſtrictly attended to.

The politician would never make erroneous combinations, without the extreme variety and ficklenefs of national character. It is requifite therefore that he beftow particular attention on this fubject, and eftimate more efpecially the poffible range of the extravagance which enters the human brain.

Such is the difficult part of his art: he muft build his plans on the character of a people viewed at large. When he fhall poffefs the true knowledge of its manners, he will obtain over the nation an afcendency which the moft fortunate warrior could never expect.

The latter rufhes like a torrent, and like a torrent paffes away. The bloody trophies of victory are always dearly purchafed; the conqueror often miffes the fruits of his fuccefs. He retains nothing, if policy does not affift him.

The greateft and moft formidable ftate may be ruined by a vigilant policy, which, protecting a neighbouring ftate of lefs ftrength, fhall be able to fteal almoft imperceptibly from its rival the fecret and vital ftrength that formed its flourifhing condition.

A body of perfect laws, with regard to what concerns policy, would be a mafter-piece of human genius. It would confift perhaps in an exquifite felection of what is moft excellent in

the

the political and civil laws, and in a ſimple and ingenious application of theſe laws to the cuſtoms of the nation to be governed by them.

It would be the buſineſs of the *ſublime compiler* of theſe laws to connect together the ancient and modern codes, in order to form a new one. If he ſhould poſſeſs abilities, if he ſhould have a profound knowledge of the human heart, and, above all, of the genius of the nation, he would maintain ſuch an unity of deſign, follow ſuch certain rules, and preſerve ſuch exact proportions, that a ſtate with ſuch laws for its guidance would reſemble thoſe mechanical engines, all of whoſe ſprings conſpire to the ſame end.

This great man is ſtill to appear among us, becauſe the perfection of politics is an eminent ſtep to which the human powers can with much difficulty attain.

But every thing announces the poſſibility of ſuch a genius ſtarting up; and if ſo many men endued with a profound ſagacity and a ſenſible heart had not waſted their talents in the deceitful charms of the fine arts, we ſhould have found this happy junction of moral and political laws: all would have been marked out at leaſt in theory; all would have been combined, and this eloquent type would have led us inſenſibly to the practice.

Without possessing that genius, I have done what has been in my power; I have, for twenty-five years, collected ideas with the intention of their entering into the sublime plan which another should trace, and which far exceeds my abilities. To collect every idea into a focus of unity, and apply each with precision to the national genius; this is the philosopher's stone of politics. It is less chimerical than that of the alchemists, since we see governments which enjoy a certain degree of perfection, that is to say, such a degree as may be assimilated to the passions of human nature.

Happy the people who, by the help of their writers, have given to authority that knowledge which will permit it neither to step beyond the law nor to turn it aside!

Since legislation cannot be the work of political circumstances, does it not proceed from the information and conceptions of men of genius?

GEOGRAPHY CONSIDERED IN A POLITICAL POINT OF VIEW.

WHOEVER admits an orignal plan in the universe, whoever rejects the words fatality and chance, and surveys with an attentive eye the empires

empires of ancient and modern times, will perceive an order of demarcation upon the ſurface of our globe, and will not fail to recognize the hand that traced the limits and erected the ramparts. He will behold nations mutually contending till they are confined within the geographical circle drawn by nature; in that encloſure they enjoy the repoſe which was denied them when they overleaped the bounds.

When in the height of metaphyſics, we feel ſomething that reſiſts, that repels us forcibly, that defeats us in ſpite of our efforts, it is a deciſive mark that we go beyond our limits, and ſtrain to ſurpaſs our natural capacity: it is a ſecret admonition which reminds us of our frailty, and corrects a preſumptuous weakneſs. But, in the material world, when an evident principle enlightens reaſon at the commencement of its reſearches, it is a certain token that the mind poſſeſſes a fund of reſources which will enable it to draw infallible concluſions. Let us firſt be natural philoſophers: I have thought I could diſcern on the globe a decided intention of nature to ſeparate ſtates without too much disjoining them, to delineate geometrically the form of empires, and to domiciliate kingdoms; I have thought I could perceive that the globe was ſo configured as that navigation would one day be the tie to bind together the human race. Theſe ideas will no doubt pleaſe thoſe, who, ſtruck with the harmonious immenſity, believe, that the government of the univerſe preſides majeſtically and neceſſarily over all other governments. We need only uſe our eyes, perhaps, to be convinced of theſe new truths: an attentive ſurvey of geographical charts, determines in ſome meaſure the poſitive extent of ſtates; for the mountains, the rivers, and the lakes, are the unqueſtionable boundaries and guardians which kind nature has placed for the preſervation and tranquillity of human aſſociations.

But if the order of nature have viſibly ſeparated empires, it has on another hand decreed that they ſhall have a mutual commerce of knowledge; its deſign in this reſpect is not concealed. When I hold in my hand a fragment of loadſtone, and reflect that this ſtone, which appears in no way remarkable, informs us conſtantly of the direction of the north, and renders poſſible and eaſy the navigation of the moſt unknown ſeas, I have about me a convincing proof that nature intended a ſocial life for man. All theſe indications of deſign ſeem, therefore, to evince that her views tend ſimply to unite men, and make them ſhare in common the good things diſſeminated over the globe.

Whenever,

Whenever, for the preſervation of the whole, a great criſis of nature occaſions the diſruption of a ſmall portion of the globe, you ſuddenly perceive ſeas ariſe where iſlands were ſwallowed up. Never has a gulf, never has a large gap invincibly ſeparated the different parts of the globe; on the contrary, the ſoft girdle of the waters everywhere invites man, everywhere preſents to him roads more dangerous than difficult, and which his courage and genius have ſurmounted. The celebrated Engliſh navigator who diſcovered the inhabited iſlands in the Pacific Ocean, ſailed from the Thames, paſſed the Antipodes of London, and performed the circuit of the earth.—Laſtly, ſince it has latterly been diſcovered, by a never erring experience, that winds which blow conſtantly during a certain ſeaſon of the year, waft our ſhips to India, and that contrary winds, prevailing during another ſeaſon, convey them back again to our ports—it is impoſſible not to recognize certain admirable guides calculated to approximate and unite the moſt remote nations. If man has learned to conſtruct a veſſel, a bridge upon the ocean, if this frail machine neverthleſs braves the angry elements: it is becauſe the primary intention of nature was that men of all climates ſhould not be ſtrangers to each other. A dark cloud conceals from us the nations which inhabit the northern extremity of America; but a ſlight convulſion of the globe may ſuddenly form a ſea, to conduct our veſſels among theſe new nations; and in a ſimilar way, although the interior parts of Africa be nearly as much unknown as the centre of the earth, it requires only a happy occurrence to open for us the route. The great views of nature will ſooner or later be accompliſhed.

For the ſame reaſon that ſhe gives mountains a gentle ſlope, to allow a free acceſs to them and facilitate the entrance into the vallies, ſhe has diſtributed in all directions a profuſion of rivers and ſeas; every thing announces a circulation ſimilar to that in the human body. She therefore wills that all the people of the earth ſhould be knit by the bonds of union, but without claſhing ſuddenly and being too readily blended. Thus, by extending and connecting our various branches of knowledge, we ſhall find that they all tend to the improvement of the human ſpecies; and in this view art is nature.

At firſt ſight, Europe, Aſia, and Africa, form only the ſame continent. It is not certain but America has a communication near the pole with the other parts of the earth. Theſe continents, which nature has united, have a natural right to procure, by means of navigation, an eaſy intercourſe between one country and another.

If Japan forms in a manner a kind of ſolitary ſtate, it may be replied that, when the Corea and the adjacent countries ſhall one day grow commercial ſtates, the ports of Japan, becoming then neceſſary to theſe ſtates for facilitating commerce, will be opened, and that empire obliged to enter into the general plan.

Let political œconomy conſult above all the geographical chart of a country; it will perceive that happy conſequences depend on the reſources and natural advantages of a ſtate. The paſſage of the ſound alone gives exiſtence to the kingdom of Denmark: the dukes of Savoy take a moſt important ſhare in the wars of Italy, not ſo much on account of the forces they can bring into the field, as by their having poſſeſſion of the lofty chain of mountains which enables them to open or diſpute the entrance.

There is manifeſtly a neceſſary correſpondence between the political laws and the aſcendancy of ſituation; it is falſe that the ſame intereſts can equally ſuit all nations. The geographical ſituation conſtitutes a poſitive law which cannot be miſconceived. Theories are abſurd when they

they pretend to enjoin in one ſtate what is practicable in another.

Local circumſtances ſway every thing: men may enact laws, but the moſt admirable regulations can never be ſeparated from their application. When the genius of Frederic ſhall be totally extinct in Pruſſia, that country will no longer comprehend a kingdom, but marquiſates; while the mountains of Switzerland will conſtantly have in their view the ſame forms of government.

In the adminiſtration of ſtates how great is the diſparity occaſioned by the hilly or plain ſurface, the ſouthern aſpect or the expoſure to the north wind, a natural haven or a promontory, an eaſy anchorage or a road crowded with rocks? Hence ariſes an infinite variety in the political inſtitutions.

If the geography of a country be not ſeriouſly examined, if its hydrography be ſlighted, all will reſt upon ruinous foundations; for nature has ordained that the moral conduct of nations ſhould be intimately connected with their phyſical qualities, and a chart is the moſt luminous torch for ſtateſmen:—a torch which reflects a much clearer light than the idle ſpeculations of cabinets, that have ſo long been deceived by inſignificant terms. It is impoſſible to behold

 without

without admiration how great an accession the empress of the Russias could have made to the grandeur of her provinces, by uniting the rivers her empire embraces. This admirable plan, so worthy of being happily executed, was abandoned upon the event of the war against the Turks. It presented to the industry of many nations all the resources indicated or formed by nature. Catherine would have imitated the example of Alexander, had she not for the sake of personal repose, preferred the removal of her military forces from the vicinity of her throne, and the employment of them in distant expeditions.

If we may still judge from the scite of Alexandria, its founder possessed a genius superior to his success; the one passed away like a gleam of light, and outlived not the conqueror of the Persians, but the other will last for ages.

View the situation of Tyre, of Carthage, of Venice, of Genoa, of Amsterdam, and of London; you will acknowledge that nature has made these different points the centre of a vast commerce. Change the scite, and the resources, the means of strength and prosperity, will no longer be the same. Venice was formerly the emporium of an universal trade, and as it were the bond of union of the three parts of the

world

world then known. The paſſage to India by the Cape of Good Hope has cauſed that grandeur to diſappear which was the object of the jealouſy of thirty ſovereigns.

When an empire is extenſive and compact, it can ſpeedily acquire wealth and protect itſelf. The ſovereign of ſeveral disjointed ſtates, ſuch for inſtance, as the Pruſſian monarch, may command and give laws to rich but ſtraggling provinces; but he will never have the force of him who reigns over provinces united and connected in one centre. France eminently enjoys this advantage, by which the different parts that compoſe it, forming a contiguous whole, afford to each other mutual aid, ſupport, comfort, knowledge, and defence. This kingdom owes its natural dominion to its compact regions, wedged in between three great ſeas and many chains of craggy mountains: the rivers and mountains of this fine country have latterly given names to various of the departments; and it was a moſt happy idea to hit upon, that nature, in forming kingdoms, had alſo traced the diviſions, by giving them diſtinct and material limits.

Who ſees not that France, that Spain, if Porgal were again united to her, that England, Ireland, Switzerland, Sardinia, and Sicily, are in a manner placed on the foundations of the globe! When you beheld (at a time when the reſt of Europe was enſlaved) liberty extending her ſway over the Britiſh iſles, it was becauſe theſe iſles are eſpecially formed for the throne of liberty. If the Hungarians are oftener convulſed than any other nation, the reaſon is, that they occupy an abundant territory, capable of ſupplying to them every thing within themſelves. Behold Poland expoſed on all ſides; ſhe has needed inceſſantly for her defence all her valour: her children are obliged to be perpetually in arms; and her ſoldiery, far too numerous to maintain, keep her peaſants in abjection, indigence, and ſlavery. That the Poliſh territory is entirely open, is the primary cauſe of theſe miſchiefs. The well-known calamities of that unhappy republic reſult leſs from the defects of its conſtitution than from its geographical ſituation, which leaves it a prey on every ſide to the invaſion of foreign troops.

If we conſider Italy, it requires only, as was the caſe formerly, one central point; and as ſoon as the papal phantom ſhall fall with the moſt incredible of all ſuperſtitions, it will be revived by this ſingle and probable event. Ruſſia announces plainly that it will ſoon be divided into two ſtates, becauſe the capital of

that

that empire being badly ſituated, it is a giant with an exceſſive head which it cannot ſupport. The compariſon ſhows that nature has been prodigal to France; this is her favourite kingdom: it is accurately circumſcribed, and this circumſtance forms and will form its invincible ſtrength; for we have only to ſtretch our dominion to the Rhine and unite Savoy, and it will be difficult to find on the face of the globe an empire better ſituated and of a nobler and more commanding figure.

Although the Grand Signor poſſeſſes, in Europe, in Aſia, and in Africa, immenſe countries, yet the double deſpotiſm of the ſcimitar and the koran, the victories of Selim and of Mahomet, have not hitherto been able to form one whole of the Ottoman empire, becauſe nature oppoſed it by frittering too much theſe ſpacious and magnificent ſhreds. If an arm of the ſea were ſuddenly to croſs the Germanic ſtates, inſtead of being divided into ſo many particular ſovereignties the intereſts of which mutually claſh, there would certainly be no more than two, and each of theſe would be incomparably ſtronger than all the ſovereignties collectively that now exiſt. What conſtituted the force of the United Provinces, thoſe ſeven little provinces which the Spaniſh monarchy ſeemed ready to ſwallow up?

What created that republic, ſo feeble in its origin and the pooreſt in Europe, though grown the richeſt in the world? The ſea. It was the ſea that multiplied its hands to protect and enrich it; it was the herrings, which it raiſed from the abyſs of the ocean, that laid the foundation of its commerce and its opulence, that began to make its name known and reſpected in every quarter of the civilized globe. Theſe herrings gave it in Africa the Cape of Good Hope, and in Aſia opened to it the invaluable traffic of its Eaſt India company.

I form, therefore, no hypotheſis; but would it not be curious at leaſt to fix in ſpeculation the dimenſions of all the modern ſtates; to lop the overgrown empires, and meaſure them by prudent and ſage proportions; to give ſolidity to thoſe which are too ſmall; to ingraft between the great powers little ſtates which, ſerving as barriers or wedges, may oppoſe each over-violent hoſtile encounter; and to communicate the benefit of the ſeas without ſhutting up the paſſage of the rivers? In meaſuring certain ſtates according to their latitudes, a new order would ſpring up, and the auguſt deſigns of Providence would ſtill be manifeſted in thoſe vaſt maſſes which ſeemed committed to *chance*: but this opprobrious word chance, ought no longer to

have

have a place in our books. Order prevails every where, though concealed; and if it eſcapes our view in great objects, it nevertheleſs exiſts. Geography muſt give the firſt leſſon on theſe important objects. We can already trace the outlines of this grand ſyſtem in the preſent poſition of empires, and war often introduces by violence what reaſon would have brought about peaceably. Nothing is then more abſurd than the ambitious chimeras of thoſe great ſtates which ſeek to encounter and ſwallow up other great ſtates. Conſult antiquity: the Tigris and Euphrates have always defended with ſucceſs the countries through which they flow againſt the ambition of conquerors; Arabia has repelled every attack; and Egypt, though become a province, has ſtill retained the majeſty of a kingdom.

At the appearance of the Romans, the empires for the greater part had acquired their natural ſite, when the ambition of that nation deranged every thing. The world, ſtill new at that period, exhibited powerful kingdoms in Aſia alone, the true cradle of the firſt race of men. Africa, and eſpecially the weſtern world, was peopled much later, and was filled merely by a multitude of little republics or of little rival nations, jealous of each other.

They

They were, however, able for many years to contend againſt the Romans, weak as they were, and incapable of maintaining expenſive wars of any conſiderable duration. It accordingly required ages for theſe Romans to ſubdue Italy; but when once they had acquired the dominion of that noble country, Sicily and the then ſeparated kingdoms of Spain were conquered, the empire of the Carthaginians ſhaken, Macedonia and Greece invaded, and Africa and Aſia ſwallowed up.

Undoubtedly the whole world would then have come under the yoke of the Romans, if conſiderate and provident nature had not afforded ſecure and almoſt inacceſſible retreats for the liberty of the human race: ſhe had in this way provided ſo well, that theſe conquerors fell back, and certain of the ſtates were ſaved by their mere configuration. Univerſal monarchy was, even in thoſe times, a chimerical pretenſion: theſe conquerors ravaged on all ſides, but retained nothing.

Had the Romans conſulted [political geography,] they would not have reduced into provinces the great kingdoms which they conquered. Rome, content with a moderate grandeur, could have fixed certain limits within which all would have been Roman. Nothing was more

conſonant

consonant to nature than such a compacted circle of territory; and in our own days, the constituent assembly has judged well that France must be circumscribed, to double its force.

The vast conquests of the Roman empire may be regarded as one of the causes of its declension. The Romans had within their grasp the most efficacious method of securing its salvation; it was, to form small states, independant of each other, under different forms of government.

They might easily have retained over these states a superiority which should keep them always dependant in a certain degree on the empire. The people who would have formed these states would have been happier, and Rome would thence have better retained her power; the barbarians, obliged to attack separately each of these small states, must have met with infinitely more resistance than in attacking in many points at once this immense colossus, whose magnitude was such as afterwards to form the empires of the East and of the West.

A small state has its peculiar principle of existence; it sometimes successfully resists the most violent attacks, and makes head against forces which might appear sufficient to annihilate it. Rome, protected by private states, would undoubtedly have repulsed the enemy; and a conqueror

queror of the diſtant provinces would never have dared to attack the capital of the world. Of all conquerors Alexander is the moſt famous; but, in his rapid progreſs, he gave unwittingly a ſalutary ſhock to the univerſe: he ſubverted the empire of the Perſians, who ventured to paſs the boundaries which the Euphrates and the Tigris had oppoſed between them and the people of upper Aſia; and order was thus re-eſtabliſhed in that vaſt part of the globe.

Parthia, from that time included within its natural limits, reſiſted with glory thoſe Roman legions that carried their victorious arms over the moſt diſtant frontiers; and was itſelf repulſed by them when it attempted to tranſgreſs thoſe bounds.

On the other hand, Egypt, protected and enriched by the Red Sea, by the Nile, and the Mediterranean, defended by ſands which fought for it and buried whole armies; Egypt reſumed under the Ptolemies its place among nations, and has ſince preſerved an impoſing dignity, even beneath the fetters of deſpotiſm.

Arabia, bordering on fertile Egypt, and entrenched by the Red Sea, the ocean, the Perſian gulf, its deſerts and its rocks; Arabia triumphs over the efforts of all the conquerors who have attempted to maſter it. If the liberty

of

of man, dear to the Supreme Being, has prepared retreats, after the plan of nature, in the vast forests of Germany and amidst the frozen tracts of the North, it seems to have fixed its eternal empire in Arabia. The Arab, by his deserts and his mode of life, which has never varied and appears in him a kind of instinct, seems by his destiny to be the immortal child of independance. How indeed could the yoke be fastened round a wandering being who, in his immense plains, changes continually his spot of residence, who can endure fatigue and hunger, and who regards a sedentary life as a punishment? Should the rest of the globe be covered with slaves, the stamp of freedom would be still preserved among these roving tribes.

I repeat it, I doubt not but by improving political geography, people will discover sooner or later that nature has traced visibly with her finger the walls and boundaries of empires, and will be convinced that it is against the eternal order of things for a kingdom to extend itself and diverge into separate and unconnected provinces. It is by following this simple and fertile speculation that we shall probably come to know the great designs of the author of nature, who, having with profound wisdom ordained every thing, has undoubtedly not abandoned the physical

ſical form of ſtates to the ambitious graſp of a few madmen named conquerors. In proof of this it is to be obſerved that empires of prepoſterous dimenſions have periſhed, while the regular maſſes have ſubſiſted.

The geographer would therefore become a firſt rate politician, if, knowing how to eſtimate the value of rivers, of mountains, and of maritime coaſts, he were in a manner to trace in detail the felicities and enjoyments of a nation, by ſhewing that it could neither be contracted nor aggrandized without imminent danger; if he were to ſay to a nation, "*This is the ocean which confines you; this the continent which tells you to extend your territory to ſuch a mountain; this the river which forms your ſeparation from other ſtates*,—and the mouth of which cannot be cloſed up *by vain treaties, while the merchandizes of two bordering ſtates can traverſe over the extent of its waters.*" The ſovereign laws of nature are much ſuperior to the diplomatic code: they are imprinted upon the globe. When theſe laws are violated, there is a reſiſting effort which convulſes for ages, till the ſtates adjacent to each other acquire the form preſcribed to them by nature. Rouſſeau thus addreſſed the Poles: *Fear not being conquered, ſo long as they are unable to digeſt you.*

After ſo many uſeleſs treaties, it is neceſſary to recur to theſe eternal laws, becauſe, in the real order of things, the right of nature is the firſt of rights: when political right ſhall advance ſupported by thoſe beautiful and material forms which nature diſplays to the contemplative eye, it will not go aſtray. The ſucceſs of this plan appears to be demonſtrated, ſince, notwithſtanding the extravagance of family compacts and treaties of inheritance, the coalition of crowned heads, and the violence of their deſpotiſm, the phyſical maſs of the globe has withſtood the agitation of thoſe ſovereigns, who, wiſhing to efface ſome of the lines of nature's eternal graver, have only ſhown the vacuity and nothingneſs of proud imbecility.

OF THE STATE OF PUBLIC INFORMATION.

THE people form the government, and for this reaſon, that the general opinion in every ſtate regulates the adminiſtration, which never claſhes with impunity againſt the public voice, a voice that reſiſts and oppoſes an inſurmountable obſtacle to the proud will of the ſovereign.

Thoſe

Thoſe nations merit our ſcorn and contempt that would have an adminiſtration great and enlightened, and yet betray the utmoſt levity, or rather an abſolute inattention, in the weightieſt public affairs.

The moſt conſummate miniſter always ſprings from the claſs of citizens, and can carry into the national council that expanſion of mind alone which the nation has attained, unleſs he be ſuppoſed to poſſeſs ſuch an extraordinary genius as is exceedingly rare. He will have no other ideas than thoſe which have been circulated around him.

The miniſter will be heedleſs and fickle, if the nation is heedleſs and fickle; he will be devoid of genius and intelligence, if political matters ſhould by all be abandoned to chance. What uſe would he make of a genius vaſtly above his age, if the nation were to be incapable of profiting by all the ſuperiority of his knowledge? He would not be underſtood, and his political genius, in a manner inſulated, would not be able to combine execution with theory. But let this ſame miniſter, legiſlator, or adminiſtrator, placed (no matter how) in the governing body, ſee his ſyſtem, till then uncertain even in his own eyes, confirmed by the public opinion, and he will acquire confidence,

and

and advance with the train of thinking men. Thoſe who are capable of reflecting will beſtow their approbation; the weakneſs of the adminiſtrator will diſappear; and he will become ſtrong in his intellectual operations, becauſe a very great number of men will have adopted before hand his ideas. Thus is every well enlightened nation always well governed. As a great number of men can, by their united efforts, raiſe the moſt ponderous maſſes and erect obeliſks; ſo the opinion of all and the vigilance of all, meet and ſtrike out in practice the more important truths of political œconomy. For when the ſubjects which intereſt adminiſtration ſhall be publicly debated, they will be cleared up in a ſhort time; the moſt intricate queſtions will become plain axioms which the ignorance of ſome and the treachery of others can no longer obſcure.

When people complain of the adminiſtration, they often accuſe themſelves; they confeſs that they have not beſtowed on public affairs the attention theſe deſerve, and the miniſter has perhaps in the ſequel reaſon to advance this great abſurdity, *that it is lawful for the miniſter alone to examine what intereſts the general order.* The people having ceaſed to reflect, it becomes the minister, however unqualified for the task, to reflect for them.

When the sovereign or his council is not well informed, the nation must supply the limited ideas of the ministry; and this is what happens in those states over which a degree of political knowledge is diffused: the false ideas of ministers are there rectified, a general clamour is raised, and the happy effects of a well directed education among all the classes of citizens are perceived. No dastardly or servile fear is entertained; justice is rendered to the real statesman, the superficial theorist is hunted down, and if there be no city for slaves, as is observed by one of the ancients, there is always a government for enlightened men.

Every head of a society depends on the society, and is accountable to it, even in the most imperfect governments. The good citizens are the true reformers of the state; they expect from a placeman a statement of his public conduct, because men, being rational beings, are calculated to know their own interests. They submit to be in some little degree deceived, because they are sensible that administrators are surrounded by tribes of mercenaries; but, after having rejected these fractions, they discover the truth,

truth, which is destined to subsist eternally, and, what is still more astonishing, they pass sentence as posterity will do after them.

If laws were to be precise, clear, and simple, and if all the strength of human reason were to be manifested in a nervous style, the wisdom of institutions would be understood: and why has not eloquence applied itself to write with force and simplicity the sacred text of the laws?

A code in the vulgar tongue still remains a great desideratum: amidst so many bills posted up, we have never seen one which contained an ordinance replete with simple and moving reflections.

When we consider that the laws ought to be read and understood by all men, and yet that we know not where to find the national code, we are surprised at this culpable negligence; and the legislator has lost his noblest right, that of speaking to the heart of man.

Is there a single individual who cannot comprehend the conventions of which the utility is clear and known, who cannot judge that he enjoys the advantages of the law, and that, without it, other men might arm and conspire against him? The minds of the people become enlightened when an attempt is made to enlighten them, when an attention is paid to the efforts of the men of intelligence who ſeek alone to propagate knowledge. The moſt ignorant people are at the ſame time the moſt wicked; ſtupidity is the parent of every diſorder. We teach grammar and the catechiſm, yet we have neglected to teach the code of laws.

Maxims (who would believe it?) direct empires. All hiſtory bears teſtimony that there is a faſhion in the polity of nations. The Romans, who were perſuaded that the fates had decreed to them the empire of the world, looked upon every thing as juſt which conducted them to greatneſs. The treaties of the republic were always ſo many ſnares: the prince whom it was its intereſt to raiſe up, was always held to be the lawful prince. We muſt not imagine that the Romans affected even any ſenſe of ſhame; they believed that their will ought to be the rule of the world. Their perfidy towards the Carthaginians, the Rhodians, the Ætolians, and Jugurtha, is well known. The Roman republic never feared but two men, Hannibal and Mithridates; but the enemies of the Romans failed in their deſigns, becauſe they continued to employ the ſame policy when new circumſtances required a different one. Rome was invariably guided by the ſame principles; and the exile of the Tarquins and the deſtruction

tion of Carthage tended to but one object. Rome moulded itself, from its origin till the time it over-ran the world, to all the virtues which ought to serve as the basis of greatness. It watched the neighbouring, as well as the most distant states, and surprised them under such predicaments as must necessarily have hastened their fall. When the Romans had not an immediate plea to make war upon a nation, they recurred to the ages prior even to the foundation of Rome. All these heroic attacks had their foundation in the lofty maxims which promised to them the dominion of the universe. Thus a few words, when they have made a lively impression on a people, are a rallying point which supports and re-establishes their courage; and such a Power has become predominant because its standards bore such a device and not such another.

THE NEW GENERATION.

THE sentiment of liberty is universally diffused; the birds, the fishes enjoy it; it accompanies the lion in his deserts, the chamois-goat on his mountain-summits, and the rein-deer amidst his snows: and yet there are slaves so mean and debased as to dispute this innate feeling in man, and to dare assert that he is from his birth in a subjected state.

Man is born free, and has a freedom annexed to his very existence: his rights and titles are at each generation renewed, for nature bestows on all a *new title*.

If all beings are free, nature, ever the same and ever uniform, is no where in a state of slavery. Who has fancied himself able to strip man of his noblest inheritance?

Since, when they united in society, the first men framed a *contract*, this contract unquestionably cannot be revoked. Society requires common and equal rights; but this contract could only bind those who made it. A father has no lawful authority over his children, except during their minority, and before they are grown men and able to act for themselves: otherwise he would abase and degrade his posterity for ever, by a breach of justice, which is repugnant to good sense, to reason, and to paternal affection.

Nature, always entire, always new, and always a *minor*, does she not continually demonstrate that her rights are unalterable and independant? Every individual brings into the world his rights at his birth; he has therefore the liberty of examining, of approving, of renewing, and of changing the contract made by his father. The father, a fierce warrior, fixes his views on war alone; the son, a peaceful labourer, breathes only peace: the one flies to the field of Mars; the other repairs to the temple of Minerva. Can their laws be the same?

Besides, in the perpetual ebb and flow on the surface of our earth, it is impossible but that human ideas must change. How could it enter the head of man to enact stable and permanent laws, in which it was prohibited to make the slightest alteration? Are we a community of beavers or a hive of bees, that we are thus reduced to mere instinct? The sparrow, hatched to-day, will be the same as his parent, his grandsire, and all his ancestors, as high as the Adam of his race: the son is equal to his father, since their nature and essence are absolutely the same. But what matters this to me; I am neither a sparrow nor a beaver.

Besides, if man be considered as a slave, why are laws framed? How can virtues be required of him? If he were in reality a slave, then would all be in the same condition; but then would not all be equal?

Of what benefit are reason, knowledge, and

humanity, if we muſt remain ſubject to laws written with the point of the ſword, by people alike barbarous and ignorant? Are the rights of humanity to be diſcuſſed with a lance in the hand? And yet was it not in this manner that moſt of the nations of Europe received their laws? Does not the ſpirit of the Goths, the Viſigoths, the Burgundians, the Lombards, the Saxons, the Francs, and the Alani, almoſt every where prevail?

Reaſon, ever ſlow and tardy, has arrived always too late, and has not had force ſufficient to deſtroy old prejudices rooted by long habit, and ſupported by obſtinacy and ignorance. Hence the abſurd code of barbariſm, which endeavoured to make man a ſort of beaſt of burden, by attaching him to the *glebe*.

But, if our anceſtors ſought thus to degrade the human race, on the other hand they ennobled the ground. With them it became a fief, a marquiſate, a viſcounty, a county, a barony, &c. Ought ſuch an extravagance to be ſanctioned by us becauſe it originated in the brain of our forefathers? Had the Egyptians, the Greeks, the Romans, and all the moſt enlightened nations of the univerſe, ideas ſo fantaſtic? Aſſuredly they never ennobled the ground, even that in which they planted their gods,

gods, the bean, the onion, the garlic, and ſuch other divinities.

And what is there in common between us and our forefathers? They were ignorant and barbarous, we are enlightened and civilized; they were enemies to the fine arts, we derive luſtre from them, our mode of life being diametrically oppoſite to theirs; if their code was reaſonable for them, it is abſurd for us; and if it was irrational when they formed it, how much more irrational is it that we ſhould ſuffer ourſelves to be governed by it!

Ought not this noble ground to be trodden, cultivated, and reaped by nobles only? Ought it not to be manured with noble compoſt alone? Ought it not to be tilled by no other than a noble plough, and noble horſes? In that caſe, all muſt be ennobled, not excepting the dew which ſhall fall from heaven to fertilize theſe noble fields.

The only noble ground, in my apprehenſion, is that which yields moſt food to its inhabitants. The land only exiſts and has a real value, by the labour of the peaſants: and the nobleſt of all lands, were it peopled with dukes, and earls, and barons, with pride and indolence, would be ſtrewed by their noble carcaſes, and inhabited by birds of prey and fallow-deer, allured thither

to

to devour the noble carrion, if none but noble hands were allowed to touch the noble domain.

To ennoble the *ground* and to degrade the nature of man who renders it fertile, is one of thoſe cruel follies which could only be fallen upon in times of barbarity, when the human underſtanding was totally debaſed and eclipſed. It belongs to the divinity alone to ennoble the clay, by animating it with his breath; nor is it more poſſible for men to change the nature of things and to ſuppreſs human liberty, than to preſcribe another road to the chariot of the ſun.

Man, being free, has on that account preſerved all his rights, and no one could contract for him without having been fully authorized. As ſoon as age permits him to enter into ſociety and to form a part of the public, he has a claim in the *public concerns*. This is the moment nature has aſſigned him for the complete expanſion of his organs and of his intellectual powers: let him ſtipulate his intereſts; he is maſter of them. But, ſince it is proved, by the moſt accurate calculations, and by the experience of ages, that ninety years compoſe three ages of men, we ſhould thence conclude that in every thirty years there ought to be a gene-

ral

ral aſſembly, to eſtabliſh a reviſion in great ſocieties.

What a truly auguſt ſpectacle would a new generation preſent, exerting its moſt inconteſtible privilege, that of ſettling, in its own name, the rights of humanity, and thus correcting, in the face of heaven, all ſorts of outrages committed in every corner of the world! *This ſocial regeneration*, to be renewed every thirty years, would ſtamp on government a majeſty that would no longer allow it to adopt thoſe pitiful little laws which public reaſon would treat with contempt; for many old laws are only the teſtament of cruelty and inſolence. A new generation can annul the revengeful or abſurd edicts which are contrary to the immediate and general intereſt.

MUNICIPALITIES.

A MUNICIPAL government is the one the moſt conformable to the happineſs both of the nation and the ſovereign *. Each city has its own intereſts more eſpecially in view, and there

* What I mean by the term "Sovereign" cannot but be well underſtood: it is moſt unqueſtionably not a ſingle man.

are an abundance of things which depend on locality. The ſovereign is therefore intereſted to hear the repreſentations of the various corporations which compoſe the nation, ſeeing that each of them has particular obſervations reſulting from its ſituation to make. A bridge, a river, a mountain, conſtitutes either the riches or the indigence of this or that city. In nature the great whole is compoſed of parts infinitely ſmall; and in politics this general rule is ſtill clearer obſerved.

A municipal form * ſtrengthens the ties which attach the people to the ſovereign, whoſe eſpecial duty it becomes to direct to the general intereſt the intereſts of individuals. He facilitates the gathering of taxes, and diminiſhes both the expenditure, and that ſwarm of uſeleſs beings who would otherwiſe be a burthen to, and in the pay of the ſupreme authority. The ſovereign whoſe aim is to accompliſh every thing, and to leave every where the traces of his power, is not an enlightened ſovereign. Love and confidence know how to make ſacrifices; and the people fancy themſelves free when they are placed in a line with their magiſtrates, of the

* Here I proteſt that this chapter, as were alſo the preceding ones of the preſent volume, was firſt publiſhed by me in 1786.

juſtice

juſtice of whoſe awards they are then perſuaded, as well as that the magiſtracy is calculated to favour liberty.

The people, while they ſee the power in the hands of the ſovereign, perceive at the ſame time the laws confided to thoſe of the magiſtrates, by whom the prince and his ſubjects are united. The ſtrength of the ſociety reſides in its well-informed, laborious, and zealous citizens. Nothing can therefore be better conceived, nor more wiſely eſtabliſhed, than provincial aſſemblies, by which the people will of themſelves be led into a faith and confidence of the goodneſs of the government, and their view, wearied unceaſingly with the diſplay of military preparations, will be guided towards the patriotic functions of this happy magiſtracy.

The municipal government gives, in a manner, a higher policy to the political government, renders knaves of no utility, beſtows additional reſpect on men of worth, and makes the citizen ſtill freer. Taxation is managed in a direct way: it paſſes immediately from its ſource into the hands by which it is to be expended, a ſimple mode which is certainly vaſtly preferable to the ſyſtem of farming out the taxes. Were ſuch a plan to be adopted in France, the revenues of the ſtate would be as conſtant as ever, and that kingdom would be delivered from its greateſt ſcourge, the farmers-general, who heap up riches, obtain a miſchievous credit, and multiply the agents of their avarice and the accomplices of their extortions; who, while they vex and torment their fellow citizens, live at their expenſe. By employing the municipal body in the collection of the taxes, the latter become ſimple, equitable, and little burthenſome, at the ſame time that all the inconveniences which are now dreaded, and have been ſo ſorely felt, are avoided.

The municipal government is a ſtranger to all commerce except that which is uſeful, or, in other words, that which tends more to the advantage of the ſtate than of the merchant. A more limited commerce which beſtows eaſe, not riches, which gives a value to the productions of the ſoil, not foreign productions, is preferable to that external commerce by which money is accumulated without commodities being multiplied, and which brings in its train a luxury deſtructive of cultivation, to favour the importation of certain ſuperfluities reſerved for the rich. Mercantile proſperity is not always the criterion of the proſperity of the ſtate. An excluſive commerce, a commerce in which there ſhall be no competition, is one of thoſe extreme vio-

lences

lences more detrimental to him by whom it is obtained than to him who ſubmits to it. All the *good* it can produce is an accumulation of pernicious money. The municipal government at once retains the cultivator and the artiſt, encourages them without enriching them too much, and above all prevents them from tranſporting elſewhere their talents and their induſtry. All theſe opinions are founded on facts; and it is to be wiſhed that every oppoſite opinion ſhould be laid aſide, in favour of truths either certain or evident.

Laſtly, Municipalities lead to the perfect organization of the different parts of the ſtate, and enter into an harmonious combination with monarchy, which they gradually and effectually improve. Each province, that is to ſay, each municipal diviſion of the kingdom, has an *interpreter* to explain its wants and its true ſituation. Municipal adminiſtrations form the political bond of union, by giving to the people an apparent liberty: they are eſtabliſhed to prevent great abuſes. In politics every benefit reſults from a concurrence and union of intelligences. Men conſtantly gain ſomething when they are interrogated on that which intereſts them in a direct way; and obedience thus becomes more ready, even confounding itſelf with love. In France

the

the pens of generous writers have juſt effected the happieſt plan of provincial adminiſtrations, as well as that of the intermediate aſſemblies of the cantons and dioceſes: ſuch a ſervice rendered to the nation could not without a moſt abſurd ingratitude have been paſſed over in ſilence.

A good internal economical adminiſtration therefore depends on theſe municipalities ſo fruitful in local advantages: it is impoſſible that the eye which embraces the politics without, can ſuperintend all the details of the towns, villages, and ſmall cities.

We ſee then that the part which inſtructs has taken a form and conſiſtence; and the more it ſhall be diſperſed among the people of the provinces, the more will it, in entering into a ſtill cloſer intimacy with them, be enabled to bring about very uſeful ameliorations.

PERPETUAL OSCILLATION.

WHO does not ſee (this applies, however, to thoſe who know how to ſee) a *real* oſcillation in each government? Here the abuſe of the power termed monarchical has given riſe to the idea of republics; and farther on the abuſe of of liberty has reſtored the monarchical ſtate. The Danes, to extricate themſelves from a monſtrous government, ventured to eſtabliſh and legalize a deſpot, becauſe, ſuffering as they then did, it was the ſmaller evil of the two.

He who thinks, examines, and judges by effects ſhould not be the dupe of thoſe vague notions, expreſſed by terms ſtill more vague, which every one underſtands in his own way. The names we are pleaſed to beſtow on different governments, can in no way change their relations to each other, and theſe relations are what it is important for us to know.

The blind admirers of the conſtitution of the republics of antiquity will not give to theſe a new birth among us, becauſe men can merely correct and not change the nature of things. States, like individuals, will undergo continual modifications, but will never loſe a certain character.

The particular circumſtances of the poſition of every ſtate determine on the more or leſs extenſive employment of its means. Run over all the ſyſtems of the different governments, and you will ſee that the ſame cauſes conſtantly produce the ſame effects. If the people are happy and tranquil in a ſtate, of what import is it that the denomination of the government is held to be bad, when the ſyſtem is a better one than is to be found elſewhere?

To pretend to ſubject ſtates to certain adminiſtrative principles, while the ſcience of politics is no other than an aſſemblage of facts inceſſantly varied by cauſes which man is permitted neither to foreſee nor to ſhun, is to place the remedy for the evil in impotent hands, and to deprive man both of his reſources and his means: to him it belongs, by an unceaſing labour, to correct the *minutiæ* of the political economy.

Upon the ſlighteſt examination we perceive a multitude of governments, which, carrying as they do the ſame title, ſtill differ from each other. The term *monarchy* alone calls up ſeveral ideas. *Abſolute* monarchy; *limited* monarchy; a monarchy *tempered* by a ſenate, and modified by ſtates general; a monarchy *modified* by a national diet, (not merely compoſed of the grandees of the nation, but in which are blended the magiſtrates or deputies of the ſecond order, ſuch as the *communes*, theſe laſt by their profeſſion and their moral habits having a ſtronger inclination towards the people and their intereſts;) and a monarchy chiefly *tempered* by the prevailing manners.

The republican ſtate of government is ſplit

into

into as many divisions, and sub-divisions, as its form has from age to age been varied, at times by the ascendancy of some citizen of extraordinary talents, at others by its own intrinsic rudeness, and, finally, by the insensible passage of a nation that loses its liberty, into a submission to monarchical authority.

There is a servitude so pleasant and so natural, that under its yoke liberty is forgotten. A nation may be found that will not govern itself, because it fears being exposed to commotions of a nature and magnitude not to be borne. It dreads an energetical constitution like that of England; and resists that economy and that gravity which found the basis of free governments. It neither thirsts after universal dominion, as did the Romans, nor after an universal system of commerce. It wishes to taste, if I may be permitted the expression, every species of legislation; and as it judges its character incompatible with the republican constitution, it adopts a reasonable but reserved obedience. It preserves a love and a respect for the sovereign, provided he does not bear too hardly with his sceptre. It cherishes a delicate idea, the point of honour, which it will never allow to be wounded, while a severity of discipline is not suited to its courage. It fancies itself posſeſſed of more freedom than it chooſes to expreſs, and, contented with its lot, envies not other nations, depending equally on its own fidelity and the moderation of its monarch. Is not this the picture of the French nation *? It feels within itſelf that ſublime ardour which would be ſo excellent a principle for the formation of an Engliſh liberty, but as that would be too great a tax on its gaiety and its pleaſures, it pants after tranquil movements alone, and, to ſecure its glory and repoſe, will never ceaſe to pay its court to the genius of monarchy.

To judge aright of the different conſtitutions of ſtates, their effects muſt neceſſarily be ſeen. When a legiſlation is purely ſpeculative, it is changed by the phyſical poſition of the country and the character of its inhabitants. Every nation has within itſelf ſome cauſes which require particular regulations. If the legiſlation be inflexible it will be turned againſt itſelf: if it be ſagaciouſly contrived it will adapt itſelf to the

* When this fragment was penned, the author had perhaps a right to think ſo. Louis XVI. diveſted of an abſolute ſway he had always been too good to exerciſe, but the right of which, abandoned as was its uſe for a ſeaſon, had been notwithſtanding a grievance, was then the idol of his people—of ſubjects who ſeemed to be bound in an eternal obedience to him and his deſcendants; how ſtrangely has the picture been ſince reverſed! *Tranſlator.*

physical and moral character of the nation by which it shall have been received; and as every national character is subject to variations, the legislation will follow these movements, and will never thwart the propensity of the national spirit.

TRIBUTES.

"*TRIBUTES,*" observes the author of the Spirit of Laws, "*should be so readily collected,* "*and so clearly established, as to render it impos-* "*sible for the receivers either to augment or di-* "*minish them.*"

In these few words every thing is comprehended. The tribute will not be burthensome when limited and defined by law. The legislator, therefore, to avoid being forced to be equitable, will aim at being clear and precise;—he will frame laws of easy execution.

Edicts of exemption from tribute have never been promulgated. "*Princes,*" as Montesquieu further observes, "*speak constantly of their own* "*necessities;—never of ours.*"

Can a man bless the laws of the society in which he lives, when in reality he derives from them no advantage whatever; when in their name he is obliged to make full and abſolute ſacrifices; and when, in common with himſelf, the greater part of the kingdom is borne down and oppreſſed by theſe very laws, which by every impartial obſerver muſt be held to be arbitrary? There is a certain burthen which I am ſenſible muſt neceſſarily incline more to the one ſide than the other, but it ought to be ſupportable to all.

The happineſs of man, and the property he has acquired, attach him to the ſoil, the foſter-mother that provides for all our wants, and diſcharges all the coſts of our ſtay here below. Man brings nothing with him into this world but his nakedneſs, a poor ſecurity, and but badly calculated to fill the *royal treaſury*. The earth therefore is to be our paymaſter, and to diſcharge the taxes.

Monarchs make war to ſubjugate a province and augment the ſtate revenues, not to ſubdue men who can fly and eſtabliſh themſelves elſewhere. The man who has his hands alone gives us our rich harveſts, builds our houſes, and defends our frontiers; but if the enemy approach, I aſk whether he has any thing to loſe, and whether he can be made to carry a *ſtaff* in each hand to the conteſt.

He has nothing then to dread, and the terror

belongs

belongs to the landholder alone. To the latter the conqueror may ſay: this is mine; *hinc migrate coloni.* The holder of contracts is expreſsly in the ſame predicament, ſince he lends his money on no other pledge than that of houſes or fixed revenues: he has conſequently every thing to fear when the enemy plans the ſeizure of the domains on which his ſecurity repoſes; and he ſhould therefore be made to reimburſe the royal tax paid by the property pledged, which has a value annexed to it to diſcharge his claim. Man in himſelf owes nothing: the earth is bound to pay both for him and for herſelf. France can exiſt without Frenchmen; a German carries thither his induſtry, and gives a new value to the deſerted territory: the produce is the ſame, and the ſtate has loſt nothing.

Ought land to be taxed according to a rate of eſtimation, according to the leaſe at which it is granted, or in proportion to the productions it affords?

The mode of eſtimation is liable to a thouſand errors; and, putting man and his labour entirely out of the queſtion, the ground changes and degenerates, either through accidents, ignorance, or the unſkilful management of the cultivator. It ſupplies every one with a pretext that his land is over-rated, and enables thoſe who have weight and intereſt at all times to obtain favour and have their contribution leſſened, while the great weight of the tax falls on the weak. How many opportunities does it create to torment the people!

A taxation proportioned to the leaſe is ſubject pretty nearly to the ſame inconveniences. Leaſes at an under rate are colluſively drawn up, and others are diminiſhed by a yearly *preſent* of ſome part of the produce. The farmer in the mean time is not favoured a ſhilling: the whole of the gain flows into the purſe of the lordly landholder, or perhaps, to ſpeak more correctly, into thoſe of his receiver, ſuperintendant, and domeſtics in general.

The tax in kind, which fulfils all the conditions required by Monteſquieu, is therefore the only one that can be efficaciouſly adopted. It is a kind of tribute eaſy to collect, and ſo clear in its eſtabliſhment, that it can be neither augmented nor diminiſhed by the receivers. A law to this effect will give no ſcope to the will and caprice of individuals, and it would be very eaſy to prove that on that account the tribute will not be *burthenſome*.

But to the end that this tax may be juſt, its uniformity is a neceſſary condition. I am far

from

from admitting thoſe erroneous proportions which exact from the good lands twice as much as from the bad. It has been for a long time ſaid, that the good has no greater enemy than the better; and ſuch a regulation as the above would open the door to every deſcription of abuſes, and expoſe France to an arbitrary law.

My idea is that the great, urged by the noble deſire of contributing, ought to forget their titles, their privileges, and their exemptions, ſhunning every expedient which can prevent their paying leſs than the pooreſt peaſant. But are all the lands of a vaſt empire equally calculated for productions of every deſcription? Does not every one know that our lands are for the greater part more or leſs good or more or leſs bad, according to the genius or induſtry of him who gives them their value, whatever it may be? This field, which has hitherto produced bad wheat only, will be excellent for the vine, and *vice verſâ*; while ſuch a one will yield more in wood, in trefoil, in ſainfoin, &c. &c. Certain lands are very good in years of drought, and others in rainy years. This land which has yielded nothing for want of manure, will turn out of the beſt quality in the hands of a labourer who ſhall take care to manure it, and beſtow on it other attentions. I think I have ſaid enough to demonſtrate that an eſtimation of lands, ſuch as I have hinted at, is a chimera which can only occaſion much expenſe, difficulty, and clamour, and all for a pure loſs. The culture, the manure, the ſeaſons, the highways, commerce, the ſpecies of productions in the growth of which the land is employed, &c. &c. changing its value inceſſantly, it is clear that no determinate value can be aſſigned to it with any degree of equity. We muſt therefore reſort to the tax in kind, and collect it in the ſame way that the eccleſiaſtical tythes are raiſed. In the latter caſe no attention is paid to whether the land is good or bad, and whether the labourer has beſtowed more time or ſeeds in the cultivation of this land than of that; and ſtill we do not ſee that this omiſſion excites any clamour, or meets with the ſmalleſt difficulty.

As to the objections drawn from the expences of culture, ſeed-crops, &c. to prove that more attention ought to be paid to good than to bad lands, theſe objections are remarkable on this account, that they are the very reverſe of what is now practiſed, with reſpect to the poor who are made to pay, while the rich accumulate wealth under ſhelter of their privi-

leges,

leges, exemptions, titles of nobility, &c. &c. Nothing is ſo eaſy as to prove that they belong to the claſs of thoſe reaſonings, or rather mental deluſions, which are to be found in each page of the books of the economiſts.

For example, I ſuppoſe myſelf in poſſeſſion of a farm of thirty *arpens* of wheat, ſix of which *arpens* are of the beſt quality, ſix of an inferior quality, ſix middling, ſix below mediocrity, and ſix of a bad quality.

The firſt ſix produce me each of them two hundred ſheafs: at a tithe rate each of them will therefore pay of theſe ſheafs 20 - 120

6 at 150 - - - - - - - - -	90
6 at 100 - - - - - - - - -	60
6 at 75 - - - - - - - - -	45
6 at 50 - - - - - - - - -	30

It is eaſy to ſee that the good *arpent* pays more than that of an inferior quality, and infinitely more than that of a bad quality.

The expenſe of culture, ſeed-crops, &c. ought to go for nothing, for this reaſon, that the land itſelf pays all the coſts. When I hire two *arpens* of ground belonging to M. B———, he lets me one of theſe at 60 livres and the other at 10: here is a difference of 50 livres in the rent. Theſe 50 livres of abatement on the bad land are to indemnify me for my expenſes

and

and the ſmallneſs of my crops. Thus has M. B——— paid for the latter *arpent* 200 livres only, while the other has coſt him 1200 livres, which to him comes to the ſame thing. If, by my aſſiduities, this bad *arpent* yields me as much as the good one, will not my caſe be a very ſad one? And ſhall I not have good reaſon to exclaim againſt the injuſtice done me, and to ſay: this *arpent* paid but five ſheafs, when it produced fifty only, and now that I have ſucceeded in making it produce two hundred, I pay twenty of them? Would not this man whom you pity have an hundred and thirty-five ſheafs more for himſelf, ſufficient to recompenſe him amply for his pains and attentions?

Have you much? you ſhall give much. Have you little? you ſhall pay little. If I pay much, it is becauſe I gather much, and am rich; and on the contrary, if I have little, I pay little. By ſuch a regulation the fortune of our monarchs would for the firſt time be wedded to that of their ſubjects, whom it would become their beſt duty to enrich and protect from the voracity of financiers.

I am fully perſuaded that every other impoſt beſides that of a tax on the ſoil is a ſource of errors: but I lament at the ſame time that ſuch

a law

a law ſeems calculated for a pure and virgin ſtate alone. The regeneration of impoſts in France hinges on another regeneration *; and the code of proſperity can only be engraven on tablets from which there is nothing to efface.

With reſpect to the impoſt on the conſumption, it is in every point of view bad, becauſe it is at once cruel and unjuſt. To the end that it might be equitable, men ſhould all of them have an income proportioned to their wants, to the end that the tax ſhould not be ſenſibly felt unleſs by thoſe who ſhould conſume more than they ought. *Peter* would have enough to ſatisfy the demand upon him; and *Paul*, in paying more, would not have to complain, ſince it was in his power to pay leſs. But is not the taxing of *the firſt neceſſities of life*, condemning the multitude to the hard lot of miſery? The rich ſmile at it: they do not dread ſuch an impoſt, becauſe they never find any difficulty in procuring what is neceſſary. If they retrench, it is at the expenſe of the artizan alone, who

* This chapter was penned by me in 1786, to which period many others muſt be referred. I am very indifferent about the charge of ariſtocracy, having frequently ſaid that I ſhould prefer the *deſpot of Morocco* to thoſe vile little ariſtocratical ſenates with which Switzerland abounds, notwithſtanding that country has the character of being free!

on that account gaining lefs, becomes oppreffed by want, and fells his articles at a lower price, to be enabled to prolong his life and provide for the prefent moment. The tax on confumption is evidently a burthen on the poor; and there is nothing more cruel and more barbarous than to fay to him who is famifhing, *Begin by paying me, and you may afterwards take a fmall fupply of nourifhment*; *if you are not able to do fo, die.*

The gains of workmen are befides not the fame, there being a very great difproportion between the wages of a day labourer, and thofe of an artizan or of an artift. Their wants are notwithftanding the fame; and among thefe there are facred ones, which nature has ordered, and which muft be refpected. Lay a tax of 200 livres on a load of wood: a fourth part of the inhabitants of Paris will ftill warm themfelves; but the reft will die of cold. Moreover, as men gain more in proportion to their inutility, and as what they produce is an object of luxury, if the confumption of articles were to be too highly rated, all the ufeful and neceffary arts would no longer be able to fupply the wants of thofe who cultivate them: the country would be deferted; mifery would feek a refuge in the cities under the defignation of *lackeys*, *milliners*, and *fempftreffes*; and the ftreets would be filled with wretches, vagabondizing round the palaces of ſloth, luxury, and libertiniſm! Then would misfortune be the lot of the many, at the ſame time that pity would fly, becauſe incapable of affording any effectual relief. Probity would be no more than an empty name; and while neceſſity would overturn every thing, there would be no barrier to ſtay its mercileſs courſe.

In 1654 a tax was laid on baptiſms and burials.

In 1695 the capitation tax was fallen on.

In 1721 came the tax on all the hereditary titles to property. And

In 1751 the tax named *induſtry* was brought forward.

Theſe four impoſts are ſcandalous, becauſe they deſpotically tax the exiſtence, life, and death of thoſe whom poverty has already made wretched; and puniſh the labour of aſſiduous citizens who are deſirous to make themſelves uſeful.

The capitation tax ought to have ceaſed at the peace of Riſwick, that is to ſay, a year after it was laid on; but it ſtill exiſts [in 1786], 97 years after its creation.

A woman engaged in a laborious occupation, or in trade, who becomes a widow with four children,

children, pays her own perſonal capitation tax and that of her helpleſs infants. They are puniſhed for having loſt that which gave them bread. To tax misfortune and wretchedneſs! without doubt this was the dernier reſource of cupidity, for ſuch an impoſt was aſſuredly fallen on in the firſt inſtance for the rich alone. But was it neceſſary to make it bear on indigence?

The control over all the heirs of families is not leſs tyrannical, ſince it is demonſtrated that in the courſe of the ſucceſſion from grandfather to grandſon, a full third of that ſucceſſion was already ſwallowed up by the ſucceſſive rights which prey upon inheritances.

The tax on induſtry carries with it the air of ennobling the idle, uſeleſs man, without talents, and without profeſſion. It is a ſecond perſonal capitation tax levelled excluſively at the laborious man.

If to theſe impoſts we add the aids and gabelles, diſadvantageous to ſociety through the inequality of their rate and ſervitude, we muſt acknowledge that the taxation, already ſo terrible in itſelf, is rendered ſtill more ſo in France by the arbitrary will which directs the partition.

To bring about the neceſſary reforms, a profound inquiry muſt be made into what is due to the ſtate, and every vile, odious, and tyrannical procefs muft be banifhed, to render the impoft conformable to phyfical nature, by requiring of the earth and what it bears the neceffary tribute.

By *what it bears* is to be underftood, not only its fruits and productions of every defcription, but alfo the houfes, mills, taverns, &c.

I fhall without doubt be told that a tithe on the revenues of the land, an unique tax, would not fuffice at a time when the ftate is fo burthened as it now is. This is evident; but before I reply, let me in the firft place afk how much a tithe on the productions of the kingdom, and a proportioned impoft on the houfes of the cities, towns, &c. would produce? Nothing on earth can be eafier than this operation, which would coft the ftate nothing; and in lefs than fix weeks the neceffary information might be come at, by taking the commencement of May or the end of April, when the earth is rich in productions.

But I already hear the modern doctors exclaim that this is impracticable. To prove their fkill in arithmetic, they will fay that the granaries to hold all thefe tithes would coft more than 33 millions of livres—a monftrous burthen to the ftate. But I maintain that, in imitation of what is daily practifed in the provinces, it would not be neceſſary to conſtruct a ſingle barn: and thus againſt all their economical figures I place a zero which would certainly coſt the kingdom nothing.

When it ſhall be known how many hundreds of millions ſuch a proceſs ſhall have produced, and which will beſides aſcertain all the deſcriptions of the reſources and riches of the kingdom, it will no longer be difficult to come at the number of millions which will be ſtill required to make the receipts agree with the expenditure. But as it is not merely ſufficient to pay the current expenſes, and ſeeing that a ſtate ſo rich and powerful as France ought not to be in the ſituation of a workman who lives from day to day, and whom the ſmalleſt accident plunges in difficulties, the ſovereign ſhould be enabled to liquidate the debts, to extinguiſh thoſe rent-charges with which France is ſo heavily oppreſſed, and to maintain the wars which happen at the moment when they are leaſt thought of. Men of intelligence and information, who know the chapter of events and the poſition of the kingdom, will undoubtedly think with me that an hundred millions more than the annual expenſe will not be allowing too much.

It will therefore only remain to claſs all the inhabitants of the kingdom, beginning with the

church

church and the nobleſſe, for with reſpect to the *tiers-état* no difficulty can ſurely ariſe from that quarter. Vanity will pay, induſtry will pay, and ſloth itſelf will not be exempted. The dukes, the marquiſſes, the counts, the fief lords, and the chevaliers, will be ranged each in his claſs, as will the notaries, advocates, and proctors, in theirs, &c. The claſſes once formed, and the numbers in each claſs preciſely aſcertained, it will be very eaſy ſo to lay on the general impoſt as to procure the neceſſary ſums; and by this expedient France will be in a ſituation worthy of herſelf and ſupported by the prop of her own reſources. Then will the rich have a juſt claim to the title of the columns of the ſtate; they who are of all others the moſt intereſted to maintain and defend a country in which they find themſelves ſo much at eaſe, and where they enjoy ſo many brilliant advantages. Loaded with ſtate benefits and recompenſes, does it become them to adduce their old titles in proof that they owe nothing to the ſtate? What would it beſides coſt them? the ſurrender of the enjoyment of a party of *vingt-un* for one day in the year, which aſſuredly cannot be conſidered as a very great grievance.

But again, with all their exemptions, titles, and privileges, is it not in truth they who pay?

The poor, who poſſeſs nothing, can certainly ſurrender nothing to the royal treaſury: they can give their induſtry alone; and if it is not the rich, who is it that pays? All the difference that I can find, is that the poor live badly, and the rich at a great coſt. In ſpite of all the prerogatives of the latter, they are on every ſide environed with taxation. Their hats pay, their coats pay, their linen pays, their ſtockings, and their head: their horſes pay for their corn, their hay, and their ſtraw; their kitchen utenſils, their ſpit, their fire, and their wine, every thing, in ſhort, pays: and who does not ſee, that, loftily as they carry themſelves, they are every way beſieged? By the mode I have ſuggeſted they will pay each in his claſs, and they will aſſuredly be great gainers. They will no longer be ſearched at the barriers; while the armies of commiſſaries and financiers who devour France will be more uſefully employed, and, inſtead of laying the baſis for the ruin of their country, will become its beſt riches. The treaſures of the ſtate will ceaſe to be altogether buried in the coffers of finance; and the frontiers no longer infeſted by ſmugglers. The ranks being perfectly diſtinct and well marked, the nobility will no longer ſee themſelves confounded with the ſwarm of newly created gentry

try who diſhonour them. The impoſt will no longer attach itſelf to the commodity; and a multitude of individuals now engaged in plunder, again reſtored to themſelves, will apply to commerce and induſtrious employments, which will more than ever flouriſh among us. France will become the rival of England, and will even poſſeſs a far greater ſum of happineſs, ſince with a much greater extent of territory and population, ſhe has certainly within herſelf many more reſources.

The tax on conſumption neceſſarily eſtabliſhes the odious adminiſtration of farms and the army of commiſſaries at the barriers: it ſeems to view the citizens in the light of ſo many ſwindlers, and degrades the nation that it oppreſſes, as well as him who is the ſource of the oppreſſion. Now, can there be a calamity greater than the degradation of the human ſpecies? Jews and Lombards were formerly the inſtruments of the public miſeries of France.

The tax on conſumption is a long ſharp-edged weapon, which plunges itſelf into the body of the poor, while it juſt ſcratches the ſkin of the rich, whom it cannot effectually reach, and who ſtation themſelves behind the wretched as a bulwark of defence.

Men have equal wants to ſatisfy. Lay a very heavy duty on wine, and water will become the ſole drink of the poor: it is true that the rich will drink leſs of the former liquor, but they will not diſpenſe with its uſe. Who in this caſe will be the ſufferers? the poor in the firſt inſtance, and the vine-planters, who will ſell leſs wine than before. Under whatever point of view we regard it, the tax on conſumption is always an evil; and, beſides, as each production pays by rent, tallage, and capitation, it is extremely unjuſt to make it pay alſo for the grant of the right of conſumption.

OF THE MULTIPLICATION OF THE HUMAN SPECIES.

THE multiplication of the human ſpecies is to be dreaded according to the circumſtances which attend it.

There are countries, ſays Monteſquieu, *where a man is worth nothing; there are others where he is worth leſs than nothing.* This muſt be underſtood of countries poorly civilized, where food is wanting to man.

And even in civilized countries, when the reſources are diſproportioned to the inhabitants, and conſequently many of them are unemployed

or

or uſeleſs to the ſtate, men are obliged to migrate into other regions, eſpecially if, living wholly by the chace or on the milk of their flocks, they require a vaſt extent of ground to ſupport them.

Theſe emigrations are ſtill ſeen in our own days; men continually reſort to countries where the arts and ſciences afford them the means of ſubſiſtence.

Seldom a year paſſes but Switzerland ſends abroad ſeveral thouſand men. A very great number alſo leave Germany.

The American colonies will become valuable to the human race, becauſe they alone are capable of opening immenſe retreats to the ſurplus population of Europe.

Is there then a degree of multiplication deſtructive to ſtates? If life be the great end of the creation, ſubſiſtence is indiſpenſably neceſſary. But it appears that nature has left to polity the charge of completing this great work; the arts and the laws hinder men from devouring each other.

War has unqueſtionably its horrors, but the ſpectacle it preſents is far from being ſo terrible as that of famine: in this conſiſts abſolute diſorder, a ruin which ſcandalizes, the laſt term of wretchedneſs, and the diſgrace of humanity.

The teeth of man fixing upon the fleſh of his fellow creature! This image makes us recoil with horror more than all the thundering cannons which ſpread carnage from a diſtance.

To man are ſubjected the air, the earth, and the ſea, that from theſe he may draw his ſubſiſtence; and the multiplication of the human ſpecies will not affright the contemplator, when man ſhall call to his aid the means which ſecure and increaſe ſubſiſtances.

How immenſe is the quantity of living matter diffuſed over the whole face of the earth!

I ſhall here lay aſide metaphyſical ideas: when we treat of nature, it is the effect alone that can inform us of the true ſtate of things. All devour and all are devoured; animal life is a fire which conſumes but does not extinguiſh; the whole earth is for the convenience of the human race, which in reality will never be too numerous when it ſhall be enabled to ſelect its food by an aſſiduous toil and an enlightened induſtry.

Who would have believed that the ſwarm of men who ſought a refuge in Holland in the time of the duke of Alva, could have ſubſiſted there? It was ſufficient for theſe people to poſſeſs a knowledge of the arts and the ſciences, and to have found a ſpot where they could apply themſelves in ſafety to procure by their induſtry that ſubſiſtance which their marſhes could not afford.

The carnivorous beaſts, whom nature has ſubjected to the power of man, are deſtined in their turn to ſerve as a barrier to the multiplication of the granivorous tribes: and thus are all creatures dependant on thoſe general laws which nature has eſtabliſhed for the production and preſervation of that immenſe quantity of living matter which circulates in the world.

Some ſtates have dreaded the propagation of the human ſpecies, and have enacted laws to reſtrain its multiplication. But if certain nations not yet emerged from barbarity made no regulations to check the too great exuberance of children, it may in general be aſſerted that civilized ſocieties ought ſtill leſs to dread this ſuperabundance; ſince, beſides the reſources which ſurround them, they are ſubject to coercive cauſes; ſo that, in every ſituation, there is always ſome one of theſe cauſes which acts, and favours this retrenchment, equally neceſſary in animal and in vegetable life.

Nature throughout employs a multitude of powers which, in all the ſpecies of beings, oppoſe the production of too great a number of individuals: ſhe has expoſed men to war, to peſtilence,

peſtilence, to diſeaſe, to melancholy; ſhe has divided the human race into different bodies, which encounter each other often without a cauſe, and which loſe invariably ſome part of their maſs in this reciprocal action and colliſion.

If Ariſtotle adviſes to procure the wife an abortion before the fœtus is quick, when the father has children beyond the number preſcribed by the law; if, in China and Tonquin, the parents are permitted to ſell or expoſe their children; if, in the iſle of Formoſa, religion prohibits the women from bearing children until the age of thirty-five years: it has been becauſe theſe people and theſe legiſlators conſidered nothing ſo terrible as the ſpectacle of famine. But a larger ſum of induſtry, a more attentive huſbandry, will ſhew that famines are not inevitable ills, and that polity ſhould leave the human race to general laws; theſe will confine the multiplication of the ſpecies within due bounds, and the equipoiſe will be maintained by the wonderful œconomy of nature, for its laws are all mutually connected.

If there are ſtill countries in Europe which are inſufficient to the multiplication of the human ſpecies, they ſuffer not from this penury, becauſe their ſurplus inhabitants paſs continually into the neighbouring countries, where the arts

dependant

dependant on cultivation and thoſe reſulting from them, afford them the means of ſubſiſtance. We no longer behold theſe inundations and theſe emigrations marked with continual ravages and maſſacres: the ancient inhabitants of Europe, warriors and robbers by inclination, became ſuch in a manner through neceſſity.

The poets imagined gods who had arms, legs, and in a word a body like that of man; but who had not blood like men, and required not food like them. Others came afterwards and made human fleſh and blood invulnerable, inviſible, and immortal. They next deſcribed thoſe happy times when men lived ſolely on acorns, and when the tygers, the lions, and the bears, were ſo courteous as to lick the feet of thoſe who played on the lyre.

I eſteem theſe fables as much as thoſe which teach that the lives of animals ſhould be revered and exempted from all deſtruction. It is with this law of nature which ordains the deſtruction of one part of animal life for the good of the other as with all the laws which Providence has eſtabliſhed for maintaining order in the univerſe: this law does not conſult partial benefit, and yet it is wiſe and equitable, even with regard to thoſe beings whoſe felicity it

ſeems

ſeems to oppoſe. It muſt happen that general laws, laws which have for their object the preſervation of the univerſe, and conſequently that of an innumerable multitude of beings, will from time to time claſh with ſome particular good; and as the preſervation of the whole ought to be preferred to that of a part, the general laws of nature ought for that reaſon alone to be fixed and immoveable: a truth which is not comprehended, becauſe men uſually do not comprehend what is beyond the ſphere of their particular wants, and becauſe each requires for himſelf the well-being of the part, conſidered independantly of the whole.

But without that phyſical law which directs the living ſubſtance to feed on animals, without ſuch an appointment of nature, the equilibrium would be broken, and life would extinguiſh of itſelf. It would have required a world proportionally vaſt to ſupport the vital flame. The caſe would have been ſuch as if the earth were ſtocked with gigantic tribes, as if individuals were admitted into the animal ſyſtem which the ſeas could not ſwallow and which the mountains could not cruſh: the maſs of the world would then have been ſubject to them; but what is mortal and corruptible cannot at the

ſame

ſame time be immortal and incorruptible. All the inhabitants of this world, formed of duſt, muſt neceſſarily be re-converted into duſt.

Animal life moſt neceſſarily ſuppoſes new generations; and we obſerve nature follow up one generation by another, and multiply them ſixfold, tenfold, an hundredfold, and ſometimes more, that, when the different ſpecies ſhall have ſuffered conſiderable loſſes by the cataſtrophes which happen in this world, they may quickly repair themſelves, and leave in life no vacuum whatever.

No vacuum in life, what an expreſſion! Be prepared then to die, proud man; thou who believeſt thyſelf the centre of all, while thou oughteſt to obey the laws general and phyſical.

Nature ſeems cruel in thus eſtabliſhing the law of multiplication. We blame the ſhort ſpace of life; but the natural fragility of animal life calls for the ſhort duration of its exiſtence. This rock ſtood in paſt ages, but it ſees not, it feels not, it is one of the members of nature.

I ſhall carefully avoid attempting to explain the origin of phyſical evil in the world: all the philoſophers have bewildered themſelves on this theme. They have endeavoured to reconcile certain

certain phænomena in nature with the idea of infinite wiſdom and goodneſs; but in ſuch abſtruſe diſcuſſions, as in the calculations of Algebra, the miſtaking of the denomination of a ſingle term is enough to make the concluſion for ever falſe, however juſt the reaſoning may otherwiſe be.

What reaſoning canſt thou frame: *worm, be ſilent!* Thou haſt called evil what was not evil.

But while the law of propagation maintains animal life in all its plenitude, it multiplies pleaſures. Can we otherwiſe term thoſe ſweet affections, and thoſe ſtill ſweeter returns of tenderneſs, which, in the train of ardent deſires, complete felicity? Theſe amiable illuſions form the tranſports of life; for nature, that powerful ſpring, while ſhe ſubjects us to ſome afflictions, has created the bonds of love which unite all individuals: hence the reciprocal commerce of aid, of conſolation, and of good offices. In the law which ordains the multiplication of individuals in each ſpecies nature has placed the moſt exquiſite pleaſure, that which comes neareſt to ſupreme felicity; for it obliterates ſorrow, and is the ſovereign mover of human actions. What indeed are they not capable of performing, whom love inſpires? It gives ſtrength to the weak, boldneſs to the timid, activity to the

 indolent;

indolent; it ſoftens the moſt ſavage manners, it ſtamps animation on the calmeſt tempers; and, laſtly, it blends itſelf with all the ſentiments of the ſoul, and communicates a certain air of nobleneſs and grandeur. If love be not the cauſe of the faireſt virtues, at leaſt it diſpoſes to them. We may obſerve that the period of life when men are acceſſible to the emotions of benevolence, of generoſity, and of compaſſion, is that in which this paſſion reigns imperiouſly over the mind. The moment this fire begins to be quenched, the heart of man contracts, and its utmoſt ſallies ſurpaſs not certain private virtues.

Thus is there a fixed end to which all nature tends; this conſiſts in the production and conſervation of life, and, by the univerſal conſent of animated beings, life is a bleſſing.

Yes, a bleſſing! it is fondly cheriſhed by all. Men love life, and are attached to it; it is a ſort of gratitude paid to him who has beſtowed on them their exiſtence. If there are melancholy ſpirits who conſider it as a burden, they labour under diſeaſe; and their judgment ought not to overbalance that of the human race. The pooreſt of individuals has the pleaſures of ſentiment: as lover, huſband, father, the meaſure of his happineſs always ſomewhat exceeds that of his miſery.

If,

If, by eternal and immutable laws, every thing is converted into living ſubſtance; if all ſecondary cauſes, all events, and all beings, are ſubſervient to the reproduction and preſervation of life; if the time of the exiſtence of theſe individuals is confined within certain limits, it is in order that the multiplication may not be exceſſive in the different ſpecies, which would deſtroy the ſcene of the univerſe.

We may boldly pronounce that the contradictions which appear in the plan of Providence are only apparent; that ſhe could not employ more effectual means towards the full accompliſhment of her ends; and that the contemplation alone of her works muſt raiſe us to admiration and confidence.

God has given us underſtanding to know, reaſon to diſtinguiſh, and a heart to love truth; we ought then to admire his works, to reſpect the general whole, and to humble ourſelves before what we do not comprehend. Of what avail would be our mental obſtinacy? Only to conceal ſtill more the great deſigns of Providence, and to deprive us of hope.

But nature has leſſened in ſome degree the empire beſtowed on man over other animals. The thouſandth part of theſe is not conſumed as food: they have much ſagacity in diſcover-

ing

ing the ſnares laid for them, and great addreſs in avoiding them; they have a multitude of diverſified retreats over the ſurface of the earth; and the woods, foreſts, mountains, and inacceſſible rocks, ſhelter by far the greater number from the hunger of man. The ſpecies which are ſubſervient to the wants of others are beſides extremely prolific.

But nothing can releaſe us from the pity which we owe to animals. They ought to ſhare the happy emotions that flow from our beneficent diſpoſitions; and when the deſire of our own preſervation obliges us to exert our rights over them, attentive to their ſufferings and their groans, we ought to ſhorten their pains, and not to ſtifle that ſentiment of grief which ſwells in our breaſt when we perpetrate thoſe acts of neceſſity connected with the totality of nature, and which compaſſion ought at leaſt to render prompt and as little cruel as poſſible.

POLITICAL ENTHUSIASM.

ENTHUSIASM in matters of religion has had its day, and the public mind is now led by the word *liberty*: but can political enthuſiaſm be attended by effects equally fatal with those that have sprung from religious enthusiasm? Authority is viewed under the aspect alone of the restraints it prescribes, and in governments we still obstinately refuse to see the power which strengthens individual liberty. We perceive the necessity of a power which may restrain audacity and repress injustice, and we are at the same time desirous to enjoy liberty in the fullest extent of which it is susceptible, that is to say, in the state in which it degenerates into licentiousness: this is a manifest contradiction. Wherever the powers are accumulated, political danger exists: let them be placed in the hands of the people, it is all over with liberty; and place them in the hands of a government, tyranny ensues. In an enlightened state, however, the rare union of extreme authority and extreme mildness may be found; but nothing good can be expected from absolute authority in the hands of the people. In such a case fanaticism has too great a scope, and each individual, enthusiastically jealous of his power, pushes it to excess. Every democracy plunges itself into the most imprudent enterprises: each individual acts as a sovereign, because all the citizens are so when legally united; but they recollect it too well when separated. It is on this account that

every

every ſenſible man will ſhun a democratical, or what is ſtill worſe, an ariſto-democratic government.

The conſtitution of democracies is ſubject to ſo many cauſes of agitation, that their tranquillity is a kind of conſtant miracle. Their delicate organization tends to diſconnect the chain that ſhould link together all the parts, which naturally ſeek a ſeparation. How can good order and harmony ſpring up where there is an eternal tendency to diſcord? and how, where there is ſo much diſſonancy, can concord prevail?

The conſtitution of ſtates engenders in the brain of man chimerical ideas: the ſubject of a monarch fancies himſelf a ſlave, while a republican believes himſelf to be a monarch, for want of having obſerved ſociety in its great and immutable relations.

The people feel themſelves not a little flattered by thoſe who recommend to them to puſh liberty to its higheſt degree; but were they to proceed from enterpriſe to enterpriſe, they would annihilate this liberty of theirs, and the ſtate would be diſſolved. If the ſpirit of moderation could reſide in a nation, that is to ſay, if it knew how to eſtimate in the conſtitution the law which bounds its power, it would not be dangerous to live under its empire: but in its blind paſſion for liberty, it breaks through the boundary which ſeparates the latter from licentiouſneſs, and fancies it exerciſes its legitimate rights alone, while it vexes the other bodies of the ſtate.

A truth which no one will conteſt is that the national authority never ceaſes: every deſcription of power emanates from the nation; but at the ſame time it is next to an impoſſibility that a very numerous nation ſhould exerciſe in a body this ſupreme power.

Thus is a patient and vigorous ſtruggle, when the government ceaſes to be tolerable, more conſiſtent at the early onſet than the burſting out into a civil war. Authority never becomes arbitrary when the nation attends carefully to the ſuppreſſion of certain abuſes; and an unreſtrained power can never be ſuddenly eſtabliſhed. It is the long ſlumber of the people which emboldens tyranny; but if the nation is watchful in the recollection of its prerogatives, and in reclaiming them under a variety of circumſtances, the depoſitaries of the public authority will never exceed the limits preſcribed to them by the laws.

Deſpotiſm is ſo monſtrous that it even terrifies the man by whom it is exerciſed: he will

never

never dare of himſelf to make any violent attacks, unleſs he ſees men formed for ſervitude, and diſpoſed to pardon his attempts.

If all governments have the ſame aim, namely, the maintenance of the laws which are to reſtrain the paſſions of the citizens, there muſt be in every government, as a neceſſary conſequence, a *primum mobile*, that is to ſay, a power which ſhall aſcertain the neceſſary ſubordination. The citizens of no ſtate whatever have reſerved to themſelves the right of diſobedience: from one end of the earth to the other, every nation has perceived how neceſſary it is that private paſſions ſhould be ſubjected to the laws; and this aim excites in the mind the idea of an exact ſubordination, and conſequently of a ſupreme and inconteſtible power in thoſe who govern.

The word *liberty* cannot be other than relative, ſeeing that it would have no ſignificant import if it were to be applied to all the private acts of individuals. The freeſt nations have the moſt deſpotical laws; and in a republic there is at leaſt as much reſtraint as in a monarchical government. Provided each part be not diſunited from its whole, and does not find, or think that it finds, its particular advantage in the weakneſs or ruin of the other parts, the government, by whatever name it may be called, will unite all the qualities which are eſſential to it.

Governments therefore differ from each other merely by the various combinations of which the ſame thing is ſuſceptible: they diverge from or approximate more or leſs nearer to the degree of perfection which policy requires, according to the relations that ſubſiſt between the part which governs and that which is governed. A barbarous government is corrected by the progreſs of knowledge, and the improvement of morals: by degrees the confuſion of laws, and that anarchical equality which invariably terminates in the oppreſſion of the weak, diſappear.

The paſſions are the ſoul and ſtrength of ſociety, but they muſt be governed by a dexterous policy, ſince they would otherwiſe tend to the deſtruction of the ſociety itſelf. The ſocial rights become equivocal, and the laws inefficacious, if knowledge does not eſtabliſh the true ſubordination, that is to ſay, the one which enjoins obedience in the ſubjects, and the niceſt vigilance in thoſe who govern. It is thus that circulating knowledge and ſcience eſtabliſh as much diſparity in ſtates, as education places between the different orders of citizens of the ſame kingdom.

THE GREEKS.

THE Greeks entertained a nice ſenſe of honour; and this delicate idea, to which they ſacrificed for a long time, was national among them, while the Tyrians and Carthaginians applied themſelves to the cultivation of the principle of private intereſt.

The Phenicians were the firſt who colonized Greece: at the time of their arrival they were more enlightened than the aborigines of the country.

The mythology of the Greeks was the chronicle of their heroes. This theological ſyſtem, connected with the national intereſt, contributed rather to elevate than to depreſs the courage of individuals. The ſecrets of civil polity, as well as thoſe of the polity of war, were entruſted to the flowery imagination of the poets, by whoſe verſes each citizen was inſpired with an heroical enthuſiaſm, inſomuch that the plan of defenſive ſtate polity may be ſaid to have been formed and executed by the genius of literary men.

The Greeks were better acquainted than any other nation with the value of the cultivation of the fine arts, and with the ſcience of rendering them ſubſervient to the public weal. Policy, obſcure and enigmatical among their neighbours, was with them both luminous and practical.

Their miſcellaneous knowledge was productive of a variety of characteriſtics, which, when blended, ſerved to ſharpen the underſtanding and to correct the morals.

If the Greeks, notwithſtanding the very limited ſtate of their national power, daringly undertook to give laws to other nations, their arrogance is juſtified by the zeal they manifeſted in diſſeminating knowledge, and in ſerving eſſentially the cauſe of humanity.

Inferior in population and riches to the oriental nations, they eſtabliſhed public and national ſchools of honour and the art of war. Gymnaſtic exerciſes were in high eſteem among them; and in thoſe warlike ſpectacles to which the youths from all the cities repaired, they were placed, by the glory of which they entertained ſo high an idea, above the other nations that were ſo ſuperior to them in force.

Thus did the ſentiment of honour produce an infinite number of great effects among the Greeks, who were the more fertile in expedients, in proportion as they had better ſupported the dignity of citizens, and combated in defence of the true intereſts of humanity.

The idea of the public weal, like a ray of light, illumined on all occaſions the liberties and advantages of the people: the civil virtues might be ſaid to approximate moral perfection, becauſe each Grecian, ſtimulated by honour, was deſirous to be loved and applauded, and on that account prided himſelf in being really good, honeſt, and magnanimous. Greece was a new free world which had for its baſis the principle of the public weal; and it was therefore not ſurpriſing, that while the ſight was gladdened by a multitude of agreeable images, the beauties of civilization and thoſe of nature ſhould have belonged to the Greeks, who taſted in their fulleſt extent the ſweets of a new beneficence.

The city of Athens, altogether different from Sparta, was founded on the intuitive idea of liberty. Its conſtitution was formed on the ſpirit of induſtry; and in this city all thoſe who could labour with the head or the hands were received with open arms: the reſult was that commerce brought in its train the arts and ſciences, which flouriſhed in a pre-eminent degree, while the mind muſt have received the higheſt poliſh of which it is ſuſceptible.

To the preſervation of their national character no people were ever more attentive than the Greeks. The enthuſiaſm of liberty, diffuſed in the ſoul of each citizen, did not diminiſh that nice diſcriminating feeling which ſhould characterize the magiſtrate: juſt in their eſtimation of truly illuſtrious deeds, the Greeks accuſtomed themſelves to appreciate merit nicely, to diſtinguiſh the faults of genius and the ſucceſſes of chance.

This ſpirit of civil equality maintained the conſtitution of Athens, a conſtitution by which the people, intelligent and enlightened, were permitted to be in a conſtant ſtate of agitation. They were inquiſitive, unquiet, and argumentative; and this mental ferment tended to prolong the epoch of liberty, the principles of which were inculcated, in a flowery and ſonorous language, by the orators, poets, and individuals of all ranks. The theatre, the harangues from the tribunal, every thing, in ſhort, favoured the only democracy which, throughout the whole world, was truly enlightened: the fine arts employed, for the laſt time, the delicacy of the pencil, and the elegance of the chiſel under the direction of a government in which the ſimple citizen was equal to the chief magiſtrate.

In the hiſtory of the world Athens forms an exception; and the Athenians paid dearly for this rare authority, ſince they were perpetually miſtruſtful and ſuſpicious, as if ſuch a democracy had been a preternatural effort, and an unique moment unknown to any other nation.

EGYPT.

THE Egyptians have ever formed a diſtinct people in the hiſtory of nations. Egypt is the richeſt of all countries in natural curioſities. The grandeur and ſingularity of the ſoil, and its amazing fertility, filled the minds of thoſe who dwelt on the banks of the Nile with ſtrong and gigantic ideas. Their imagination roſe to a pitch of ſublimity, and delighted only in powerful and extraordinary impreſſions. Their religion was emblematical, and their edifices awfully majeſtic. Adminiſtration, conſtantly taking a higher flight, reared temples and pyramids: and proceeding from wonder to wonder, framed the ſtructures of the Egyptians in a maſſy ſtyle, as it had wrapped their religious notions in venerable and myſterious ſhades.

The more the mind is prone to admiration, the more it cheriſhes confuſed ideas, and the more it becomes timid, diffident, and ſuperſtitious. The Egyptians, extreme in every thing, ſoon

ſoon aſſimilated their ideas, even the grandeur of that tyranny which their maſters exerciſed over them. The pomp of their monarchs ſerved to feed national vanity; but it was becauſe the Egyptian monarchs, flattering the character of the people by exciting ſtrong ſenſations, had conſtructed thoſe immenſe works which regulated and directed the inundations of the Nile. The kings of Egypt acted in the fine arts as the prieſts had done in religion: the multitude obeyed none but ſupernatural impreſſions; they were amazed rather than inſtructed. Placed on a theatre of natural and artificial wonders, every thing that came in their way was to them an object of veneration. Divinities multiplied before their eyes; and as every thing was become an object of public adoration, innumerable gigantic images and unintelligible ſounds ſerved to add ſtrength to the ſentiment of terror. They proſtrated themſelves alike before the throne and the altar. Surrounded with prodigies, the Egyptian had all the weakneſs of a child of morbid ſenſibility, whoſe mind is credulous, and whoſe imagination is haunted with fear.

Thus people, caught with whatever produces vivid and forcible ſenſations, are unfit for cool reflection on their real political intereſts.

Monaſtic

Monaſtic life took its riſe in Egypt, and the rage of dogmatizing paſſed from that country into all the regions of the Eaſt and of the Weſt. The Copts ſtill retain the timid and ſuperſtitious character of their anceſtors. They have disfigured the chriſtian religion in the ſame manner as the Egyptian prieſts had accumulated hieroglyphics, thoſe myſterious ſymbols which the people never comprehended, and of which the true ſenſe has eluded every reſearch. The influence of climate has always been more felt in Egypt than in other countries, becauſe the ſands of Africa and the rocks of Arabia form the moſt ſtriking contraſt with that happy region, where the ſoil yields an hundred fold.

The Egyptians paſſed through all the degrees of curioſity, from the ſimpleſt to the moſt complicated. This was a ſingular national character; but in the earlier ages curioſity was unqueſtionably a livelier paſſion than at preſent.

In this way, the Egyptian was led by admiration to regard the aſſemblage of the objects around him as a ſyſtem of wonders and prodigies.

Pleaſurable ſenſations left him undetermined in the choice of a divinity. It was thus that he adopted religious cuſtoms, which with him were ſentiments equally ſolemn and profound.

Hence thoſe vigorous and extraordinary ideas which characterize that people:—and it may be obſerved that when religious ſentiments are once eſtabliſhed in a nation, they maintain an aſcendency over all others of a public nature.

We have loſt the traces of thoſe ancient governments where deſpotiſm reigned with unlimited ſway. At Rome and Cathage, at Athens and at Sparta, religion was entirely ſubordinate to the ſtate. The oracles were conſulted merely from curioſity, from policy, or from deſpair. But we find religious deſpots eſtabliſhed in the remoteſt antiquity, particularly among the Tartars, the Peruvians, the Jews, and the Japaneſe; and upon the ruins of the Jewiſh, the Chriſtian, and the Arabian religions, there has ariſen among the Mahometans a deſpotiſm more imperious ſtill.

What was the ſocial origin of religious ſtates? I know that there were every where men of ſpeculation in phyſics and in morals, theologians of all countries, who formed an abſtract and ſyſtematic idea of the government of the univerſe. But theſe notions, being out of the reach of the people, could not powerfully influence either the political order or the manners of a nation.

It is neceſſary, therefore, to go back to ſome great calamity which overwhelmed men's minds with terror, or to ſome imminent danger from which a nation ſuppoſed all human means incapable of delivering it. Such was the caſe of the Jews, who could not eſcape from the ſervitude of Pharaoh, unleſs encouraged by the idea that they ſhould receive miraculous aid from heaven. In this ſituation, a legiſlator gave them the wiſeſt and ſublimeſt idea of the Supreme Being, by inſpiring them with a probable hope of ſafety and deliverance: but having to govern a people degraded by a long courſe of ſlavery, he was obliged to call in all the rigour of religious legiſlation.

The modes of conſtraint which he employed were derived from the fundamental ideas and ſentiments of the Jewiſh nation. That people conſidered the land of Canaan as its inheritance. This legiſlator promiſed to a poor, wandering, and fugitive nation the poſſeſſion of a country flowing with milk and honey: a country which, defended by mountains and deſerts, was well ſuited to a people hated and deſpiſed by all the Arabian tribes.

Their legiſlator alſo ſtrengthened the religious principle of the Jews, by rendering them dependant

dependant on the juriſdiction of God. *Jehovah* was the true and only ſovereign of the country, and the office of his prime miniſter was filled by the ſovereign Pontiff.

Jehovah exerciſed, therefore, the rights of ſovereignty; and the police of the Jews being entirely religious, every crime by which the Divinity was attacked was neceſſarily puniſhed with death. Every act of idolatry was treaſon againſt the Majeſty of heaven. The legiſlator gave an infinite variety to religious cuſtoms, and extended them as much as poſſible, that a true Iſraelite might have his mind perpetually overawed by the preſence of *Jehovah*. After having fixed the religious polity upon the firmeſt foundations, he found means to guard the land of Canaan againſt too great an inequality of conditions. He reſtrained avarice by the unalienable partition of lands, which like thoſe of the Spartans, were handed down to all the deſcendants of the head of a family; and in default of theſe, they were transferred by marriage into the family of him who eſpouſed an heireſs, and who was always the neareſt of kin.

An Iſraelite could mortgage his perſon and property; but, at the end of ſeven years, he recovered the poſſeſſion of his perſonal liberty; and,

and, after a term of forty-nine years, he might claim the reſtoration of the eſtate of his forefathers.

If we coolly weigh the equity and wiſdom of this inſtitution we ſhall perceive it to be profound, and derived from the very nature of mankind.

With regard to divorce, he accommodated himſelf to the genius of the age and the intereſt of the nation, which required that population ſhould in no way be impeded.

In a country which belonged to God, no perſon diſputed with the ſovereign pontiff the exerciſe of the moſt abſolute ſway; nor did any one murmur at the rigour of the penal laws. The judges were the lieutenants of the God of Iſrael in time of war, and the judges of civil cauſes in time of peace. But ſoon the Jewiſh people, haraſſed by the incurſions of the Canaanites and Arabians, deſired to have a military governor under the name of *king*. The nation therefore appointed a commander in chief, and the religious government changed, becauſe the military authority ſerved to aboliſh that of religion.

The Arabians had in reality a religious principle ſimilar to that of the Jews. Mahomet commanded the Arabians to wage war againſt all who maintained a different doctrine from that of the Koran. The Arabian lawgiver proclaimed to all nations his divine miſſion. He went to heaven for the fire with which he burnt all the temples that were not dedicated to the Muſſulman faith. If, in our days, we are aſtoniſhed at the temerity of a man who forms his monarchy according to that of God, and maintains it to have the ſame extent, we may obſerve, that it was this aſtoniſhment itſelf which in a former age ſubdued the ſpirit and the will.

The Sophis founded a religious monarchy in Perſia upon the ſingle idea of ſchiſm, or religious party. As the origin of their authority was religious, no perſon durſt queſtion the lawfulneſs of the uſe which they made of it.

But we ſee that the legiſlator of the Jews as well as of the Ottomans, inſpired the people with moral, religious, and civil ideas, and compoſed books which were received as ſacred: obedience has ever been the tribute of ſalutary ideas preſented to mankind. Men are ſubmiſſive only when they perceive univerſal reaſon addreſſing them for their own good. It is the ſentiment of admiration rather than the ſword of the conqueror that has reduced them to obedience. Lawgivers have ever employed religious ſentiments to gain the moſt powerful aſcendancy

ascendancy over the national mind; because these sentiments are the dearest to man; and because he is eager to feel and to know.

Religion was, among all nations, the first species of civilization.

OF THE ARABS.

THE Arabs are the true Tartars of the south; but the natural richness of their peninsula kept them at home, nor were they ever tempted to quit their mode of life. They continued divided into tribes, and wandering with their flocks.

The revolution of the prophet of Arabia had its centre in Mecca, from whence it spread over the whole peninsula. We presume that Mahomet would not have heated the imagination of the Tartars as he did that of the Arabs: the latter took fire for religious principles, because their manners and customs approached nearer to social life. They grew fanatical, and declined from their past grandeur, the abject wrecks of a nation that was once most renowned.

Yet the Arabs are still in our own days a free people, merely because they have not neglected their national manners. That nation, formerly the maſter of Aſia, ſeeks at preſent its ſafety in deſerts and on the ſummits of mountains. But what is worthy of reflection, this people, unqueſtionably the moſt ancient and moſt illuſtrious on the face of the globe, has ſunk to ſuch a pitch of meanneſs as to ſupply the wants occaſioned by its ſlothfulneſs, by plundering paſſengers. We may compare the glory of the Arabian nation to an old caſtle, once the reſidence of kings, now become the retreat of robbers and the haunt of wild beaſts.

The poſſeſſion of the temple of Mecca, the object of all the devotion of the Muſulmans, conſtitutes its whole wealth. But the Arabs, ſomewhat like the *modern Italians*, know how to eſtimate the idol of which they have a nearer view. They are not over ſcrupulous in the article of religion, either becauſe religious principles are never ſo fervent in free as in poliſhed nations, or becauſe the unconquerable love of independence has made the Arab reject with horror fetters of every kind.

Behold the Tartar.—Having no lands to cultivate, no mechanical arts to improve, he enjoys abundant leiſure for the bodily exerciſes. It is for him that the horſe exiſts; he is the centaur of ancient fiction. He is always in the open air; he paſſes over a vaſt extent of ground; his

ſpeed

ſpeed is great, and his body robuſt. Migrating from place to place, he is of all men the moſt dexterous in the management of his ſteed. Nothing approaches to the natural equality which he enjoys, becauſe the whole nation, being only an aſſemblage of hordes, it behoved them to elect a deſpotic chief, on condition that he ſhould be active and experienced; for the more internal irregularities ſubſiſt in a ſociety, the more it is fitting that external regularities ſhould obtain.

A chief inveſted with abſolute authority, was evidently neceſſary among a people at war with all the world, and whoſe ſafety conſiſts wholly in the promptneſs of attack and the celerity of retreat. If the leader of theſe hordes was not a monarch, how could the Tartar give to his violent aſſaults the rapidity of lightning? How could he make his haſty incurſions into the adjacent countries? What would courage avail without exact diſcipline? There can be no conqueſt, no victory, without a firm and undivided authority, eſpecially when recourſe is had to hazardous enterpriſes, for nothing ſhould equal the vigilance of a people which diſturbs the repoſe of all the earth.

Thus every warlike nation ſubmits naturally to an abſolute chief; and the greater his authority is, the leſs riſk does the nation run of periſhing or of falling into ſlavery, becauſe if the chief is weak, fooliſh, or cowardly, events will produce another in a few days.

We ſee the greateſt conqueſts, marked with devaſtation and blood, achieved by this turbulent nation, although ſubjected to a maſter retaining the power of life and death. All the north of Europe, and perhaps that of America, was peopled by Tartarian hordes. It required order and conduct to put thoſe military caravans in motion which interſected the globe, and made of the Tartars a ſingle national body. Tartary collected under a ſingle leader, twice gave law to Aſia; while the Tartar nations which over-ran Europe, fixed their ſeal, as may be ſaid, upon all the cuſtoms that prevail in the courts of the monarchs of Tartarian origin.

Religion and policy have changed many things; but amidſt all theſe changes, we behold that the greatneſs of ſeveral European kings was built on the plan of thoſe conquerors of the world. The deſpotiſm of the Tartarian monarch is mollified among us, and his character is only retained by the head of the armies. Laws, cuſtoms, and forms, reſtrain and modify that abſolute authority; as in China the character of the people has controled the Tartarian genius,

genius, polished it, and led it to adopt ancient and wise laws. With the sword in its hand the savage nation has yielded to the civilized; and the Mantchews, respecting the moral character of an enlightened nation, submitted in their turn to the force of *reason*, the only arms that were opposed to them.

OF THE VENETIANS.

THE Venetians, flying from the fury of the Huns, sought a shelter on rocks intersected by canals. Of all governments that of Venice is *in its principle* the most truly despotical, if we except the government of Berne, of which, perhaps, it is the model. It speaks through the organ of a senate, and has neither the stern caprice of a sultan, nor the ferocity of a chief of an army. The laws alone are inexorable at Venice; but what old laws! they bear harder than they do in any place elsewhere on the *grandees* and the ministers of state. Rigour being equally exercised *on all*, secures to each the part in the management of public affairs he possesses in this government; and there results from hence, under this venerable despotism, a kind of liberty.

This republic has discovered the rare secret of securing its independence, by being particularly attentive to restrain the ambition of the nobles and the licentiousness of the people. Never was a senate more sagacious nor more friendly to national liberty than that of Venice. It is the government alone that inflicts the blow, and never without a just cause. If the nobleman is the sovereign of the people, he is at the same time ready to sacrifice himself for them: he is the first to venerate the republic, as a son during his minority respects the despotism of his father; he maintains the decency of a magistrate, and has all the pride of a Roman, without possessing his ambition.

These sage patricians having remarked that republics had for the greater part fallen through the want of an executive power, have remedied this imminent danger by the admirable establishment of a *council of ten*. Acts of heroism, similar to those among the Romans, embellish the annals of Venice, the subjects of which are perhaps as happy as any people on the surface of the globe: they are forbidden to intermeddle with a single object only, and their felicity is after that better secured to them than they could secure it to themselves.

The defect of this government resides in its political

political inquisition, which is pushed too far, and has a tinge of cruelty. Let this terrible inquisition be abolished, or let it never be employed without an extreme reserve, and Venice will present the spectacle of one of the finest governments in which the human race can pride itself.

OF THE NORTHERN NATIONS.

WHILE the orientalists, amid their sensual enjoyment and the perfection of the arts of mere luxury, never ceased to be cruel to the vanquished, to pay an absurd adoration to their sovereign, and to establish *slavery*, which began with them, on all sides, the northern nations, rude and uncultivated as they were, were not unacquainted with the rights of man. It may be said that our ancestors, the *Francs*, in pillaging and ravaging, and even in turning their victorious arms against themselves, preserved the *sacred fire*, liberty: it has indeed been extinguished for a time in Europe, so contagious was the influence of the south.

The immutability of the modern thrones, the good laws of succession, those fixed establishments the associations against the Normans in

favour

favour of the *communes*, and the ſecurity of the highways, are due to our anceſtors. They poſſeſſed that noble idea of the natural dignity and equality of man which is in a manner innate in the courageous, free, and warlike nations of Europe.

ECCLESIASTICAL BODIES.

IT is commonly ſaid that in all religions the clergy are alike. Few proverbs are ſo ſtrikingly true. The character of ſoldiers is leſs ſtrongly marked than that of prieſts. The fulcrum of their lever is placed in heaven, and they muſt have nearly the ſame ideas. They can leſs bear contradiction than other men. If we carefully ſtudy the eccleſiaſtical life of one prieſt, we may form a judgment of almoſt all the reſt. Their character is uniform.

Man dreads all that he knows and all that he does not know: his imagination is little elſe than the faculty of diſcovering on every ſide the concealed cauſes of fear and of ſorrow.

The experience of the ſenſes confirms his apprehenſions. He beholds diſeaſes, wild beaſts, conquerors, the conflict of the elements, and the fire of heaven. He is the only being that has an idea of death; and he perceives it in every object. Alarmed at the countlefs evils which affail his fhort exiftence, he fought for recipes againft the accidents of life; and adopted moft whimfical and various ones, with a confufion equal to the prodigious diverfity of calamities which he ftrove to avoid.

Crafty knaves took advantage of this univerfal terror, and infpired weak and diftempered imaginations with new alarms. They collected together in difcourfes the inftances of paft difafters, and prefented them in a fingle point of view to the trembling eye of fear.

Amidft thefe multiplied terrors which diftracted the human breaft, religion naturally infufed itfelf into the character of each nation. More or lefs cruel, it bathed the altars of its gods either with the blood of men or of animals.

The picture of human fuperftitions is only the picture of the timorous ignorance of man. Hence proceeded the chaos of thofe dogmas and of thofe abfurd inftitutions which weighed heavily upon the heads of all nations, till they became enlightened, that is, till they received the vivifying beams of found philofophy.

The Catholic faith has a fatal influence when

mingled

mingled with maxims of government; the ſacerdotal order diſturbs and mars the political. Italy and Spain have witneſſed the diſmal effects of this interference. The proteſtant ſtates, deſirous that their clergy ſhould always be quiet and ſubmiſſive, have in general prohibited every eccleſiaſtic from enjoying a ſhare of civil adminiſtration.

It muſt be confeſſed that the French, in adopting the Catholic religion, have not entruſted the ſacerdotal order with that power which might tempt abuſe. Celebrated writers have remanded the prieſt to the altar, and confined him to his proper office. By theſe means, extraordinary abuſes have been prevented for the laſt fifty years; and the popes, who owe their temporal greatneſs to our kings, are very ſolicitous to exalt their perſonal authority over that of the whole church, and receive from us enlightened ideas in politics, which are very beneficial to them.

The refugees who eſcaped from France, deſpoiled it to people the neighbouring ſtates. This emigration was a loſs to the nation in proportion to its extent; but what was ſtill more dangerous, they carried abroad their hatred to their perſecutors, and fomented the antipathy of foreigners to ſuch a degree, that we have ſeen children ſhudder at the very name of French Catholics.

One fault in politics always involves another, commonly more dangerous. The dragoon miſſionaries far from ſtopping the migration, only lent it new force; revenge and hatred kindled on both ſides a fanaticiſm which knew no bounds; nor was there in France a ſingle man of ſuch enlightened reaſon as to point out, in the revocation of the edict of Nantes, an error doubly monſtrous, as it attacked at once humanity and ſound policy.

Cardinal Richelieu, ſenſible of the importance of retaining the Proteſtants, propoſed to give them the communion in reality, under appearances; ſo that by this expedient he left them a choice. This anecdote is true, though it muſt appear extraordinary.

QUAKERS.

BEFORE the eſtabliſhment of ſocieties there were combats: one man attacked another and killed him; his brother, his neighbour, his friend, avenged his death, and blood was ſhed. But theſe fights, however frequent, probably carried off a very ſmall portion of mankind in compariſon of modern wars, the intermittent fevers of the political body. It would require many private broils to equal the deaths occaſioned by thoſe general quarrels which arm five or ſix hundred thouſand men at once to ſpread deſolation over Europe, while ſtanding themſelves at the door of death. If they periſh not by the ſtroke of violence, they fall miſerable victims to hunger, fatigue, inclement-ſeaſons, and epidemical diſtempers. Murderous war, which at once attacks the aggreſſor and the defender, that double edged ſword which wounds him who wields it, is then the fruit of political ſocieties. Men unite to ſecure repoſe and felicity; and yet the ſhock of their calamities ſtops not at a ſingle empire, but convulſes the whole of Europe. A flag inſulted in the regions of the Baltic ſets the whole ſouth in conflagration, and millions of men loſe their lives for the honour of an enſign! Here then we behold mankind a prey to ills an hundred times more numerous than what they wiſhed to avoid. They deſigned to preſerve their exiſtence; to ſave their property; and to guard againſt aſſaults: and in ſo doing they crowded together in ſuch a manner that the ſhock extends to every individual. It is thus when one ball of ivory is ſtruck, the impulſion is propagated through all the reſt in contact. The remedy is worſe than the diſeaſe, and ſtrikingly exhibits the moral of that fable, where the horſe implores the aſſiſtance of man to revenge an affront. The chiefs of the human race have ſaddled and bridled it; and to ſeduce the imagination of mankind, it behoved them to ennoble war, to deck that hideous monſter, to encircle it with the palms of glory, and to pronounce the ſwelling words of *valour*, *fortitude*, and *patriotiſm*. How otherwiſe could men be incited to ruſh into ſcenes of blood? What could perſuade them to leave their peaceful fire-ſide, to forego the tender careſſes of their wives, and the endearing ſmiles of their children, to court abroad the loſs of eaſe and of health, to receive frightful wounds, and be expoſed to all the ghaſtly forms of death? But kings have ſurely a magical taliſman. The greateſt of crimes, the ſubverſion of all law, is termed *the ſupreme law*; and the contempt of honour is called *honour*. It was ſaid to be great to butcher ſoldiers while aſleep, to lay ſnares for them, to aſſaſſinate women and children; and, brutal ferocity, having maſked its grim viſage, claimed the name of juſtice, and the people believed it; a fatal blindneſs which nothing can diſpel!

There is a nation in Europe eſteemed virtuous,

ous, which, under the name of auxiliary troops, gives real aſſaſſins indiſcriminately to all princes that will purchaſe them. This execrable traffic, contrary to the rights of nature, and the laws of nations, is performed under the ſpecious name of liberty. But what dependance is more vile, what ſervitude more diſgraceful, than, without feeling rage or reſentment, and without taking any intereſt in the diſpute, to ſell one's ſelf deliberately to the higheſt bidder, and to fight indiſcriminately on either ſide? And what appellation ſhall we beſtow on the trade of murdering in cold blood at the command of him who has firſt engroſſed the mercenary butchers?

Never did hiſtory exhibit men ſo perverſe. They take hire in the face of the world for committing maſſacres; brothers and fathers appear in oppoſite regiments, and ruſh into mutual conflict.

Thus this nation is at war with the human race; and it requires only gold to procure their children and their courage. Are they citizens, when they deſert their homes? Do they merit the name of ſoldiers, when, ſerving under foreign enſigns, they have no intereſt in the country which they aſſiſt, or in that which they attack?

Open

Open the volume of hiſtory, and ſearch among the ancients for a nation capable of ſuch an outrage upon humanity. Alas! what difference is there between dogs bought and trained for the chaſe, and theſe men of blood? They are only free that they may be the gladiators of Europe. How diſgraceful this privilege! and what ſhame ought it to caſt upon an unfeeling nation, that perceives not its conduct to be baſe, criminal, and even adverſe to the true wealth of the country!

What ought to demonſtrate the inutility of all the blood ſhed in battles, is that no great power was ever really enriched by the deſtruction of a neighbouring people. All the great ſtates have kept nearly their firſt limits; they are what they were ſeveral centuries ago, the conqueſt of kingdoms being now impoſſible. France, Spain, Germany, Great Britain, and the northern ſtates, occupy the ſame extent. Poland alone has ſuffered a partition, ſtill incomprehenſible though performed before our eyes; but perhaps, before a century has elapſed a reaction will take place.

If we turn our views to the Aſiatic nations, we ſhall ſee them vanquiſhed without melting into the common maſs; it is the ſame with the ſtates of Africa. Thoſe bloody commotions derange the policy of nations, but neither alter their extent nor their character.

I cannot pardon geometry for promoting that execrable art which points the thunder of artillery, and teaches the moſt certain way of killing the greateſt number of men in the leaſt poſſible time. It is geometry, then, that has diſcovered a more deſtructive evolution, and the method of charging a cannon thrice in the ſpace of twelve ſeconds! Wretched geometers! you have laboured coldly at the ſolution of ſuch problems!

In his youth, Hannibal, at the cloſe of a battle, ſeeing a ditch overflowing with human blood, kept his eyes long fixed on the ſpectacle, and exclaimed, *how charming!* The great Conde (for this is the name he bears in hiſtory) ſaid, on beholding the bodies of twenty thouſand men lying in gore, *one night of Paris will repair all this.* Demetrius uttered a like ſentiment: he was beſieging a town, and though he had no hopes of carrying the place, he commanded an aſſault to be made every day. His ſon having expreſſed a regret, that the lives of ſo many valiant ſoldiers were unneceſſarily ſacrificed—*Do you owe rations of bread to the ſlain?* was the reply of the father.—Such are warriors! Almighty God!

A very ſingular contradiction of the human mind, is the right of nations eſtabliſhed amidſt the horrors of war. Yet I admire this convention; it reſtrains the barbarity of plunder, ſo atrocious even in ſoldiers; and though it conſoles not the philoſopher, it will extort from him a ſigh of pity at the inexplicable conduct of men. A trait of beneficence *then* touches him more than the virtues practiſed in peace; he recognizes the human character, though horribly disfigured; he beholds, in that moderation, a generous principle which will ſtop the progreſs of hatred. The charms of reconciliation preſent themſelves amidſt the thunders of war, which will ſoon be huſhed at the voice of amiable concord. Then the philoſopher breathes awhile, and ſeems diſpoſed to pardon human nature.

LOANS.

A STATE borrows, either to *acquire*, or to *preſerve*. The loan to acquire takes place when a ſovereign buys a province, a city, &c. But if, on the one hand, potentates are always eager to purchaſe and to increaſe their poſſeſſions, on the other, by the reaſon of contraries, they are all very little diſpoſed to ſell. Hence the firſt kind of borrowing hardly ever occurs in ſtates.

But there is another ſort of acquiſition which may ſtill oblige to borrow. I mean great commercial eſtabliſhments, the clearing of lands, the draining of marſhes, the cutting of navigable canals, and the conſtructing of new harbours, which invite or protect trade.

This ſort of debt, incurred through a love of public proſperity, is infinitely leſs pernicious than the debt contracted for *preſerving*, which is always dictated by neceſſity, and which always brings loſſes and damages in its train. Yet, though it has good for its object, it is ſtill a loan, and we ſhall find that every loan is in its nature pernicious.

To *borrow*, is to aſk aſſiſtance; and no one aſks aſſiſtance unleſs compelled by real neceſſity. Every borrower is therefore placed in a diſagreeable predicament, and expoſed to receive the law from the lender, who will not conſent that another ſhall become maſter of his property but in conſideration of advantages offered to him. Borrowing therefore is in itſelf prejudicial to the perſon who has recourſe to it.

Every wiſe ſtate, a friend to its own welfare, will ever carefully avoid the expedient of borrowing.

rowing. It is besides contradictory that the sovereign power, from which all law ought to emanate, should submit to laws composed for it, and act a part so little becoming its dignity: its essence is to be sovereign and not subject.

But is it then never prudent to recur to loans? I do not assert this. Wisdom condemns equally all extremes, and its mighty ægis is not always successful in protecting great nations from accidents, and disasters, to which, notwithstanding the breadth of their base, they are no less subject than humble individuals. A calamitous war makes a breach in the frontier; famine and pestilence carry their ravages from one end of the empire to the other; the raging sea destroys formidable fleets; the earth, shaken to its foundations, swallows up spacious cities and sometimes whole provinces. Lisbon and Messina are reduced to a heap of ruins; and the wretched Calabrian seeks, amidst the wrecks of his country, the places which witnessed his birth.—Pardon, Oh! sovereign power, Oh! mother of our country, pardon my temerity! But it then behoves thee to descend from the majesty of the throne, to solicit, to urge, to borrow; go, pledge your crown; go, with your sceptre in mourning to beg succour for your children, and the universe will fall at your feet. So true it is that the love of humanity can ennoble actions which appear the least becoming the majesty of the throne! It was hence that Marcus Aurelius deserved to occupy one of the first places among the few princes who have been the benefactors, or rather the fathers, of the human race.

It is therefore proper to have recourse to loans for the relief of great calamities, or the formation of establishments useful to the country; and the more so, as its preservation and welfare concern alike the present and the future generation. But, unless in uncommon circumstances, the greatest misfortune that can befall a state, is borrowing; since if it be not able to answer its wants before borrowing, still less will it be capable when it shall have to repay the loan with accumulated interest. Borrowing necessarily requires imposts; and the coffers being drained, recourse must be had, on the event of a new war, to additional loans, which will draw on a multitude of taxes more and more burthensome, and will quickly end with devouring the state and the power itself.

But, in absolute monarchies, the fatal effects of borrowing are beyond all calculation. Ministers, accustomed to extricate themselves from difficult situations by loans, act without œconomy,

nomy, and ſquander what comes to them in ſo eaſy a way. They are little diſquieted about the fate of the ſtate, which, after twelve or fifteen years, will feel itſelf overloaded, becauſe a miniſter is a bird of paſſage, and transfers the burthen to another, who throws the weight off his own ſhoulders by new loans. Meanwhile as the public debt increaſes, the lenders, who entertain juſt apprehenſions of loſing their money, become more backward; and in order to tempt them, it is neceſſary to offer higher intereſt, and, therefore, more ruinous to the nation. The loans of the needy treaſury make money ſcarce; commerce languiſhes, and induſtry declines from day to day. The lenders, who engroſs the ſpecie, make bargains favourable to themſelves and injurious to the ſtate. That rapacious tribe get the management of affairs into their own hands, and every thing muſt ſubmit to their control.

But the moſt deplorable conſideration is, that the citizen who lends to government augments the power which oppreſſes him. All the ſtockholders become ſlaves of the royal treaſury; they are ever under apprehenſions for a deficiency. Individuals have henceforth nothing but ideal wealth, ſince the produce of the land

and induſtry of the kingdom is not increaſed, and yet the lenders live upon that produce.

A nation which lends to an abſolute ſovereign is, therefore, the moſt improvident in the world; it reaſons not, and it foreſees nothing. By lending its money, it ſuffers its energy to melt away; it loſes its ſpring, and incautiouſly commits its gold to the ſame hand that already holds a rod of iron: blindneſs inconceivable! it forges its own chains! How can avarice lead citizens to a ſtep ſo unreaſonable? Indolence and ſloth ſoon creep upon the annuitant, accumulating the intereſts of his capital; he becomes a ſtranger to all active induſtry. He loſes the heart of a citizen for that of a financier; ſelf becomes the only object of his narrowed affections; and the love of his country and of the public good is extinguiſhed in his boſom.

It ſeldom happens that one ſtate lends to another; but if it does, it expoſes itſelf to a ſort of ſlavery. When Genoa granted a loan to Spain, it was conſtrained to receive the law from that crown, and to enter into its views of ambition, though contrary to its own intereſt. If individual foreigners lend, the ſtate that borrows becomes tributary to them. Thus France pays tribute to its neighbours, to its enemies;

 and,

and, during war, ſends away ſums of money which ſerve to feed the oppoſition of its adverſaries. What a ſtrange contradiction! who can eſtimate the loſs ſuſtained by paying an enemy in time of war! how formidable the yoke which ſeems then to oppreſs the borrower!

Thus the plan of borrowing not only humbles and degrades the citizen, but, by transferring ſtrength to a hoſtile ſtate, enfeebles and cramps the ſovereign.

All political diſaſters may be ſaid to originate from the facility of borrowing. Is it not this that multiplies wars, which have now grown ſo much more burdenſome than formerly? But for the dangerous facility of obtaining loans, we ſhould not have experienced the fourth part of theſe that have ravaged Europe, ſince the diſcovery of the new world; we ſhould not have ſpread our fury over the whole earth. Without the expedient of borrowing, France and England, ſo rich in their internal reſources, would not have approached the brink of the precipice. They have been led to ruin by their bankers. Theſe mighty nations would have been obliged to enjoy in peace the genuine boons which nature has liberally beſtowed on them, if the plan of procuring loans had not ſupplied the means of bathing the world in blood; for nature has done

done us a moſt ſignal ſervice in rendering the art of butchering ſo expenſive as in a manner to exceed the abilities of contending powers. But the practice of funding ſupplies an hundred arms and an hundred hands to the dæmon of war; and two hoſtile ſtates then attack each other at all points, and mutually inflict every evil in their power.

I put the queſtion, what ſtate would have made war, if it had been obliged to wait till its revenues were ſufficient to defray the extraordinary expence, and if it had not borrowed the means? Oh! deplorable ſpectacle! Nations bending beneath the weight of debts and miſery, have, in ſpite of their weakneſs, the madneſs to ruſh into mutual combat, ſtill more to increaſe their debts and their taxes; for this generally is the iſſue of all wars. Nay, when too poor to exterminate each other, they ſolicit money from all quarters to fetch at a vaſt expence calamity from a diſtance!

It was by means of loans that Spain, France, and England, procured the arms of which they were in want, and with which they inflicted thoſe deep wounds that ſtill bleed and will require a long time to heal. Theſe three noble nations, if deprived of the facility of borrowing, would not have been rich enough to ſupport the

fourth

fourth of the ſtrokes under which they groan; and while forced to remain in peace, would have enjoyed their local felicity. But ſince battles are fought by dint of money, they have borrowed money to multiply them in the four quarters of the globe.

The practice of funding, after giving the war fever to the preſent generation, entails poverty and wretchedneſs upon poſterity. We are groaning to this day under the debts occaſioned by the martial pride of Louis XIV.; and our deſcendants will pay for our numerous political errors, ſince we ſhall tranſmit to them an inheritance encumbered in the moſt cruel manner. This load of taxes and miſery will then fall upon the race yet unborn, and will deſtroy the bounties which nature had provided for it.

Who does not ſee that loans, which cruſh the exiſting race by fomenting wars and producing every form of wretchedneſs, lead the future generation between two precipices equally dangerous, and equally fatal; evident ruin, a dreadful ſtate of miſery, or a diſhonourable bankruptcy, the ſad effects of which extend to the remoteſt futurity.

Loans are, therefore, equally injurious to the ſovereign power of the monarch and to that of the nation, ſince they render the latter the ſlave

both

both of the gold they have lent, and of him who has received it. In reality, loans are alike pernicious to the present and to future generations. He who advises or accedes to the contracting of public debts very nearly resembles a pilot, who, to escape a storm, should steer his vessel amid the rocks. Every minister who can command only that easy but sad resource, and who displays no other talents, ought never to enjoy any portion of esteem ; he ought to be ranked among those ordinary mortals who have risen to high offices only to repeat the faults of their predecessors, and who, notwithstanding the goodness of their theory, proceed in practice along the same roads of destruction.

Every one knows that the individual who has recourse to borrowing, most frequently makes a miserable end. Prosecution, disgrace, and poverty, flight or a prison, become his portion. But, if at last, he die insolvent, all his debts die with him ; death, less rigorous than his creditors, gives him a general acquittance, with which his ashes repose in peace. If he leaves nothing to his children, they are at least under no obligation to discharge the debts which they have not contracted. The law has chosen, in this instance, not to offend nature, by robbing them of that liberty which this tender mother

has

has beſtowed as the inheritance of every human being.

But it is not ſo with a ſtate, which, notwithſtanding its age, is always young, always a minor, and which has not the melancholy hope of dying to pay its debts. Years, and ages, and generations may paſs away, but the ſtate is for ever the ſame, and its obligations perpetually binding. The men, nay the cattle, the trees, the fields, and the very air, are debtors. Nay, the creditor himſelf, if not a foreigner, becomes his own debtor, ſince he muſt pour his money into the treaſury, if he wiſhes the treaſury to make him payment. He and his heirs will remain for ages ſticking to the public treaſury; nor can any thing abſolve theſe wretched coffers, for the creditor is no longer a patriot. The lenders are always inexorable; they are indifferent to the welfare of the country, and only ſolicitous for the punctual diſcharge of their annuity. The ſovereignty, perpetually occupied in ſatisfying its creditors, loſes its majeſtic character, as it is in the dependant ſituation of a debtor; and being unable to liquidate its debts, it is continually tormented in loading the people with impoſts, to fill the royal coffers. Can the ſovereign power then be called one, entire, the

ſignal

ſignal protector and the pledge of public felicity?

Without the practice of borrowing, the rich poſſeſſor of Peru, the ſovereign of one of the fineſt kingdoms in the world, the ſon of Charles V. would not have been reduced to the neceſſity of diſhonouring his name by bankruptcy, nor forced to cover his diadem with a *green cap.* Spain, once ſo formidable, would not have experienced, ſince that diſgraceful æra, a ſtate of languor and diſtreſs, ſo unbecoming one of the moſt valiant and moſt generous nations upon earth.

A ſtate firſt reſolves to borrow during ſome critical juncture. The nation, ſenſible of the neceſſity of the meaſure, cheerfully ſubmits to a light impoſt, for the purpoſe of ſecuring payment to the lender. A certain term is appointed at which the loan is to be diſcharged; but thoſe through whoſe hands the money paſſes, always deviſe means to withhold it, and the debt and the impoſt ſtill remain.

If a nation were made thoroughly acquainted with its true intereſts, it would moſt anxiouſly provide for the liquidation of its debt, ſince while this exiſts, it is a memento that, on the firſt emergency, recourſe will be had to a new loan;

loan; it is an infallible thermometer which tells the people, *there is no money in the treaſury, becauſe the debt is not diſcharged; if a war break out what will become of us? Shall we not be placed between the hammer and the anvil? We muſt create new loans and new taxes, and thus will the nation be burdened more and more.* But a nation is a nation, as a ſhip is a ſhip, as a mule is a mule; and after theſe have received a certain load, any additional weight will ſink the one to the bottom, and bring the other to the ground. The lands of a ſtate are capable of yielding only a certain produce; the induſtry of the inhabitants can be carried only to a certain point, and any attempt to go beyond will ſoon prove that it cannot turn every thing to gold: *eſt modus in rebus, ſunt certi denique fines*, &c.

A nation is not a ſpunge; but admitting the compariſon, it is well known that the humidity may be ſqueezed out. The extremities, or the common people, are firſt drained, and the centre, or the grandees, though always puffed up, ſoon contain nothing but wind. We ſhould be ſtrangely miſtaken if we took this appearance of plumpneſs for vigorous health. The multitude of taxes are like a crowd of men who impede one another

another in ſtriving to reach a particular ſpot at the ſame point of time.

The practice of funding may, therefore, be regarded as the heavieſt ſcourge of modern ſtates. Who has ever fully comprehended it? Not you, aſſuredly, O miniſters! who have ſought only temporary expedients, and who, under a ſpecious title, have taken what would have been refuſed you under another; you have entrenched yourſelves behind tranſient illuſions, and you have filched renown with a dexterity that may attend you through life. But the terrible day of truth will arrive, and you will be rigorouſly called to account for adminiſtering only deceitful and dangerous palliatives; your diſſimulation will even haſten the criſis of the gangrene, for the calamities interwoven with the national debt have never perhaps been eſtimated, for want of attending to its progreſs and extenſion. What a vaſt field opens before me! How I could enlarge!—But we ſhould be in poſſeſſion of the remedy before we exhibit all the magnitude of the evil.

OF THE DISSOLUTION OF STATES.

GREAT ſocieties periſh notwithſtanding all the ſprings of policy and the ſupport of real patriots. These revolutions are, however, ſlow, when great ſtates are conducted by vigilant principles. They muſt fall in the event, becauſe to accidental cauſes are annexed thoſe other ſecret cauſes which nature ordains, to renew the face of the earth. Even were there nothing more than the declination of the plane of the ecliptic, the combination of which with the centrifugal force cauſes the ſurface of the ocean to circulate around the globe, who does not perceive that what the ſea gains from the land muſt ſucceſſively ſubmit to the empire of the waves the moſt habitable grounds?

Such is the effect of the hand which regulates every thing, and which by an unerring circle brings back every thing to the point from which it ſet out.

States that are too extenſive will neceſſarily be partitioned out: thoſe which are better proportioned will have a duration relative to their prudent limits.

Here the ſociety diſſolves without noiſe through the relaxation or extinction of the national character imprudently wounded by weak adminiſtrators: and there it periſhes, either laid waſte by barbarians, or mutilated by conquerors. Thus the aged oak, in the foliage of which ſo many birds had neſtled and died, decays in its turn, falls, and crumbles to duſt.

Great ſocieties have their infancy and their decrepitude; and politicians may readily diſtinguiſh whether they poſſeſs the fire of youth or the froſt of age: in their youthful ſeaſon they are actuated by a lively ſentiment and are little argumentative; in their old age they are profuſe in harangues and ſparing in action.

It is not uncommon to ſpeak of the diſſolution of ſtates, when that diſſolution is ſimply confined to the ruling dynaſty. Becauſe an empire is disjointed, it is not on that account deſtroyed: the advantages nature has beſtowed on it ſubſiſt; the number of the inhabitants is the ſame; their induſtry, their talents remain; the luxuriance of the ſoil, its extent, and poſition, are not annihilated by the conqueror. If the political body no longer makes a proud and oſtentatious ſhow, the ſubjects may in ſome caſes be the gainers: the hands which formed the coloſſus of the armies return to the cultivation of the land; and ſeveral nations have profited

fited by difplaying a lefs confiderable figure on the grand fcene of the globe.

The falfe image by which ftates are compared to the human body has reprefented the word *diffolution* as the greateft danger which can befal a nation: even the chronical difeafes of an empire have been fpoken of. Thefe extravagant figures engender the falfeft and moft puerile ideas; as long as the foil exifts, the people and the political body exift under another denomination. A ftate may change its mafter and its name; but it dies not. If we pay attention to fome writers, the phyfical exiftence of empires depends on the reigning houfes: nature is nothing, the fovereignty every thing. But becaufe there is no longer a Roman empire, is Italy deftroyed? If the ancient territory of Poland has three mafters, has corn ceafed to fpring up in Poland? Becaufe her quondam North American colonies are feparated from England, has England felt the fpafms, the delirium, and the fever, which fucceed the cutting off of an arm? When a family changes its name, are the individuals which compofe it changed?

By earthquakes, and by the devaftations of fire, ftates are diffolved. The barbarians have in the moft inconteftible way effaced empires, and having put themfelves in the place of thofe who occupied them, have been obliged to preſerve in one way by deſtroying in another.

But ſo long as human ſocieties preſerve their laws, their inſtitutions, their opinions, and their manners, of what moment is it that the government is deſtroyed? Another leſs brilliant perhaps, but not on that account leſs happy, will be very ſpeedily formed. A monarch may loſe his power, and the nation be the gainer by it. The perpetual action and re-action of phyſical bodies neceſſarily produce more or leſs conſiderable commotions; but ſo long as the ſoil ſhall not be condemned to ſterility, moral beings will ſurvive theſe tranſitory concuſſions; and the great ſhocks of nations, in ſhaking thrones, are unable to touch the immobility of ſtates, provided phyſical revolutions are not blended with political ones.

Nature has ordained that human ſocieties ſhall be ſheltered from the ſanguinary caprices of ſovereigns: they may divide them, but their deſtruction is not within the ſcope of their authority. The diſſolution of ſtates is therefore altogether chimerical: they change names and forms; but when diſmembered by an extraneous force, their independance, provided the inſtitutions and manners ſubſiſt, is not to any conſiderable degree changed.

The true diſſolution of a ſtate occurs when the citizens, detached from each other, ceaſe to reſent an affront or an injuſtice done to any one of them; when they no longer have their eyes fixed on the public operations; and, finally, when they entertain a contempt for themſelves. The danger is then imminent becauſe the general will is impaired; but this diſaſter does not befal enlightened nations which keep up an intercourſe by the means of the preſs. Nations may oftentimes deſpiſe authority, but it very rarely happens that they deſpiſe themſelves: they do not loſe ſight of their adminiſtrators, whom they either celebrate or ſtigmatize; and ſo long as the different bodies of the ſtate contend againſt degradation, nothing is loſt. Men are not annihilated unleſs when they ceaſe to figure among moral beings: when they are ſenſible of their chains, there is an end to ſlavery, and inſurrection cannot be far off.

The citizen is to be commended when he bears with a variety of ills, in preference to the riſk of a dangerous rupture: but there is a certain point at which an enlightened nation, when it has once entered on its career, never retracts.

Nature, by an inevitable courſe, produces certain changes. Thus the exiſtence of the ancient empires which figured ſo conſpicuouſly on the face of the globe three thouſand years ago has ceaſed, and from the ſame cauſe that has influenced the alterations which have been wrought in the form and height of mountains. All the genius of legiſlators, and all the prudence of ſovereigns, cannot prevent nations from preſenting one day, to the view of the univerſe, their grand and awful ruins. But a veneration will at leaſt be entertained for a power which is no more, when its laws ſhall have been ſage and ſublime: theſe will be meditated on; and the name of the legiſlator who ſhall have yielded to time alone, the vanquiſher of all ſublunary things, will be reſpectfully mentioned.

POLITICAL QUESTION.

HOW happens it that the people are ſo happy in their choice of the men who are to act, and ſo little fitted for action themſelves? Among the people the miniſtry was never altogether corrupted; the genius of the multitude does not form villains. The people do not allow their eſteem to be ſurpriſed: they require at leaſt the maſk of great virtues; and thus, in

free

free ſtates, the truſt and management of public affairs are beſtowed on celebrated men alone. It is on this account that theſe ſtates produce a greater number of extraordinary men than are to be met with in pure monarchies: in the troubles inſeparable from a republican government the mind is forcibly agitated, and the imagination imperiouſly ſwayed; it is a beam of light added to the regard man has for his preſervation.

But when it becomes neceſſary for this multitude to act, the love of the country engenders a brilliant and capricious virtue perfectly well fitted to produce confuſion, inſomuch that, notwithſtanding all the heroiſm which is diſplayed, a point of unity is needed. Free ſtates are calculated for defence, not for attack.

OF CLIMATE.

GOVERNMENT commonly performs more than climate; but government ought never to oppoſe the climate, for then it would ſplit upon the national character.

Animals and vegetables are modified by the climate, but it is government that imprints all moral ideas. It can produce courage and virtue in every latitude; but at the ſame time we muſt acknowledge the influence of climate with regard to manners and habits.

The climates of Egypt and of Greece are not changed; and yet a barbarous government has converted the Egyptians and Greeks into a ſort of barbarians.

How could the Engliſh conſtitution, by taking root in the Britiſh iſles, do otherwiſe than beſtow a ſingular energy on thoſe very Engliſh, once ſo ſuperſtitious, ſo patient under the yoke of deſpotiſm, and ſo ready to become the prey of the firſt invader?

Polity can, therefore, mould the moſt debaſed and moſt ſtubborn people; it can metamorphoſe them entirely, for men well governed will ceaſe to impute to climate what was the fault of government: they are ennobled or degraded by the virtue or miſconduct of their rulers, and the vices of a nation will always be a reproach to its adminiſtrators.

If the influence of climate on the government or the legiſlation is felt, it is chiefly in mountainous countries: a clear and pure air, and plants of great virtue, give the inhabitants vigour of mind and calmneſs of temper, without dimi-

niſhing

nifhing the fenfibility of their organs or the acutenefs of their intellect.

Among thefe people, youth is flower in ripening; they are ignorant of the diforders occafioned by incontinence. A mild government feems naturally to fpring up among thefe men, whofe blood flowly circulates through their veins, and whofe cold temperament forms an invincible rampart againft the turbulence of the paffions.

Add, likewife, that mountaineers are religious: it fhould feem that the fublime objects around them raife the mind to devotion, and that thofe vaft fummits, which loudly teftify their Creator's power, keep cheerlefs and frigid incredulity away; being nearer heaven, they feem to accept its favours with more gratitude. Their liberty, prepared by the hands of nature, becomes more precious to them; and they grow enamoured of thofe fnowy heights which protect them from tyranny. Thus, they find in the ftructure of the earth the pledge of their felicity, being always ready to hurl their rocks upon the heads of the inhabitants of the plain who fhould attempt to difturb them in their happy retreats: their precipices are their ramparts; their flocks their riches; milk is their food;

food; equality their law; charity and the adoration of the ſupreme being, their religion. They are bleſſed with the incapacity of underſtanding the catechiſms of our theologians.

The eternal ice of their tranſparent lakes, that heightens the ſublimity of the landſcape, impreſſes their minds with chaſte ſentiments, which are reflected on their freſh and ruddy complexions.

The libidinous paſſions have not disfigured thoſe calm countenances on which are depicted ſerenity, and, to ſay all in a word, the true phyſiognomy of man.

The ſpectacles which they enjoy are tranquil, ſtriking, and worthy the ſanctuary of nature: they hear the cry of eagles, the roaring of foamy caſcades, which, pouring from the rocks, daſh wildly below, and fill the ear with awful ſounds. Their cottages, the abode of innocence and liberty, founded on ſteeps, and rocks, and ruins, ſeem to tell us that a guiltleſs people has taken poſſeſſion of a criminal and ruined world, to regenerate the earth and ſtock it with a mild and happy race of men.

Theſe mountaineers, grown familiar with ſuch grand objects, do not always admire them, but they ſometimes fix their thoughts on the

ſcenery

ſcenery about them, and have moſt aſſuredly diſpoſitions analogous to the climate in which they live.

It is ſaid that the Japaneſe, who live under a ſky perpetually embroiled with thunder and hurricanes, are tormented with violent paſſions, and are haſty, cruel, and vindictive; their mind is ſhaken by their propenſions, as their territory is by volcanos; and, while their coaſts are aſſailed by the daſhing of a ſtormy ſea, ideas equally impetuous agitate their brain.

Theſe are phænomena in the political order of things. I am far from denying it; but, at the ſame time, I believe that a wiſe and happy conſtitution of government will always reſtrain the tumultuous paſſions; for I am diſpoſed to aſcribe more to the effect of government than to that of climate, notwithſtanding a few unaccountable exceptions.

The influence of climate is alſo perceivable in the fertile plains of Meſopotamia, which reſemble thoſe of Egypt. A great number of rivers interſect the country, and at firſt hindered population from ſpreading. The overflowing of the rivers cut off all communication, and the art of guarding the country againſt theſe inundations was ſtill unknown. Each tribe, ſeparated from the reſt, was obliged to elect a chief within

within its narrow territory. Hence the origin of the numerous princes who occur in the annals of the earlier ages.

That multitude of petty princes muſt have been divided, by the great oppoſition of their objects and views, and muſt, in the iſſue, have melted down into a ſingle monarch; which really happened.

The Aſſyrian monarchs, deſirous of extending their empire, conceived the plan of extinguiſhing the courage of the people by the taſte for pleaſure on which they were conſtitutionally bent. Theſe princes eſtabliſhed the capital as the centre of luxury and debauchery. This expedient obtained all the ſucceſs that could have been hoped for. The authority of the kings of Aſſyria, being that of effeminacy and voluptuouſneſs, was the longeſt and the moſt peaceful of all. Agreeable ſenſations, diverſified by the aſſiſtance of the fine arts, enchain all the faculties of man; after he has once drank out of the cup of pleaſure, he imagines himſelf following the inſtinct of nature; he contracts the ſtrongeſt and moſt invincible habit of indulgence, and he becomes reconciled to the moſt diſorderly paſſions. The depravation of public morals totally ruins the firm and heroic virtues. The voluptuary is a

man

man of repose; he shudders at the mention of the word fatigue; he is incapable of undergoing patriotic toil; he knows not, nor does he wish to know, the epoch of the decline of a state.

The taste for pleasure having become the predominant character of the Assyrians and Babylonians, and the fertility of the soil favouring their luxury, the monarchs of Assyria were careful not to disturb the tranquillity of their subjects by alarming attempts; they lulled them into voluptuousness, but, at the same time, without sinking them to debasement and disgrace; for if the people are willing to be amused they will not suffer themselves to be degraded. The kings of Assyria sought only to render the nation effeminate, and to take away from their subjects the possibility of revolt.

When the last king of Assyria, disdaining the policy of his predecessors, affronted the body of the Median and Babylonish nation, the Arabs and Belesians planted their standard on the walls of Nineveh, to wash away the outrage in the blood of the monarch; for a voluptuous people must not be too much provoked, since their hatred will be as immoderate as their other unbridled propensities. The Babylonish monarchs who succeeded did not forbid the pleasures and comforts of life to a people fond of

licentiousness;

licentioufnefs ; and thefe monarchs, who exacted divine adoration, and who iffued fo many extravagant orders, were tolerated by a nation which was permitted to indulge without referve in all the caprices and all the refinements of a voluptuous life.

CONNECTION BETWEEN NEIGHBOURING STATES.

POLITICAL bodies have not been ftrangers to a mutual affiftance: in times of calamity London has relieved Lifbon, and France has fed Italy. For a century paft the moft effectual fuccours have flown to a nation, which, in its diftrefs, implored the aid of a neighbouring or even diftant kingdom. Thefe offices of humanity, which trench on the rigid policy of cabinets, confole the friend of the human race, and lead him to prefume that the natural law will one day become the law of policy. Ah! what a fource of happinefs to nations, to the great bodies of fociety, which will then, like fimple individuals, exift by a mutual fuccour and fupport! So confolatory is this image, that the great fcourges of nature, famine, peftilence, civil discord, and every concomitant horror, seem to vanish under its controul.

These reciprocal duties, scarcely known to the ancients, if duly extended, would place every nation under the protection of the neighbouring state, and preserve from total ruin a territory laid waste.

Oh! should these amiable precepts of nature be at length fully developed! should nations, already communicating to each other their knowledge, maintain a similar intercourse of aid and support, as we have every reason to trust may in time be effected, then would a profound peace reign over the earth, and a mutual gratitude, resulting from these disseminated benefits, no longer allow war to point its homicidal lance!

Europe would then become a great republic. Instead of the fervid hatred now manifested, the essence of man and his noble nature would be recognized, seeing that he is an intelligent and feeling being, and has a right to exact from another what is essential to his well doing. His preservation and perfection depend on these important relations; and the love of duty consists in promoting in the most effectual way the felicity of whatever has an existence.

FORCE OF INSTRUCTION.

WHENCE arose the great influence of the Brahmins over the Indians, of the Druids over the Gauls, and of the clergy over France? It was from the circumstance of their having the charge of instruction: they taught the people all that relates to religion and morality, and to eloquence, which inculcates them.

The Brahmins still practise medicine; they are skilled in the science of numbers, and calculate eclipses of the sun and moon; they perform the most difficult operations in arithmetic without pen or pencil. It is from their knowledge, that they are highly respected by the whole nation, and enjoy the greatest privileges.

In France, the ecclesiastics have long presided over education; they filled all the colleges and occupied all the chairs. Without their support, the arts and sciences would, at certain eras, have been lost; they have obtained their great prerogatives from the service rendered the nation by their religious and moral functions. When all the rest of the world was plunged in deep ignorance, it was very proper to bestow on them that respect which man never refuses to knowledge, that is to say, to him who teaches.

All

All the inſtructive and valuable books have been preſerved from age to age by the care of prieſts, the true legiſlators in times of barbariſm. And when philoſophers came at laſt, they were only in the office of inſtruction the ſucceſſors of men attached to the prieſthood, and the reſtorers of opinions in which falſehood and extravagance were mingled with truth and utility.

The body which inſtructs has no longer the *ſame name*; its privileges are not ſo extenſive, but its power is equally real. Its wiſe and ſalutary deciſions command univerſal attention and regard. If the clergy and certain men of genius are now at war, it is becauſe the latter diſpute for pre-eminence with the former.

Among the Perſians, the Magi formed the moſt valuable part, that which communicated inſtruction, the arts, and wiſdom to the people. The Magi ſtill ſubſiſt; they are repreſented by the eminent writers of Perſia.

The Peruvians were better informed than the Tartars; they were accordingly cultivators, and had views of induſtry. The worſhip of the ſun begot the ſocial virtues, cheerfulneſs and ſerenity of mind, while the apotheoſis of men engendered, in the old world, nothing but hatred and ferocity of diſpoſition.

The law of Moſes which forbade the eating of unclean animals, was calculated for the climate and conformable to the laws of nature.

Numa cauſed his inſtitutions to proceed from the mouth of the nymph Egeria. Lycurgus aſſerted that his laws were dictated by the oracle at Delphos. When the object is to render men better and wiſer, polity may employ an innocent artifice, provided it be neither ſavage nor cruel. As the firſt want of man is an enlightened legiſlation, if in his way to wiſdom he muſt be led along the paths of extravagance, he ſhould be led with care.

The ſage Locke, employed to legiſlate for Carolina, placed under the protection of the laws every man who ſhould inſert his name in the regiſter of ſome communion, whatever it might be; and thus laid the firſt foundations of religious toleration in the new world.

The American Lycurgus, Penn, inſtead of taking poſſeſſion of the country by deluging it with the blood of the natives, purchaſed from them the tract granted to him by the crown of England. He acquired the confidence of the ſavage tribes, and exhibited to the world, in Pennſylvania, the model of a government founded on juſtice. What force of inſtruction!

Moſes among the Hebrews, Mercurius Triſmegiſtus among the Egyptians, Solon among the Athenians, Lycurgus among the Lacedemonians, Anacharſis among the Scythians, and Numa Pompilius among the Romans, have given laws to men, and theſe laws are in our own times ſtill ſubject, if I may ſo expreſs it, to the moſt deliberate diſcuſſion.

Why then, in this enlightened age, does not ſome ſovereign lay claim to that kind of glory, the moſt fit to command the admiration and reſpect of future generations? Many good laws are already made; it is only neceſſary to apply them with diſcernment.

OF THE EMPEROR OF CHINA.

THE Emperor of China enjoys an unlimited ſway; all power reſides in him and in him alone. His empire is the moſt extenſive in the world, and requires an authority ſuited to its magnitude and capable of maintaining order throughout. The emperor has the ſole diſpoſal of all the offices in the ſtate; he has a right to chooſe a ſucceſſor to his mind, while in other monarchical ſtates the preſumptive heir is regarded as a kind of ſovereign.

Here we ſee the will of the deſpot in its full extent; but here you may alſo behold the reaction. The lettered Mandarines ſhare with the emperor the veneration of the people. The Mandarines of letters have the favour and preference over the Mandarines of arms, becauſe China has more need of laws and inſtruction than of ſoldiers. The internal adminiſtration devolves on them; they obtain the homage of the public, morality being the baſis of Chineſe polity: this ſyſtem of government has given to the literati an aſcendancy which overrules the management of public affairs. Theſe literati compoſe a tribunal which carries its inſpection over the whole empire, and preſents to the emperor the ſtrongeſt and moſt effectual remonſtrances. If the monarch ſtrike one of them, he ſtrikes all; their voice reſounds through the empire, nor is it appeaſed till he yield to the laws. The tribunal of hiſtory takes under its care the heir of the throne; and, ever incorruptible, it intimidates the emperor by holding the inflexible graver of truth. In ſhort, he is conſtrained to reſpect the national laws, for every infraction of them is recorded in hiſtory, and even the perſecution which he might ſet

on

on foot to punish them for their noble employment.—This government is, therefore, not subject to the opprobrious yoke of despotism, as I am about to show.

In China most of the imposts are paid in kind; two hundred millions of men contribute only about a milliard of our money (somewhat more than forty millions sterling). France pays more than the half, though containing only twenty-six millions of inhabitants. The register of lands has long subsisted in China, notwithstanding the prodigious extent of that empire.

In China, the public treasury is not in the hands of the emperor, but is intrusted to the care of a sovereign tribunal. This charge makes a notable difference in the distribution of power: take from the monarchs of Europe the privilege of disposing freely of the public treasury, and they will no longer have soldiers for purposes of oppression.

The emperor of China lives on his patrimonial possessions set apart for the maintenance of his household: he never touches the revenues of the state, which are deposited in the public treasury, for the regular payment of the troops and officers of the empire. What wisdom in this skilful separation!

The emperor is rich in cattle. China has to provide againſt the calamity of famine: accordingly the emperor is a farmer and cultivator, and agriculture is every where in high eſtimation; for there are two hundred millions of mouths to be fed. Hence the annual ceremony in honour of huſbandry, in which the emperor holds the plough and turns up a furrow. The Chineſe cultivate even the bottoms of rivers and lakes, their public gardens abound with aquatic plants, which are eatables ſtill unknown to our induſtry.

The appellation of *father of his people* is evidently derived from the patriarchal authority, ſuited to primitive and narrow ſocieties. But in great ſtates, an immenſe family cannot regard a king as a father; for this father often chaſtiſes his children very cruelly, and exacts money for governing them. There, the monarch is an eſſential and indiſpenſable piece in the machine of government, and nothing more; except from his perſonal qualities, which may be agreeable or uſeful to a few perſons: but no individual, with whatever genius he may be endowed, can exerciſe a paternal care over many millions of men.

The abuſe of terms confuſes the ſcience of politics

politics and renders it obſcure. If the Grand Signior cuts off heads, they are the heads of his Pachas, the heads of his domeſtics. The muſſulman ſubject is not at the mercy of a maſter; and the leaſt attack upon the property of the people fires their indignation and produces a revolt.

If the Sultan exerciſe an abſolute power, it is not legal; the laws of the Turkiſh empire are a reſtraint upon his will. This ſhould be repeated to the ignorant and the daſtardly, who comfort themſelves amidſt grievances and oppreſſions, by ſaying it is much worſe in Turkey.

There ought to be many laws of police, but very few political laws; all thoſe operations, which are conducted with mighty noiſe and a vaſt apparatus only diſturb ſtates. The laws of police, the municipal laws are what ſupport life. The peaceful defenders of the fortunes and honour of their fellow citizens, the organs of juſtice which eſtabliſh its throne; theſe are the roots which nouriſh the tree: theſe maintain the vaſt empire of China, and reſtrain the emperor from abuſing the greateſt power ever entruſted to a mortal.

OF THE MULTITUDE.

IN every ſtate it behoves the people to intereſt themſelves in the government, ſince this is the ſureſt means of attaching them to the ſtate, and urging them on to the greateſt ſacrifices, when theſe may be called for by the public order: but it is altogether repugnant to good ſenſe that the people ſhould be the executors of their own wills.

The people have a knowledge of mankind, and in the choice of certain of their magiſtrates are uſually happy; at the ſame time that their deciſions, made with arms in their hands, are always dangerous. The emotions of the people are characterized either by languor or audacity. We know the ferocious exceſſes to which the people were carried at Athens and at Rome.

In the ſmall Swiſs republics I have obſerved the quality of *City Bourgeois* inſpire in low and weak individuals an inſupportable pride; and this abſurd fanaticiſm has ſpread among the little inhabitants to ſuch a degree that they fancied themſelves ſtrong and redoubtable: having no knowledge of the objects by which they were ſurrounded, they drew from intoxication, the goblet in their hand, their courage, and

and more efpecially their *fcience.* The little bourgeois is, in Switzerland, always ready to become ferocious, becaufe he is to fuch a degree infatuated with certain privileges, that he metamorphofes them into an abfolute fovereignty. In feveral of the Cantons a very trivial caufe would induce the Swifs to encompafs their ruin and annihilate their profperity.

The people therefore, notwithftanding all fovereignty emanates from them, ought never to be invefted with the executive power: they may fometimes be the avengers of their wrongs; but it would be the greateft of all calamities to fee them in the pôffeffion of an exorbitant power, the confequences of which could not be other than fatal in the extreme. It requires no great political forefight to predict that all thefe little Swifs republics, or principalities, will be ruined by the infolence and foolifh *hauteur* of the *bourgeoifie* of the fmall cities, the capitals more efpecially. They refift every amendment, and repel every political advantage.

Pure democracy is the worft of governments: if it agrees with an ifolated, poor, and almoft naked people, it deftroys every germe of emulation, each partial affembly becoming at the fame time a focus of contradictions. When men aim at being free in defpite of the laws, all liberty

liberty muſt be at an end: democracy begets a frightful anarchy; it is a true chaos in which there is neither order nor ſubordination.

As the inviſible mind gives impulſion to the human body, ſo ought the ſmall number to rule the greater. If we change to-morrow what has been eſtabliſhed to-day, nothing will be either ſtable or permanent.

A popular government is tumultuous, indiſcreet, and ſlow: the people, who do not know their true intereſts, require repreſentatives.

The evils of pure democracy are almoſt incurable. Men of low extraction are commonly more violent, more peremptory, and more intractable, than men born in a ſuperior claſs. The nation which miſtakes independence for liberty ſoon becomes delirious.

A SENATE.

A SINGLE man, a Frederic, was able to carry a ſtate to a high degree of ſplendour: but he died, and the cement which connected all its parts diſſolved with the body of the ſovereign.

A ſenate ſubſiſting conſtantly, and animated by a ſage and profound policy, ſuch as was that of of Rome, elevates an empire of a very ſmall extent to a formidable height of power and energy. Policy rather belongs to a body of men than a ſingle man; and at all times and in all places, ſays a writer, human nature, put in action under the government of ſeveral, has performed prodigies, and has riſen to the *maximum* of its force and dignity.

The character of nations changes and depends much on government. View the modern Greeks, what have they in common with thoſe of antiquity? Formerly the Spaniards were warlike, the Engliſh ſuperſtitious, the Dutch ſoldiery intrepid, the Pariſians grave and ſerious. When the people have abandoned all their rights to the public adminiſtration, it is of little import to them by whom they are governed. The Romans, familiarized to ſlavery, refuſed the liberty, an offer of which was made them by Trajan.

But if the character of a nation changes, its original ſtamp is not loſt: it conſtantly and after ſeveral ages retains what it has derived from climate and atmoſphere. The character of a nation may ſuddenly recover its primitive energy, and this is what the regenerators of ſtates, if men worthy of that name are to be found, ought conſtantly to have in view. The

tree

tree cramped and diſtorted for ſeveral years by ligatures, recovers itſelf and reſumes its natural form.

It is important therefore to ſtudy the national character, which ought not to be cruſhed: if it is deprived of its originality, its ſtrength and peculiar virtues are deſtroyed.

By proceeding with the national character or genius, the ſkilful adminiſtrator will ſave himſelf much pains and labour; but he muſt not miſtake appearances for realities. The true character of nations ſhould be ſtudied in their focus; and the truth will be come at by a comparative eſtimate of the judgments repeated from books to books, which were originally merely opinionative, and which are conſidered as eſtabliſhed facts by the third and fourth generations.

It is this ſtudy which conſtitutes the rational politician, who will never force the national taſte. It requires ages, and the reiterated efforts of a different education, to deprive a nation of that by which it is pleaſed and flattered.

A republic will not promulge a decree which will not be advantageous to all: a body ſo conſtituted cannot act againſt itſelf; it reflects, it embraces the future equally with the preſent, and generation ſucceeds generation. But in the monarchical ſtate, the chief, whoſe life is tranſitory,

ſitory, draws towards himſelf what his ſtrength will permit him to graſp before he deſcends to the tomb: he dies and another form ſucceeds.

The Roman empire had for its boundaries, towards the eaſt the river Euphrates, towards the weſt the ocean, towards the ſouth the regions of Africa, and towards the north the Rhine and the Danube. This nation, which covered the ſurface of the known globe, was at the commencement poor: now, nothing can be more dangerous than a poor and warlike nation; poſſeſſing nothing itſelf, it ſeizes on the property of others; and thus Rome ſet out. Its ambitious maxims were the reſult of its poverty; and had it been rich, it would not have poſſeſſed ſuch a ſpirit of conqueſt: the ſpirit of the Roman conſtitution would not then have been an open and inſatiable ambition.

The grand principle of confederation, the *chef-d'œuvre* of ſenatorial policy, having been ſucceſsful in Italy, the Romans applied it to Gaul, Spain, Africa, Greece, and Aſia.

Their alliances were as ſkilfully conducted as their conqueſts; and with them the ſcience of negociation ſurpaſſed the military ſpirit.

Employing every occaſion which appeared to them to be calculated to ſeize the ſpirit of a

country,

country, they concluded by putting themſelves in poſſeſſion of it.

With all the force of Italy they fell on each of the nations they were deſirous to plunder: they ſubjugated theſe by the care they took to foment a party, to unite it to their intereſt, and to intimidate the reſt of the nation.

No nation was then capable of inſtructing the Romans with reſpect to their conduct, or of counterbalancing the ſpirit of order and combination which prevailed in all the decrees of the ſenate, while that nation had its eyes open on what was paſſing in the eaſt and in the weſt.

Hannibal, whoſe penetration was profound, was the only man intimately acquainted with Roman polity: by detaching the colonies of higher Greece from the intereſts of the republic, he attacked Rome with her own weapons, and was within an ace of encompaſſing her deſtruction. Driven from Italy, and exiled from Carthage, he ſtill contrived to unite againſt the Romans very formidable powers; and this one adverſary was more terrible to them than the reſt of the world collectively.

ELOQUENCE.

LET thofe great and auguft national affemblies in which the high interefts of the ftate were difcuffed be renewed in France, and we fhall again hear the eloquence of the fine ages of antiquity. Grand objects elevate and enrich the mind; and accordingly when the ftates were convened under Charles VIII. very fine harrangues were made. A noble fubject commands talents; while gravity and a noble diction flow from patriotic ideas, as the majeftic rivers by which the earth is fertilized flow from the cavities of high mountains. The auditor makes the orator: never have folly and pufillanimity dared to fpeak in the prefence of an auguft affembly, on fubjects they have neither felt nor underftood. As foon as circumftances fhall permit, our orators will pufh forward in the noble career of emulation; and, finally, our frivolity will vanifh, whenever the important caufe fhall manifeft itfelf, and fhall enable each writer and each fpeaker, as he very naturally will, to affume the tone which becomes him.

Defpotifm is merely the degenerate offspring of monarchy; but why has the latter degenerated? It is becaufe the monarch, heaping together riches, and ſecuring to himſelf immenſe authority, more eſpecially when his reign is of a conſiderable duration, tries his ſtrength, and ſets out by ſaying, *it is my will.* If in the iſſue the nation is enervated, he ſtretches onwards towards deſpotiſm; but if on the other hand it manifeſts virility, not decrepitude, he then retracts, and ſpeaks of his paternal clemency.

What is entitled deſpotiſm is never eſtabliſhed till after a conſiderable lapſe of time, when by inſenſible layings up the monarch has amaſſed great riches, and conſequently great authority, for when he is rich he ſoon becomes the only one that is ſo; and it is ſometimes fortunate for the liberty of nations that the monarch feels thoſe wants for the ſupply of which he ſolicits the love and attachment of his ſubjects.

A national aſſembly is well fitted to keep a monarchy within juſt bounds, becauſe it balances in itſelf all the parts of the government, and becauſe it is itſelf intereſted in maintaining the equilibrium. The monarch becomes the centre from which the wiſhes of all branch out; and the ſeparation of the legiſlative from the executive power renders the laws majeſtically intereſting. The monarch is then truly uſeful to the monarchy, becauſe the third eſtate, enabled to ſpeak out freely, tears off the veil under

which

which the most dangerous and most vicious of all aristocracies was concealed. The monarch ceases to lend his name to a multitude of famished wolves, who rend asunder the state and his dominion to divide among themselves the shreds. His name becomes more venerated and respected, when, assembling around him all the members of the state, he speaks in the name of that general will which cannot be bad, and which is calculated to remedy the greatest calamities.

The monarch then destroys his worst adversary, the frightful monster that conceals itself behind the throne, whose maw is an insatiable gulf, whose talons are blood-stained, and which, like one of those mystical figures that terrify us in the apocalypsis, bears on its forehead, written with diamonds, *personal interest*. The monarch, aided by his people, has killed the horrid monster which allowed the yoke to be put round its neck, merely to be enabled the better to devour the power of its master.

In China imperial visitors go through the provinces, questioning the people whether it is their wish that such a mandarine should be continued in his office, or on the other hand punished. In the diets of Germany, not only the college of the electors and that of the princes are

 heard,

heard, but alſo that of the free cities, which ſpeak by their repreſentatives.

Sweden, in her national aſſemblies, includes the *order of peaſants*. Our forefathers themſelves, until the reign of Louis XIII. were of opinion that the people were entitled to a place in the ſtates general.

We are not unacquainted with the power of the Houſe of Commons in England: in Holland and Switzerland we find the popular ſpirit prevail every where; and the very extenſive American colonies have adopted a government diametrically oppoſite to deſpotiſm. Why, after ſo many examples, ſhould it be ſaid, that republics form an exception in the order of governments?

Man is placed at the head of the works of the creation: his relations with nature and ſociety are immenſe; while his ſenſations give him a dependance on all that ſurrounds him, and hence ariſes his thirſt after knowledge. Curioſity is the latent ſpring which preſided over the early eſtabliſhment of the arts: in the abſence of phyſical neceſſities, the moral neceſſity of providing againſt *ennui* led man to develop the mechaniſm of his flexible hand. The delicacy and perfection of his intellects commanded him to labour; and his intelligence, by its faculty of reproducing, aſſociating, and comparing the impreſſions of his ideas, did not allow him to leave in an abſolute ſtate of inaction his memory, his ſenſibility, and his imagination: had he done ſo, many a weary day and hour would have been his lot. Man is formed for the life and motion of ſociety: his eſſence evinces that in nature no being is iſolated, and that all human creatures are connected with each other, and manifeſt a reçiprocal action.

From this relation ſpring up the natural laws, the foundation of all legiſlation. Man, to follow them, muſt therefore be acquainted with theſe laws: he muſt inſtruct and enlighten himſelf on what is beſt fitted for the eſtabliſhment of public authority. The ſame law which obliges him to be attentive to his own comfortable exiſtence, commands him to ſtudy the happineſs of his fellows, to the end that his own may be enhanced, inſtead of being interrupted.

As it is by intelligence that man is diſtinguiſhed from animals, ſo is it by ſpeech more particularly that he has been enabled to form eſtabliſhments, and to puſh them onwards towards perfection: he is fitted for a conſtant ſtate of advancement, and for the production of new relations between himſelf and the univerſality of beings; he ſeizes on what is paſſed, and, to lengthen the chain, takes advantage of preſent and future truths. Thus to man the ſtate of nature is the ſtate of ſociety; and to this latter ſtate he is conducted by each propenſity and each natural affection. Agriculture is the true deſtiny of man: by its aid he is enabled to convert a wild, barren, and diſmal ſpot of earth into fertile and ſmiling fields; through agriculture he tames, directs, and forms animals, enables them to bear a tranſplantation from climate to climate, almoſt changes their nature, diſpoſes of their life, and converts their ſpoils to his uſe; and by its means he has changed his own taſtes and wants, has extended his power and his ideas.

As an agriculturer, not as a hunter, he feels that all men are united by the bonds of fraternity: and indeed as ſoon as the huts are erected, and the little colony formed, a ſecret and powerful tie unites all the individuals; each one ſubmits to it, and it is proved by the effect.

The ſocieties which are not ſenſible of theſe primitive bonds, puniſh themſelves: thoſe that ſubmit to them are themſelves happy, and, even without knowing it, eſtabliſh the happineſs of the human race. It is in vain that you extend a kingdom ideally; all the portions of an immenſe ſtate, ſubdivided even into the ſmalleſt

towns,

towns, will be no other than particular provinces of the vaſt empire of nature.

Primitive ſocieties originated in domeſtic ſociety, which is on that account entitled to tranquillity and repoſe; for it would be terrible that human legiſlation ſhould be inferior to the rude laws of nature: the aſylum, the laſt aſylum ought never to be violated. The truſt of future generations, of children, belongs to the mother, and the father belongs to them. The woman, by her deſtination, her weak frame, her faculties, and her duties, ought to be ſedentary. Perſonal property is inalienable; and nothing can inſpire more indignation than the laws which violate the laſt aſylum, and which, urged on by a miſerable thirſt for gold, ſeize on the citizen, the father of a family: civil ſociety having been formed for the protection of property, cannot attack it in the perſon of any individual without defeating its own aim, Society cannot be conſidered as ſeparated from its members, every attempt on whom, by whatſoever name it may be decorated, tends to the deſtruction of the ſociety itſelf. Thus impriſonment for civil debts is a moſt cruel outrage, invented and maintained by avarice, on the primitive compact: when a man ceaſes to have any property whatever, he belongs to

 himſelf,

himſelf, and the law which renders his hands inactive reſiſts every amends on his ſide; it is at once erroneous and unjuſt.

In proportion as time introduces a change in things, a change ought to be made in the laws. Every thing now calls for a legiſlation in ſeveral reſpects new, becauſe we have attained the point of force, civilization, and experience abſolutely neceſſary to bring about ſuch a work. It is time to aboliſh from our code the various contumacies, all of them gothic, minute, diſcordant, and embarraſſing.

The laws ought to be grand, clear, and few in number. If directed to property, this ought to be rendered independent, to the end that it may be the better reſpected and guarded by the proprietor; and it ought to be transferred with facility, to the end that there may be a free circulation of riches, and that the love of labour, unceaſingly in activity, may produce the poſſibility of acquiring. If the laws regard perſons, the higheſt reſpect ought to be paid to man.

Such are the intereſting objects which point themſelves out to thoſe who are born for a diſplay of eloquence, or who have received from heaven the talent of ſpeaking well on political ſubjects.

IGNORANCE.

IGNORANCE.

WHAT can be more ridiculous than to ſee one pope excommunicating thoſe who believed in the Antipodes, and another beſtowing countries, of which he knew neither the poſition nor exiſtence, on two nations ſcarcely better acquainted with them than himſelf?

When at laſt there was no denying the exiſtence of a new world, it was not admitted that the inhabitants were men; they were ranked in the claſs of *ourang-outangs*, or great monkeys; and the conſcience of the Europeans being quieted by that fine diſtinction, they hunted theſe animals in human form as we hunt wild beaſts.—Such was the bleſſed effect of ignorance.

An oppoſite conduct will be diſplayed in the following paragraphs.

It is only among a free and enlightened people that there can ariſe a Doctor Turnbull. Animated by a paſſion much ſuperior to that of glory, by the love of liberty, Turnbull ſaw with grief the deſcendants of the Spartans and Athenians groaning under the yoke of the Turks, and conceived the generous plan of reſcuing theſe unhappy Greeks from their chains, and of tranſplanting them into a free country. Florida, ceded by Spain to England in 1763, was the field where he wiſhed to rally that oppreſſed race, and to preſent them with the freedom they enjoyed in ancient times. He haſtened to their country, offered to tranſport them to America at his own expence, to purchaſe for them a tract of ground, and to furniſh them with proviſions and utenſils. A thouſand Greek ſlaves accepted theſe generous propoſals, embarked, croſſed the ſeas, arrived and founded a town, around which ſprang up a colony that ſoon perceived the ineſtimable advantages of liberty.

Never could a like idea have entered the head of a Spaniard, of a Frenchman, or of a German, impreſſed with falſe political notions. It required the glowing enthuſiaſm which a free conſtitution inſpires, to feel compaſſion for the ſlaviſh condition of the modern Greeks, and to exert in their behalf a ſpecies of generoſity ſo new and ſo ſingular.

Benezet, a quaker, ſpeaks againſt the ſlavery of the negroes; he preaches every where for their liberty; he converts at firſt ſome of his countrymen, and theſe convert others in their turn. The emancipation of the negroes reſounds on the footſteps of this apoſtle of humanity,

manity, who travels over all the United States, and awakens in the heart of mankind thoſe dormant virtues which need only to be put in action. Benezet demonſtrates to the Americans that they will be gainers by the abolition of that ſhameful traffic, and that, having become free by the viſible protection of heaven, the Americans are deſtined to regenerate the dignity of man. At the voice of this virtuous orator, the emancipation of the negroes gains ground in every ſect and throughout all the ſtates. Thoſe who were ſlow in being rouſed, enacted the ſevereſt laws againſt the ſlavery of the negroes, and ſcrupled not to diſavow their old barbariſm. Thus, a ſingle man, by the majeſty of the cauſe which he defends, by his noble and generous purpoſe, gains an unconquerable aſcendancy over his nation, over the age he lives in, perhaps over the whole world; for the Europeans will never hear the name of *Benezet*, or read the humane code of the United States in favour of the blacks, without reſpecting virtues ſo new, which they muſt admire if they cannot attain.

The body which inſtructs will ſecond every uſeful and generous idea; but, inſtead of ſnatching the helm from the hands of well-meaning ſtateſmen, and of precipitating a meaſure of which

which the maturity does not as yet warrant the ſucceſs, it will arm the voice of ſentiment, and turn the eyes of the Weſt Indian planters upon the virtuous and peaceful inhabitants of Pennſylvania.

A ſincere and eloquent voice will ſhew the fertility that crowns ſuch fields as are cultivated by the hands of freemen, and will point to the happy and flouriſhing proprietors: theſe will no longer have to dread the ſtifled rage and the dark revenge of the ſlave, whoſe louring eye ſeeks the poiſonous herb that may enable him to deal back death to his oppreſſor.

It will exhibit humane maſters dividing with their ſervants the precious fruits of their common mother, without being the poorer, and above all without being obliged every day to repreſs the workings of remorſe; for I am ſtill diſpoſed to believe that remorſe pierces, with its inevitable point, the tyrant, who having made man a ſlave, and degraded the whole human race in his perſon, makes a property even of his children, and holds in chains, by an inconceivable aſſumption of power, the exiſting generation, and generations yet unborn.

OF THE LEAGUE.

AS no league is comparable to the confederations that were formed in the civil wars againſt the hateful Henry III. and againſt Henry IV. whoſe good qualities were not yet known, from the year 1576 to 1593, the denomination of *the league* was particularly applied to the combats that reſulted from that noble union, which, under the pretext of religion, was at bottom no more than a ſtruggle between tyranny and liberty. What proves this is, that an article in the act of the confederation ſubſcribed on entering into the league, preſented to all the orders of the kingdom the hopes of ſeeing reſtored the *liberties*, *franchiſes*, and *privileges* which the provinces and nobility enjoyed *under the reign of Clovis*. Let us throw new light on this intereſting part of our hiſtory. I know not any ſubject better adapted to elucidate what is tranſacting at preſent: we perceive the ſame people, the ſame genius, and the ſame courage, as well as a ſingular coincidence in the occurrences of theſe diſtant periods.

This love of liberty which agitated the minds of our foreſathers was marred by theology; the arguments

arguments of the Sarbonne blunted the pikes of patriotiſm. Let us profit by the faults of thoſe who have gone before us; let us not be deceived by words, nor forget that kings never acquire ſo much power as at the cloſe of a violent civil commotion. We ſhall ſee what melancholy conſequences flowed from the prejudices of our brave anceſtors. Let us take care not to be dragged into the ſame abyſs by the miſtaking of fantaſtic terms for realities.

Civil war is never ſo dangerous in a monarchy as in a republic; in a monarchy, it always begins with deſtroying ſome uſurpations and a number of abuſes; the people better their condition by force of arms, and one or two victories give new vigour to the laws. But a republic torn by civil war, continues in an everlaſting ſtate of agitation.

Every nation reſembles a vaſt ocean of which the waves ſtill remain in motion after the action of the winds has ceaſed. The ideas of the *league* and of the *fronde* * have re-appeared with all the luſtre which reaſon in a more perfect and enlightened ſtate muſt produce among a people far advanced in improvement; and their

* The appellation given to the country-party in the civil broils during the minority of Louis XIV. *Tranſlator.*

triumph

triumph is to be aſcribed to the ripeneſs of men's minds. They have had time to know and to feel all the calamities inſeparable from an unlimited monarchy.

How happened it that France did not then aſſume another form and a combination totally different? Every ſpirit was ardent and fiery to exceſs, and actuated by a vigorous and determined will. Every limb was nervous and clad in armour; ſtrength, obſtinacy, enthuſiaſm; all beſpoke the life of the body-politic. Why was that immenſe force not directed in that age of ſuperſtition, by ſalutary ideas and by principles reſtorative of liberty? Why did a people wear out its conſtancy by contending for chimeras, inſtead of obtaining the real advantages which were then in its power?

Thus, by a fatal oppoſition, but too well evidenced by hiſtory, courage and knowledge ſeldom meet together *. Habitual intrepidity belongs to ſuch an age, but it is only a blind force which acts by chance. Political and juſt ideas ſpring up in another age, when men are ſoftened and enervated, and their weak and degraded minds equally deſtitute of vigour and character.

* The immortal year 1789 has happily belied my firſt propoſition; for I wrote all this, word for word, in 1781.

The

The times of our civil wars, in ſpite of fanaticiſm, are thoſe in which the philoſopher loves to contemplate bold, intrepid, and impaſſioned ſouls; and he regrets that ſuch rare virtues were not applied with more diſcernment to cauſes truly great, patriotic, and worthy of valorous deeds.

Thus, the fanaticiſm of that age ought to be doubly abhorred by philoſophers, becauſe it corrupted civil war, which to an oppreſſed and generous people is often the moſt uſeful of all poſſible events. England, Holland, Switzerland, &c. have purchaſed with their blood the rights of humanity; while we, after ſo many ſtruggles and combats, when theſe ſame convulſions evinced the force of individuals and the ſtrong temper of the ſtate, tired and deſponding, ſunk down again to our old level, and ſubmitted to the yoke of Richelieu twenty-two years after ſo many examples of firmneſs and reſolution. Five and twenty years were ſpent in butchering one another for viſionary notions; and the nation, with arms in its hands, could neither diſcover nor diſcuſs its true political intereſts.

Let us go back to the origin of that famous league, which might have regenerated the

ſtate,

ſtate, and yet only haraſſed it; which was inſtituted at firſt by the wiſeſt motives, and degenerated through the fanaticiſm of prieſts *; which was ſupported by great men and true patriots, and was afterwards ſhamefully loſt in the abſurdity of theological quarrels. Let us endeavour to diſcover what timid hiſtorians have, through prejudice or adulation, feared to declare. At a certain diſtance, the true cauſes of events diſappear, and we behold only the predominant colours which certain pens, either venal or miſled, have pleaſed to beſtow upon objects. Let us appeal to facts; let us inquire above all what was then the diſpoſition of the popular mind; it leaves a viſible impreſſion, and naked truth has a degree of energy peculiar to itſelf.

The adminiſtration of Louis XII. was unfortunately of ſhort duration. Notwithſtanding many political faults, he left the kingdom rich and well cultivated; and cultivation is the ſureſt pledge of proſperous population. Caſting his eye upon his ſucceſſor, this good king, whoſe memory deſerves to be bleſſed, and who was a good judge of mankind, exclaimed with a ſigh, *Alas! we labour in vain; this big boy will ſpoil*

* Thus in 1790 they diverted, marred, and brought to nothing, the revolution begun in Brabant.

all.

all. He prophesied but too well. Francis I. had none of the qualities necessary to govern a state: he possessed those which are fatal to its happiness. A misplaced bravery, a prodigal disposition, a haughty presumption, an inclination for arbitrary sway, a pompous profusion, and a criminal rapacity, separated the interests of the prince from those of his people. His love of the arts was more allied to the love of luxury than to that of humanity: nor, in reality, do pictures, statues, palaces, music, verses, and songs, the particular pleasures of exactors and public robbers, establish the felicity of a nation. Writers themselves are too frequently deceived by these equivocal marks.

But the posterity of Francis I. filled the throne only to disgrace it. Four detestable and successive reigns, stained with all the most horrid and most destructive crimes, overwhelmed the kingdom; and during the space of forty-two years, there was nothing but one continued scene of violence, cruelty, and perfidy. The effeminacy of Henry II. and his obsequiousness to the duchess of Valentinois and her favourites; the puerile weakness of Francis II. and his implicit submission to the princes of Guise and their creatures; the ferocity

city and madneſs of Charles IX.*; the infamous debauchery, the vile ſuperſtition, and the immenſe profuſion of Henry III.—All theſe wicked kings diſhonoured royalty, the French nation, and human nature itſelf. Hiſtory ought to brand with peculiar infamy thoſe moſt odious enemies of their country who availed themſelves of their elevation to tear it in pieces.

Catherine of Medicis, to extend her authority, kept poiſon on the one hand, and on the other a band of women of gallantry to corrupt and enervate the princes of the court, and to gain poſſeſſion of their ſecrets: ſhe ſought the philoſopher's ſtone with ſorcerers and alchymiſts; and, no leſs forward to trample upon the people than her Italian farmers of the revenue, ſhe ſent to the king to have the edicts

* The maſſacre of St. Bartholomew was the crime of the throne; this crime was plotted during ſeven years between the courts of Charles IX. and of Philip II. Charles IX. ſigned the maſſacre of St. Bartholomew at an age when even the worſt kings have ſhown virtues and ſenſibility. He fired upon his own ſubjects, and yet hiſtorians have ſhamefully made his youth a plea to extenuate his guilt. What proves that he was barbarous and not ſuperſtitious, is the expreſs orders he gave to ſave the life of *Ambroſe Paré*, his firſt ſurgeon. His reaſon was, that he ought not to take away the life of a man who might preſerve his own.

 fabricated

fabricated by that infamous gang regiſtered by the parliament. The king went, with a ſort of intrepidity, to meet the hatred and diſdain of the people.

Mankind are very patient; but, when they are at laſt too bitterly provoked, they exact a dreadful penalty from tyrannical power. Public diſtreſs is always a ſure ſign that the government is bad. All the orders of the ſtate, equally diſcontented, roſe at once. It was this concurrence that gave force and character to the infant league; and I think I can diſcover its true origin in the extreme wretchedneſs of the people. Men's minds were no doubt heated by different pretexts; but all ſeemed united againſt the throne. The real motive of this civil war was not *the defence of the Catholic religion*. We may learn from the writings of the times the juſt and violent hatred borne to the children of Catherine of Medicis, and the loud complaints uttered on all ſides. The people then caſt their eyes upon the Duke of Guiſe, brave, generous, magnanimous, and popular; they ſaw him lamenting the oppreſſion they ſuffered, and giving them conſolation and relief; they beheld in him the protector of the nation and the aſſertor of its forgotten rights.

There was a party of *politicians*, which, although the leaſt numerous, had not the leſs influence over the minds of men; all the proteſtants who were not fanatical, all thoſe who thought, were of this party, whoſe object was really to reform the abuſes of the crown. The Duke of Alençon put himſelf at their head; while the king of Navarre and the prince of Conde, reputed Catholics, ranged themſelves under the ſame ſtandard. Many virtuous men, eminent for their knowledge, joined this party, particularly the wiſe and brave Lanoue, who, after long deliberation, gave the ſignal for renewing the civil war. In whatever light, indeed, we view the league at its commencement, we cannot but conſider it as a conteſt between tyranny and liberty.

The moſt irrefragable proof is, that all France, from one end of the kingdom to the other, roſe in arms in an inſtant. Peaſants, citizens, artiſts, all ruſhed with ardour into this civil war; which ſhows that men were become ſo impatient of oppreſſion, that, tired of ſuffering, they ſevered their bonds with the ſword. They were ſeen to give their lives in exchange for the mere hope of relief*.

When

* While the people roſe in France, the religioniſts of the Low Countries, generous partizans of the rights of man, began

When you behold tyranny, be aſſured that inſurrection is not far diſtant.—We ſhall here offer a few reflections on civil war. It is unqueſtionably the moſt terrible of all; but it is the only war, perhaps, which is uſeful and ſometimes neceſſary. When a ſtate has reached a certain pitch of depravity and misfortune, it is convulſed by a thouſand internal diſorders. Peace, which is the greateſt earthly bleſſing, has left it; and the reſtoration of peace unfortunately can only be the work of civil war. The balance is then to be reſtored by force of arms. The nation which ſlumbered in ſoft indolence, the habitual diſpoſition of the ſlave, will not recover its greatneſs without undergoing thoſe terrible trials, proper to regenerate it. The citizen muſt draw his ſword to enjoy the privilege of the laws; a privilege which the deſpot would fain bury in eternal ſilence.

Two neighbouring nations of equal ſtrength which engage in war, only gain, after long con-

gan to hold their meeting. They were at firſt called *beggars*, yet theſe beggars ſet Philip II. at defiance and founded the republic of Holland. They took for their *device* a little porringer, an ironical attribute.

In like manner ariſtocracy ſtyled the patriots *ſans culottes*; and theſe, reſembling the *Greeks* and *Romans*, all of whom went without *breeches*, have led about the *breeched*.

flicts,

flicts, the advantage of having exhausted each other. Their disputes are always calamitous. They cannot coalesce into a single body; and, consequently, war serves but to widen and envenom their wounds. The author of the *Spirit of Laws* says, that the life of states is like that of men. Two armed nations do therefore irreparable mischief to each other, and blood is shed in useless battles. But civil war is a sort of fever which expels a dangerous stupor, and often strengthens the principle of life. The objects of this war are always clearly understood and universally discussed; and, after tyrannical attempts, it becomes even inevitable, as nature calls on each individual to maintain her indefeasible rights. A criminal neutrality becomes impossible in the meanest citizens. Ambition, folly, vain glory, family compacts, obscure or ridiculous treaties, and interests almost ever foreign to the people, occasion other wars. Civil war is derived from necessity and rigid justice: the indisputable rights of man being violated, a war of restoration becomes lawful, as no other expedient is left to the injured party. This war, which I would call sacred, is therefore really undertaken for the salvation of the state. As to the consequences, they are seldom fatal; nations rise more formidable from their internal contests. Political light is more diffused, and men are firmer and better exercised in arms. The fury and violence of this kind of war render it even of short continuance. It knows not those cruel delays which rulers calmly dictate from their cabinets; it knows not those reprisals which make hostilities eternal, and drain off, drop by drop, the blood of mankind. Here the blood flows seasonably, and spirts from generous veins; the quarrel is speedily decided, and the state either falls or recovers its pristine vigour.

Consult history, almost all civil wars, by elevating the mind, by giving greater energy to courage, by diffusing martial virtue through every bosom, and by inflaming men with the spirit of patriotism, have introduced republican liberty; and the expiring laws have revived amidst the din of arms. Each individual stipulates boldly for his own interests; and the nation, armed for that great cause, the restitution of its rights, rears a flourishing head, and becomes formidable to its neighbours, at the very time when it is imagined to be buried in ruins. Victory acquits the people from the charge of *revolt* and *rebellion*, which tyrants and slaves so liberally bestow.

This is what happened in the Roman Empire,

pire, in England, in Holland, and in all the ſtates which now enjoy ſome portion of liberty. Such will, likewiſe, be ſoon the iſſue of the revolution in America, where are laid the foundations of a new and vaſt republic, which will become the aſylum of the human race, oppreſſed in the old world. All theſe political concuſſions have everywhere produced happy changes: but, by a fatal exception, France has not reaped the fruit of its long diſcords. This was the moment for her, after ſo much inſtability, to take a permanent form; ſhe was in a criſis where every thing indicated vigour and force. But the actors in the civil war, and even the political bodies, while tending ſo many ways, advanced not a ſingle ſtep towards liberty. Indifferent, or rather blind to their intereſts, the people could neither perceive nor ſtudy, nor even divine them by inſtinct,—an inſtinct found in the rudeſt nations, which were capable of the greateſt achievements in ages of ſtill greater darkneſs. I have to no purpoſe ſought, in the writings of that time, to ſee if I could diſcover ſome trait which might indicate theſe circumſtances as favourable for operating a ſalutary revolution. But the human mind was in that reſpect totally eclipſed:

all thoſe writers diſpute only about words void of ſenſe, and, forgetting the eſſential privileges of man, talk of nothing but church ceremonies, and to them direct all their attention and their fears.

Thoſe famous ſtates held at Blois, thoſe national aſſemblies before which royalty hid its diminiſhed head, and which, in their ſolemn convocation, might have re-eſtabliſhed the kingdom, by removing the principal abuſes, waſted their time in miſerable diſputes; inſtead of defending the rights of the people, they turned their whole attention to *tranſubſtantiation* and the council of Trent. The redreſs of ancient grievances, the nobleſt, and unqueſtionably the moſt important of all cauſes, came under diſcuſſion; but the wretched ſpirit of controverſy ſpoiled all. They contended that there ought to be only one religion, becauſe there was only one God in heaven; they ſpoke however, but as if by chance, *of puniſhing minions and farmers of the revenue, and of ſuppreſſing all arbitrary impoſts.* Yet, more criminal than if they had entirely overlooked them, they abandoned theſe great objects ſo worthy examination and diſcuſſion. In reading their *papers*, we might fancy ourſelves ſitting on the

benches

benches of the Sorbonne, and hearing the jargon of cavilling-disputants instead of the language of statesmen.

The high spirited duke of Guise, the idol of Paris, and who had merited that admiration by his heroic and popular qualities, full of boldness and courage, touching with his foot the steps of the throne, turned to advantage the universal hatred towards Henry III. which was founded on the noblest motives that can actuate a nation; but he also despised his sovereign too much. He neither perceived his exalted fortune, nor all his favour with the people; and lost the opportunity of reigning over a nation which already adored him. Guise, contented with having degraded the throne by the superiority of his genius, temporized or disdained to fill it. He carried into the tomb, in the estimation of the people, the name of a magnanimous hero. It was believed that he would not purchase the crown by a crime so easy for him to commit, and from which he would have been absolved by the public sanction, and perhaps by the voice of posterity *.

* Cromwell has been termed an usurper: he rose from a much lower station than Guise. But did not the court of France go into public mourning on the death of that usurper?

The

The weak Henry III.*, during this time of commotion, appeared in public *with lap-dogs in a baſket hanging from his neck*, ſquandering away immenſe ſums for *monkeys*, *parrots*, *monks*, and *minions*: already tonſured in the public opinion, and ſhut up in a convent by the general wiſh, as ridiculous as he was deteſtable, he replied to his adverſary by cauſing him to be aſſaſſinated. He could deviſe no better expedient to retain the crown which tottered on his head; but it was an additional crime that only ſerved to increaſe the public execration. He ſeemed to have murdered his ſovereign from that moment.

* The throne of Henry III. was deſtroyed in anticipation; although young, he had no children, and had no brother alive. Catherine de Medicis believed that it would be eaſy to exclude the king of Navarre and the prince of Condé, on account of their profeſſing the proteſtant faith. She wiſhed to give the crown to the duke of Lorraine, her ſon-in-law. The duke of Guiſe on his part thought of confining the king in a convent, and of reigning in his ſtead: he would have ſet the cardinal of Bourbon in the van-guard, and have leaned upon the right of proximity; then kicking over the phantom, he would have exhibited himſelf to the people, already diſpoſed, by the love which he had inſpired, to receive him. Henry III. on his ſide, regarding the kingdom as a patrimony, as a farm which he could diſmember at pleaſure, was not far from ſharing it in favour of his minions; and Joyeuſe and d'Epernon would have had the beſt portion. Henry III. called Joyeuſe and d'Epernon his children.

The universſal voice directed the knife with which a jacobine monk ſoon pierced his vitals; and all France, in the intoxication of joy and revenge, applauded the regicide *.

What a leſſon to prevaricating kings! The children of Catherine de Medicis, as if ſmitten by the malediction of the people, all deſcended into the grave before their time and without offspring. Death, at an early age, cut off Charles IX. and Henry III. together with the dukes of Alençon and Anjou, and all that race of wicked and worthleſs princes, who were only active in doing ill. The nation immediately regarded itſelf as delivered from a ſcourge which was preparing its total ruin. All reſounded with ſhouts of joy; and this was perhaps the critical moment, during the *interregnum*, for reſtoring the rights of the nation. It was left to itſelf, and knew not as yet the heroic virtues of Henry IV. who was quite a diſtant object in

* The death of the Guiſes filled the people with ſuch univerſal and profound grief, that whoever reads hiſtory cannot help ſaying, that the people regarded theſe two brothers as the pillars of its rights and of its liberty. They loudly called on *God to extinguiſh the race of the Valois!* never did a nation vent ſo unanimous a cry. This ſlaughter of the king was conſidered not only in France, but even in Italy, as a virtuous action; and ſome compared the regicide to Judith and Eleazar, and others to the greateſt men of antiquity.

their

their eyes. The houſe of Valois was deteſted; and the houſe of Bourbon ſcarcely enjoyed more favour. All hiſtorians agree that it was conſidered as a *baſtard, ſtray, and loſt branch.*

The current of general favour ſet towards the Guiſes, who enjoyed popularity and diſplayed genius. Henry IV. was regarded by the people, only as a proteſtant who would ſoon outdo the crimes of a catholic king, and who would moreover forbid the ſaying of *maſs* in Paris. The blood of the Guiſes ſtill ſubſiſted: it was traced back to Charlemagne, and this blood, ſhed in the popular cauſe, ſeemed as if it ought conſequently to become dearer to the people. Mayenne had to revenge his two brothers ſlain at Blois. But though only a remnant of that formidable houſe, he did not conduct himſelf, as the leader of a party, with proper firmneſs and deciſion. In vain his mother demanded of him her murdered ſons; in vain did the widow of the duke and his ſiſter call out for vengeance; in vain the nation forſook the cauſe of royalty: calm, irreſolute, and moderate, he ſeemed only to dread the being elected king. Having nothing that reſembled the boiling blood of his brothers, he was not qualified to act at this great criſis of the ſtate.

Mayenne,

Mayenne, with more boldneſs and reſolution, might have put the crown on his head. The dukes and counts, in ſhort all the nobility, were ready to come over to his intereſt. By judiciouſly conferring governments, by beſtowing the principal appointments on the moſt ambitious, by uſing the moſt extreme means againſt the king of Navarre, it is probable he would have ſucceeded. The young duke of Guiſe, his nephew, confined at that time, could not have thwarted his deſigns; but Mayenne, though otherwiſe a ſkilful general, wanted activity, and knew not the value of time.

The nation, on this trying occaſion, deeply ſenſible of its wrongs, and poſſeſſed of the greateſt internal energy, waſted its courage, without eſtabliſhing, or even propoſing a form of government, that might obviate thoſe cruel oppreſſions under which the people had groaned ſo long; it never dreamt of oppoſing a juſt reſiſtance to that enormous power which ſince the reign of Louis XII. had borne down and debaſed the ſtate. Deplorable blindneſs of the age! fatal error! France, called to elect, to appoint its monarch, conceived no political idea. Armed, ſtrong, vigorous, clad in ſteel, ſhe threw herſelf into the thorny labyrinth of theo-

logical

logical diſputes; and wandering further and further through theſe crooked paths, forgot the weapons ſhe held, and neglected the happieſt and rareſt epoch for framing a ſocial contract.

Henry IV. drew his ſword to reign: but he was juſtified by the conſideration, that force only could be oppoſed to force. The ſucceſs of the pretender to the crown was more than doubtful. His claims, though juſt, might be annulled by the will of the people, by their obſtinate reſiſtance, or by the courſe of events; the terrible aſcendancy of religion and its multiplied anathemas, inviting the poignards of aſſaſſins, could alſo for ever remove him from the throne. He would then have willingly accepted any conditions impoſed on him. He was endowed with an heroic mind, and would with joy have commanded a free nation; in putting the crown upon his head, it could have dictated a generous contract, which he would have magnanimouſly ſigned. But what was enjoined him? An obligation the moſt indifferent to the government of a ſtate; *to turn catholic and every day hear maſs.* This was the only condition required; and the nation then believed it had gained a moſt important point of legiſlation,

an

an eternal pledge of the public felicity *. The grandees, more dexterous and more unprincipled, ſold for *good hard caſh* their ſervile obedience, and thought only of making private agreements. Henry IV. promiſed all they aſked †, and engaged to pay the moſt conſiderable ſums: every placeman in this tumultuous anarchy, minding only his little ſordid concerns, appeared to neglect, or rather to deſpiſe, the general intereſt.

What was the conſequence? The deſpotiſm of Richelieu, againſt the nature of things, aroſe out of theſe civil wars; it aroſe out of them to puniſh that people which had courage to take arms and to die, fighting bravely for barren opinions, without being able to form a chain of juſt reaſoning ‡. Twenty-two years after, Richelieu

* Paris is worth a maſs, ſaid he; and this maſs gave him a crown. So Louis XVI. by accepting and kiſſing the three-coloured cockade on the 17th of July 1789, changed in a minute the general diſpoſition of men's minds. Good people! you were marked out that day for ſlaughter! Good people! a trifle appeaſes you!

† The negociations undertaken at Rome for obtaining from the pope the abſolution of Henry, are really incredible; and it is equally hard to conceive the inflexibility of the pope and the neceſſity of a king of France for this abſolution.

‡ Richelieu was only capable of making ſacrifices. Henry IV. or any other great man, would have made the two religions

lieu was deſtined to reign; that Richelieu who cruſhed the very grandees that ſold themſelves and their children. This cardinal, with the audacity of a prieſt who has neither country nor children, dared to deſtroy all the intermediate powers; and Louis XIV. for whom he cleared the way with but too much ſucceſs, entered booted and ſpurred among the depoſitaries, the organs, and the guardians of our laws, who, in the abſence of the ſtates-general, neceſſarily ſupplied their place. He forbad them even to *remonſtrate*; and afterwards, when theſe bodies of magiſtrates, vain ſhadows of our ancient liberties, and blaſted by royal contempt, came humbly to repreſent at the feet of the throne his errors, oppreſſions, injuſtice, profuſion, &c. the monarch replied theologically, by driving the petitioners out of the palace: *I owe no reckoning to the nation, I hold my crown of God alone.*

Let us pauſe, and conſider the condition of the people who ſuffered ſo much and gained nothing at all; let us examine the force of preju-

religions ſubſiſt together, by permitting a third or more to be eſtabliſhed. But Richelieu calculated which half of the ſtate he ſhould cruſh, to ſubject it to the other half; and the aſcendant of his cruel character was miſtaken for genius: fatal genius, which could only chooſe between crimes!

dices in that age, the ſlow progreſs of true knowledge, and what it is that occaſions the debaſement of the human mind: this view will abundantly evince the neceſſity of the light of beneficent philoſophy, which, with all its power, may reſiſt national ſervitude. While, in this ſtate of ignorance, the people were performing prodigies of valour which might have been directed to a better purpoſe, the cardinal Granvelle, aided by Philip II. that ferocious enemy of all freedom, civil, political, and religious, was deſirous to lay on them the additional load of the inquiſition; and they ſtretched forth their hands to welcome this new curſe, although withered by famine and imbrued in blood. And to what were all the claims of this valiant nation then limited? To this general and inconceivable cry, *can we take a heretic into the throne of St. Louis?*

Whence then aroſe this invincible horror to the proteſtant church? Did the catholic communion ever eſtabliſh the ſmalleſt liberties of the ſubject? On the contrary, it was a new tranſalpine and ſhameful yoke, added to ſo many others. The people thought neither of a ſocial compact, nor of its privileges, nor of its franchiſes. *To be king of France,* they ſaid, *it was more neceſſary to be a catholic than a man.* All the adherents of Henry were judged *guilty of treaſon againſt God and man*; an expreſſion which has ſince grown ſo common among the fanatics of all ſects.

Henry aſcended the throne, after having fought like a true ſoldier. Paris opened to him its gates, and inſtantly bad adieu to its ardent obſtinacy, content with having courageouſly defended tranſubſtantiation. France became his conqueſt; he purchaſed the diſmembered parts from the rapacity of the great, who retained them ſome years, and bluſhed not afterwards to ſell them to him a ſecond time. We cannot ſee without ſurprize that their deſcendants have the aſſurance to ſtyle that *fidelity* and *affection*, which was nothing but rapacity diſguiſed under the leaſt deceitful appearances. Conſult the memoirs of the age. The good Henry was reduced to the incapacity of diſcharging his promiſes, ſo many obligations had been impoſed on him of a pecuniary and burdenſome nature. He had already paid thirty-two millions to that venal and intereſted nobility which had made him purchaſe its reſpectful ſubmiſſion.

Henry undoubtedly ſtood in need of the qualities of a merchant to bring over the French, the Germans, the Engliſh, and the Dutch, who ſerved in his army. He had to ſtifle the envy

and

and jealousy of those grandees who were already moulding themselves to the art of the courtier. To establish union among so many subjects of discord, became a work that demanded uncommon address: he possessed it; he pardoned, he forgot past injuries; he was a good king on the throne, because he had endured bad fortune, and had been brought up in the best school of adversity. He had often been in want of the necessaries of life; and he had afterwards a fellow-feeling for those in the same situation. He was three years a state prisoner; never did he convert his authority to despotism. He had risked his life in battles; he was clement after victory. He had more than once seen the poignard raised against his breast; he respected the blood of mankind.

If he changed his religion, it was more from policy than conviction. We have indubitable evidences of his way of thinking. Exposed perpetually to the holy poignards of the catholics; outraged by the popes, who, well acquainted with the genius of their age, hurled from the top of the Vatican those thunders which re-echoed over all Europe; censured vehemently by the frantic declaimers so eloquent among the populace, and tired of their violence and perfidy, he wrote to Corisande of Andouin: *all these assassins, all these poisoners are papists, and you are of that religion! I would rather be a Turk.* He explained the political reaſons of his converſion to Elizabeth, queen of England, and ſent to Gabrielle d'Eſtrées a letter, in which ſpeaking of his abjuration, he ſays, *to-morrow I take the perilous leap.*

It is probable that, by perſevering in the ſyſtem of war, to the excluſion of every other, Henry IV. might have aſcended the throne without abjuring his creed. The proteſtants would in that caſe have redoubled their zeal, their attachment, and their courage; and the catholics, ſtruck with his heroic reſolution, would have conceived a reſpect to him which they never entertained, for they imputed the converſion of Henry IV. to ſelf-intereſt. That intereſt was indeed too predominant not to leave in the minds of men ſome doubts with regard to the ſincerity of his change. Let us add that this valiant prince could by his firmneſs have rendered an eternal ſervice to France by delivering her from the yoke of Rome; a yoke which he could have broken with the ſword of victory; a yoke, deſpicable and yet fatal in its effects, which afterwards lighted up in this kingdom ſo many abſurd and theological quarrels, the diſgrace of human reaſon, and the cauſe of the longeſt and moſt inconceivable civil rage. The

revocation

revocation of the edict of Nantes, of which the baneful consequences defy all calculation; the persecution of the reformers; the disputes of the Jansenists and Molinists, continued down to our own days. These miserable and cruel errors make us pity the French nation, which, debased and lost in such ridiculous questions, appeared to neglect every other concern, though exposed to the eyes of all Europe, which is not yet recovered from its long astonishment. The protestant religion, stifling those shameful and dishonourable wars at their birth, would have conducted the kingdom to a degree of liberty, of population, and of force, which has passed over to our neighbours, grown powerful by our errors.

Much eulogy has been bestowed on Henry IV. * and admiration has been carried to idolatry; but this idolatry, current only for half a century past, arose from the resentment that wished to create a strong opposition to the character of the reigning monarchs. It is always well for a nation to set up a phantom decorated with all the virtues which it would inspire into its monarchs; this is a skilful, useful, and therefore

* Too much unquestionably, but this was by Voltaire, and out of hatred to Louis XV. Henry IV. was a gentleman-king, rather than a citizen-king.

fore respectable convention. Besides, this model of princely virtues serves as an indirect satire upon all malversations; and the praises heaped on a deceased king are so many lessons which may touch the inattentive minds of monarchs, and make them comprehend the general will. Let us beware, then, of weakening an opinion calculated to keep his successors in awe, and to confine them by the only rein which they can now receive. They will always be great enough, if they imitate Henry IV. in several of his good qualities.'

It was in order to show to mankind that *mistaken religious ideas lead to a multitude of political errors, and materially hurt the national felicity*, that I have undertaken this recital, which faithfully exhibits the actions and the prejudices of our brave, but deluded ancestors.

Alas! how mad is that abominable zeal, jealous of some particular mode of worship, attacking the refractory with fire and sword, sowing division in the state and discord among families! And what sacrilegious piety is that which tramples humanity under foot and makes a crime even of compassion! Can a man the most hostile to philosophy ever look on Francis I. as religious, who caused the protestants to be burnt in Paris, while he supported them in

Germany

Germany, kept them in pay, and ſigned treaties with them? But the moſt abſurd incongruities are the faireſt features which characterize fanaticiſm.

Let us then exhibit vile and deſpicable ſuperſtition in its true colours! This is the only way to preſerve man from the numerous errors into which he is ever apt to relapſe from his propenſion to make heaven ſpeak, and to mingle the moſt atrocious paſſions, hatred, ambition, and revenge, with the ſublime and pure views of religion, calm and compaſſionate by its nature.

Thus ſang the enlightened and elegant Lucretius near two thouſand years ago:—

Humana ante oculos fœde cum vita jaceret
In terris oppreſſa gravi ſub religione,
Quæ caput a cœli regionibus oſtendebat,
Horribili ſuper aſpectu mortalibus inſtans;
Primum Graius homo mortaleis tollere contra
Eſt oculos auſus, primuſque obſiſtere contra:
Quem nec fama Deûm, nec fulmina, nec
minitanti
Murmure compreſſit cœlum.———

Lib. I. 63.

Notwithſtanding the efforts of the philoſophical Epicurus, the monſter has again made its appearance in ſeveral ages. He delights in the thick darkneſs of barbariſm; he dreads the ſmalleſt ray of light, which he would be happy to exclude. There is reaſon to apprehend that he ſtill reigns triumphant in ſome parts of Europe. Does not he at this moment rear his hideous head in Spain, and endeavour to re-eſtabliſh there the infernal throne of the holy inquiſition? Has he not oppoſed in Poland the principles of civil and religious liberty? And have not the refractory prieſts been the moſt ardent and moſt implacable enemies of the French conſtitution? Have they not given the appellation of *impious ſign* to the national cockade which is deſtined to pervade the univerſe? The philoſopher ſhould always ſtand ſentinel, with the naked ſword in his hand, to watch the approaches and attempts of this monſter, to purſue and pierce him, and to plunge into his lacerated bowels the ſteel which he dreads and which he bites with foaming rage. No repoſe, no truce: the extent of paſt evils, the deep wounds inflicted upon humanity and not yet healed, the influence which deſpicable and deſpiſed ideas have had and ſtill have on many ſovereigns of Europe, the ſort of yoke which they wear with trembling, and dare not ſhake off by reaſon of the ancient frenzy with which the monſter ſtruck the whole earth; all theſe conſiderations ſhould induce the writer to lift the club aloft in the air, and diſcharge redoubled blows upon fanaticiſm, which in our own days only reſumes the language of heaven to deceive and oppreſs mankind.

As, after one ſhock of an earthquake, it uſually happens that others follow, ſo to the the commotion of men's minds in the league ſucceeded a kind of ſecond league, the *fronde.* That civil war bore a ridiculous character, it muſt be allowed, but it wanted not a ſort of energy; and if it was not in every reſpect rational, it was very prolific in diſcourſes that contained many juſt ideas, and ſeemed to prepare for a greater and more ſucceſsful exploſion.

The arreſting of a preſident and of a counſellor of the parliament excited a general revolt. Jokes were paſſed, it is true, but ſtill the people were in arms; and why ſhould we judge only from the ſucceſs of the ſtruggle? This war, becauſe unimportant in its conſequences and confined to a narrow territory, gave occaſion to raillery, ſo congenial to Frenchmen. The parliament nevertheleſs paſſed decrees which amounted to a real *declaration of*

war

war againſt the throne and againſt deſpotiſm. A biſhop was declared generaliſſimo; this was whimſical, but it was energetic: the counterpoiſe of arbitrary power might have been then eſtabliſhed. Twelve hundred barriers erected in a city in the ſpace of twelve hours, behind which the townſmen fired, might intimidate the court, and ſerve as a preſage of what the Pariſians would one day perform when they ſhould take the Baſtille in two hours. The *frondeurs* had at their head the Duke of Beaufort, grandſon of Henry IV. the coadjutor, whoſe counſels were ſurely not moderate, the prince of Conti, and the marſhal Turenne: this looked not, I ſhould think, like a riot, as M. Gaillard terms it. Hiſtorians and biographers have been ſhort-ſighted in ridiculing that war; for the revolt of the capital might have ſpread much farther, and the hour of revolution might then have ſtruck.

The people had a real motive: they oppoſed the pecuniary edicts ſent to parliament and the detention of two of its members whom it became neceſſary to liberate. This civil war, under a king who was a minor, might have turned out very ſerious. It ſtopt of itſelf; but I cannot find in it that contemptible character with which hiſtorians have wiſhed to impreſs it.

 We

We are apt to judge from events. The observer who places himſelf again in the true point of view, beholds the facts in a quite different light. I ſee Louis XIV. obliged to fly his capital: if at this juncture, Condé had been againſt him, what would have happened? Condé did not brave the throne till ſeveral years after. Imagine Condé to be then what he became in the ſequel, and judge of the conſequence.

Laſtly, the duke of Beaufort, ſtyled *the king of the market-halls*, a name which implies much in many circumſtances, might have kindled and propagated the ſedition and converted it into an inſurrection. The parliament proceeded openly againſt the miniſter, paſſed acts againſt him, baniſhed him, and ſet a price on his head.

Condé afterwards wiſhed, as may be ſaid, to have a taſte of civil war; and entered into a league with the Spaniards. Obſerve likewiſe that the daughter of the Duke of Orleans gave orders to fire the cannon of the Baſtille upon the royal army. The king of Spain created Condé generaliſſimo, It was Turenne that ſaved the king and the royal family, and chance had a great ſhare in the ſide he took. If Condé and Turenne had not ranged themſelves on oppoſite

posite sides, if these generals had united their skill, the war would have produced great and decisive consequences. It was during the same time, that Charles I. king of England, not juridically but very politically, lost his head on a scaffold, for betraying his people and his oaths. The principles of sedition and revolt in the two nations had a very different issue: the *fronde* disappeared and all the conspirators vanished, while the alliance of Cromwell was courted on all sides, and Mazarin made a treaty with him.

Although Mazarin returned to Paris as in triumph, the object of this civil war was to shake arbitrary power. But the volcano, richly fed with combustibles during the reigns of Louis XIV. and Louis XV. was not destined to make its great and successful explosion, till the 14th of July 1789. Every thing was prepared to swallow up that despotic Colossus which oppressed and debased the nation, but which fatal circumstances had always preserved from the stroke of the avenging thunder that it had provoked for five hundred years. Happy the man who has seen the flame of the volcano and the tempest which has overwhelmed the throne of despotism! He was born a subject and even a slave; he will fall to sleep in the tomb satisfied and free.

DIALOGUE BETWEEN HENRY AND SULLY.

HENRY.

COME, my dear Rosny, let us have a private conversation—They will hardly believe me to be a catholic. They persist in saying that I can be absolved only by the pope, and consequently reign only by his sufferance.

SULLY.

Sire, the way to render vain all the thunders of the Vatican is to conquer: then you will easily obtain your absolution. But if you are not victorious, you will remain for ever excommunicated.

HENRY.

I should already have vanquished; but I love my city of Paris; it is my eldest child. I am desirous of preserving it in all its splendor. It would have been necessary to lay it in waste with fire and sword *. The chiefs of the league and the Spaniards have so little compassion on the poor Parisians! They are their tyrants; but I, who am their father and their king, cannot

* He had no such intention, the good king! No prince of the blood, no man of the court durst make him the proposition, or deceive him on that head.

behold thoſe calamities without being grieved to the heart. I have done every thing to find a remedy for them; nay I have got by heart and can repeat the catechiſm * which they have given me.

SULLY.

You have done wiſely, Sire; the theologians are not to be otherwiſe appeaſed. Believe me, the action moſt agreeable to God will always be to ſpare the blood of men, and put an end to the evils which they endure, whether from blindneſs, or from obſtinacy.

HENRY.

But would there not have been more heroiſm and firmneſs in ſupporting the proteſtant doctrine, and in raiſing it with me to the throne, thus giving to my ſubjects a religion ſimpler, purer, and better calculated to deſtroy the numerous and incredible abuſes of the ſacerdotal authority?

* The archbiſhop of Bourges made him ſeveral times recite his catechiſm; they impoſed on him the perſonal obligation *to hear maſs every day*, a cuſtom conſtantly followed by his ſucceſſors, *to attend the ſacraments four times in the year, and to recall the Jeſuits.* This laſt article is remarkable. The catholic muſt look on Henry as hypocritical, the calviniſt as ungrateful, the courtier as covetous: the philoſopher regards him in none of theſe lights.

SULLY.

SULLY.

If this could have been effected without risking your crown, without plunging France into endless war, it would have been very advantageous for the state to receive from you the principle of its felicity and of its grandeur, and to destroy the bud of the fatal discords sent to us from Rome. But it is evidently requisite first to subdue the capital, that you may afterwards drive your enemies from the centre of the kingdom to the frontiers.

HENRY.

This abjuration has cost my heart a violent struggle.

SULLY.

It was necessary—It was indispensable to my entry into Paris.

HENRY.

You were the first who advised me to go to mass, and yet you remain a protestant.

SULLY.

It becomes me so to do. They hated your religion and not your person; it was requisite that you should become a catholic. But with regard to me, I was free to remain faithful to the law of my fathers.

HENRY.

I have more than once reproached myself with

with weakneſs; and only derive conſolation from the idea that my converſion will re-eſtabliſh peace. Alas! what ſhould not be ſacrificed to this great intereſt?

SULLY.

The minds of men are not yet prepared for a happy change—No remorſe, Sire! Kings ſhould be above particular ſects, and attach themſelves only to that religion which, compoſed of pure elements, emanates from the breaſt of the divinity, of which they are the images here below, when they are enlightened, firm, and beneficent: they ought to be ſuperior to thoſe ſuperſtitious practices which abaſe reaſon, degrade the people, and take away their energy and their virtues. It belongs to them to prepare by degrees for their ſubjects a rational worſhip, worthy of man, and to quaſh, either by contempt or by an attentive prudence, thoſe miſerable quarrels which have ſo often deluged the earth with blood. Thus it is, that ſublime and provident lawgivers become the benefactors of the human race.

HENRY.

Would to God that I could appear in that character, and could conduct this age to truth! But bred in a religion which has reſtored to human reaſon a part of its liberty, I am conſtrained to

go

go backwards ; dragged along by the barbarifm which furrounds me on all fides, I am obliged to embrace a mode of worfhip full of fhocking abfurdities. Alas ! what will become of my good intentions in favour of mankind ?

SULLY.

You will do much good by feeming to yield to the torrent which cannot be refifted. You ought firft to attend to what is moft urgent, and overthrow the fanaticifm that butchers your fubjects before your eyes. Give it the fignal which it requires to appeafe its rage ; touch the altar where it will fall vanquifhed and difarmed ; and take away its dagger and its torch—One mafs heard will chain the monfter down, and prevent the effufion of blood : hear that mafs, and confider this nation, fometimes mad, and fometimes furious, like a nation of children that muft be kept in order by the illufions they are fond of.

HENRY, *with affection.*

Do thou, my dear Rofny, whom nothing urges to this facrifice, do thou remain faithfully attached to the reformed religion. The weight of thy name, thy virtues, and thy manly probity, render thee head of a party which I can no longer favour too openly, but which will always retain my heart and affections: not that it is free from the filth which it has contracted by its vicinity to popery; but it will ſhake off the remains of its vile ſuperſtitions, and ſoon we ſhall ſee a religion ariſe which the dignity of human reaſon may avow before the face of the divinity.

SULLY.

Prince! if I am able to penetrate into futurity, and can foreſee the progreſs of the human mind, the idol of Rome muſt fall by degrees; abuſes and knowledge will one day conduct France to the proteſtant communion; and proteſtantiſm itſelf, having purified its worſhip, will at laſt exhibit to the univerſe the true worſhippers of God in ſpirit and in truth. Then, freed from a ridiculous and diſgraceful mixture of tenets, ſhe will riſe pure and reſplendent, and lift up her head to heaven. She will capitivate with eaſe all firm minds and virtuous hearts, who will cheriſh her chaſte and noble attractions; they who revolted at the degrading and injurious ideas under which divines dared to repreſent the Creator of the univerſe and the auguſt Father of mankind.

HENRY.

Happy the prince who ſhall preſide at that epoch, and who ſhall be aſſiſted in the mighty

change

change by national wisdom * as much as I have been thwarted by madness and fanaticism!

SULLY.

One of your descendants, Sire, one of those vigorous and exalted souls that Providence keeps in reserve, who are passionately bent on doing good, who conceive, resolve on, and achieve great enterprizes, will break the yoke of the religious tyrants who fill men's minds with mystical chimeras, and whose idle opulence saps the force of the state. France, then delivered from the secret principle of its destruction, will resume its lustre and renown.

HENRY.

May he perform what I am not suffered to attempt amidst so many fierce spirits, doting upon their servitude! This kingdom, degraded by its fatal union with Rome, will not recover the natural ascendant which it ought to have over all its neighbours till it shall have adopted the urgent reform that shall proscribe at once the immense and annual tribute paid to the chair of St. Peter, the scandalous celibacy of the priests, that useless army of cenobites, and all those arbitrary and ridiculous chains which attack alike the privileges of the man and of the citizen.

* The reader will be pleased to remember that here I only reprint word for word what I published in 1782.

SULLY.

Time and reaſon will realize the generous emotions of your heart—Believe me your children, recollecting you, will reſtore to man that freedom which the atrocity of barbarous ages has raviſhed from him; and the imaginary power of Rome, reduced to its juſt level, will no longer provoke any thing but the ſmile of the ſage.

HENRY.

I accept the omen, my dear Roſny; but will not my friends ſay that I have given way to intereſt, and to the deſire of reigning?

SULLY.

You would have been culpable, when the veſſel of the ſtate was aſſailed by ſo furious a tempeſt, not to have put your hand to the helm. It was your part alone to ſave it. Reſtorer of France, no, they will never caſt upon you that reproach. They are ſenſible that the firſt duty of a king is to provide for the repoſe of his country; that he is not a hypocrite for putting fanaticiſm off its ſcent:—My dear maſter, is it not the ſame God that we adore, the God who commands us to love mankind and to do for them all the good in our power?—It is the ſame goſpel, that is, the ſame ſyſtem of morality which you acknowledge as the rule of practice.—The reſt, Sire, is a vain diſpute about words.

HENRY.

Undoubtedly, my dear Roſny; and thoſe who adore the ſame God, who follow the ſublime morality of the goſpel, ought at laſt to unite, embrace, and regard each other as brethren.—Are they not ſo indeed, ſince they agree on the ſame duties, and honour the ſame virtues?

SULLY.

A worſhip ſo rational, ſo ſimple, ſo pure, would ſhock too much the ambition and pride of the catholic prieſts, who have loaded religion with extraneous monſtroſities. They have need of bewildering the mind of man in the dark confuſion of their dogmas and their myſteries.

HENRY.

How anxiouſly do my wiſhes anticipate the day when France ſhall be enlightened, when the ſpirit of perſecution ſhall ceaſe, when, for want of diſputants, the fantaſtic food of theſe ſhameful quarrels ſhall fail! In the mean time be aſſured, my dear Roſny, that, faithful to my principles as much as I can without rekindling diviſions and diſcords, I ſhall eſtabliſh toleration in my dominions: this alone conſtitutes the glory and the force of empires.

SULLY.

That conduct, Sire, is a duty recommended by humanity, by wisdom, by gratitude, and even by policy.

HENRY.

Ah! my dear Rosny, I never speak my thoughts aloud on these subjects unless with you—who ought more than myself to detest fanaticism? How often have I seen the knife lifted against my breast! I have ever before mine eyes the bleeding and lacerated body of the unfortunate Coligny *, whose virtues and probity could not save him from the ferocity of the catholics. They will kill me, my friend, they will kill me: but no matter; I wish to hold both religions in my hand, and I will equally protect those, to my last breath, from whom I have been obliged to part †.

SULLY,

* Coligny was the only man qualified to establish in France a free constitution. His virtue was firm, while that of others yielded to circumstances. The poignard of the assassins on the night of St. Bartholomew plunged into his tomb the most generous defender of the liberties of the people. L'Hopital was more attached to the throne than to the people.

† Henry IV. issued the famous edict of Nantes, revoked by the rigid intolerance of Louis XIV. The condition of the protestants was settled in France; they were satisfied and tranquil, and this edict was at once the work of his wisdom, of his gratitude, of his attachment, and of his toleration. What need had the blindest fanaticism to destroy that monument of concord?

SULLY.

Act and proceed always under the eye of God, and you need never fear men.

HENRY.

Yes, I ſubmit entirely to providence. *(After a pauſe.)* I require, to make my people happy, a man poſſeſſed of your knowledge and of your firmneſs; for there are many criminals to withſtand—Know you the term of my wiſhes, the deſired object of my labours? It is, my friend, that every huſbandman, even the meaneſt peaſant, ſhall every Sunday have *a hen for his pot.* From that ſource, my friend, all is derived, joy, health, force, population, and the bleſſings which are ſent up to heaven and fall afterwards upon the heads of kings—Believe me, I have your maxims deeply imprinted on my heart.

SULLY.

Generous prince, may you always have the courage to do good; for this is a very difficult taſk amidſt thoſe rapacious men, thoſe haughty

concord? The deep wound inflicted on our country is not yet healed. Alas! how wretched then is the conſtitution of our government, that a ſingle man, miſled or intoxicated with pride, could create in the kingdom ſuch long and almoſt incurable evils! Why ſhould an unjuſt and barbarous command ſtill bear ſway after him, when he has ſunk into the tomb, loaded with the reproaches of the thinking part of the nation?

 courtiers,

courtiers, who regard only themſelves, and never the people.

HENRY.

Never conceal the truth from me, my dear Roſny. I deſire it, I ſeek it, and believe myſelf born with a diſpoſition to liſten to it.

SULLY.

I will prove my abſolute devotion to you, by never diſguiſing any thing which may intereſt your glory and the happineſs of your people. *(He retires.)*

THEOLOGIANS.

MOST theologians have ſeparated what the Author of nature united, and out of one religion have made a thouſand. It was the fruit of vaſt and profound reading in theological works that perſuaded the illuſtrious Boerhaave, that religion, very ſimple as it iſſued from the mouth of God, is at preſent disfigured by vain, or rather vicious, philoſophical ſubtleties, which have occaſioned nothing but eternal diſſenſions and the fierceſt of animoſities. He was tempted to hold a public diſputation on this queſtion: *why chriſtianity, preached formerly by ignorant men, had made*

made ſuch vaſt progreſs, and now makes ſo little when preached by the learned.

If I may be allowed to inveſtigate the reaſons of this fact, I muſt refer them to their twiſted and forced explanations; to the boldneſs of their deciſions, which are often founded upon their own authority only, and dictated by pride or intereſt; to the abſurd, fabulous doctrines, in every reſpect hoſtile to reaſon and the good of ſociety; and to thoſe tenets which ſuperſtition has mingled with the pure revelation proceeding from heaven. It cannot be doubted but the errors of a great many eccleſiaſtics, though very learned, have much injured religion, and checked its progreſs. One needs only open the annals of the church to be in a manner a witneſs and ſpectator of their bitter and obſcure diſputes. With what facility do they pour upon their antagoniſts the names of heretics and of ſchiſmatics? Far from inſtructing and edifying chriſtians, they inſpire them with a horror which muſt in ſome meaſure recoil upon religion. Wiſhing to extend the empire of certain dogmas which they forged themſelves, they contracted the reign of that morality ordained by God, and which eſtabliſhes peace and order among men. Even when right as to the fact, they were wrong in the form; and

did

did we even approve their judgments, we could not help blaming their clamours, their abusive reproaches, and their violent proceedings. The ancients placed the graces in the train of wisdom; but theologians have substituted hatred, revenge, and the dark passion of envy.

ON ASSIGNATS.

TO metallic tokens nature has assigned bounds; and every industrious nation is therefore obliged to create new ones. But for *tokens*, how many things would remain unsold; it is essentially necessary to possess that which shall establish an agreement between whatever is to be sold, and the *token* by which the merchandize is to be obtained.

Without an active and rapid token productive industry cannot exist, since it is the circulation alone which constitutes riches, and without a multiplicity of changes industry falls to the ground.

Favour then such a circulation, for this is the aim you ought to have in view: and when the national assembly, to revive productive industry, offers assignats on disposable inheritances, how happens it that this magnificent ſecurity does not ſuffice? What other value can be offered, when terror, avarice, and a want of patriotiſm, cauſe the ſpecie to diſappear? Would you employ force to bring it again to light?

It enters into the *policy* of the *revolution* to have recourſe to a great and firm reſolve; and it is not a vulgar reſource that muſt now be reſorted to, ſince all the movements which have produced our ſecurity have been extraordinary ones.

Paper money has been often found to obtain a preference over gold and ſilver, by its rapid movement, and by favouring the circulation in a prodigious degree.

Silver has a *value*, and for that very reaſon cannot become a *token* of its own *value*: every *value* is therefore diſplaced and ſuperfluous. When ſilver is given, a rude truck is made after the manner of ſavages, of certain iſlanders who employ fiſhes as pledges of exchange. The perfection of a poliſhed ſtate is to introduce *tokens* without *value*, to introduce them with ſecurity, and to multiply them with the profuſion the want of tokens demands. Now, the whole of the ſpecie is inſufficient for the quantity of *labours* and of *merchandizes*; and it is not the *labours* which beget *tokens*, but the

tokens

tokens which beget labours; or, in other words, it is the *hope*, the *promiſe*, which in politics as well as in morals puts every thing in motion. Paper of every deſcription labours for the future; and even though it ſhould only ſave the *preſent quarter of an hour*, ſince life conſiſts entirely in the preſent, it would be infinitely profitable.

Gold and ſilver are not at the bottom repreſentative tokens of all properties; they are themſelves very *real properties*, but are at the ſame time *illuſory* riches, which, if too much accumulated, would become entirely *uſeleſs*. The inutility of gold is demonſtrable, ſince the chance that put it in your poſſeſſion may one day deprive you of it: by ceaſing to place the *real* againſt the *real*, a prodigious ſource of new riches would be created, ſeeing that a bit of *paper* might be much more ſucceſsfully bartered againſt the ſimple faculty of obtaining the *real* at will; and we ſhould at length be diſtinguiſhed from ſavages by this *political work*, a work that would baniſh a falſe uſage, and proportion the abundance of tokens to the extent of the need a nation has of them.

Give activity to *every hand*, and riches will ſpring up: multiply exchanges and trucks, no matter with what token, provided it be acknowledged

knowledged by the whole of the ſociety, and it will invariably effect a real payment in one way or another.

In America certain ſavages employ cacao-nuts as *pledges of their exchanges:* they would do better to eat their money, and circulate from hand to hand ſmall pebbles. We do not eat our gold and ſilver; but *elevated* opinions are ſo different from *current* opinions, that the riches are placed in the *ſtrong box*, while they merely reſide in the head, that is to ſay, in the idea that the promiſe will be realized. *Credit* therefore conſtitutes the *riches*, and is greater than the material object.

A falſe half-crown, if it has paſſed through ſix hundred hands, has abſolved its crime in the view of ſociety: ſince, if it has deceived one man, it has ſerved five hundred and ninety-nine others, who have enjoyed the phantom as effectually as if it had been a reality. This is above the comprehenſion of a vulgar mind, which is conſtantly deſirous to deſtroy the *hen* for her *golden* eggs, and to ſee the *ſource* and *depot* of the metal.

Multiply money, and let it even be of the baſeſt and moſt deſpicable kind: ſay to your labourers, this is the recompenſe of your toils; and theſe labourers, that is to ſay, the three

and

and half fourths of your population, will take your money, your contemptible money, and if it circulates for one ſingle day, it will circulate for a thouſand years. Such is the bank of England: confidence is repoſed in a monarch, but you will not repoſe the ſame confidence in a nation. With the ſoil of France for a *ſecurity*, you oppoſe *aſſignats*; and, notwithſtanding, the ſingle word *credit* puts in motion incalculable labours, which are paid for, it is true, ſooner or later, but are always performed in advance. Speak to me after this of putting yourſelves in the power of thoſe who have heaped together *metals*. Riches are waiting the opportunity to give laws to you, becauſe you will not declare that you will diſpenſe with metallic ſpecie.

And whence ariſes this privilege of *metals* which is to be exchanged againſt every ſpecies of property! Theſe *metals* are not amaſſed but by dint of time and labour; and the ſpecie will never be ſufficiently abundant to enable every man to be employed, and every merchantable article, finding one who covets it, to meet with a buyer. Conſidered as a *token*, the poverty of ſpecie is manifeſt: conſidered as *riches*, of all riches it is the moſt *abſurd*.

Throughout the extent of the French territory

tory there are thousands of things to sell which do not sell: and in every part we meet with day labourers who offer to sell their labour: for want of *tokens* every thing languishes. Create these, do not be afraid to *multiply* them, and you will in the event see them *pour* themselves over the *land*, because there the first materials are.

Without an abundant distribution of *new tokens*, millions of bargains which can and ought to be made will not be made, and thousands of men will remain without employment: public and private undertakings will be put a stop to, those who possess will not enjoy what they have, and those who might enjoy without possessing, will disturb society for want of employment.

Let the tokens of riches be precisely what they ought to be, *simple tokens:* those who confide in gold and silver alone, are *savages* and nothing better. Allow these tokens to circulate, and you will constantly see them find a level with the necessities of the nation. The true token of property is not gold, but paper; it is not a *truck*, to be employed as it is in the deserts of America, but a *promise*, a title given to a member of the society which assures him that he will one day obtain such a *value*.

Assignats

Aſſignats are terrifying to thoſe alone who ſee ſociety in one *unique* or tranſitory point of view;—to thoſe who do not perceive in the circulation a remedy for every political evil. Movement, movement is needed! it matters not what the ſtimulus be, multiply the *token*, and if the leaf of paper, the parchment, the bit of leather riſes one *farthing* above its *intrinſic* value, the ſtate is ſaved. Truſt to this token, and let it be *paper*; be careful even that it ſhall be nothing elſe. Shun the *real value*; for, let me repeat it to you, it is a *promiſe:* you muſt receive it or reject it, there is no medium. This paper ſupported by ſimple hope, has an advantage over gold; but as we are far above this ſimple hope, it will become a real and true payment of every value, from the greateſt to the ſmalleſt.

Monteſquieu has obſerved: " all goes well when money ſo perfectly repreſents things, that the things may be had as ſoon as the money is poſſeſſed, and when things ſo well repreſent money, that the money may be had as ſoon as the things are poſſeſſed."

Draw without apprehenſion the boldeſt conſequences from this fine truth, the neweſt and moſt important to be found in his book. Acknowledge with Monteſquieu the terrible and uncertain

uncertain domination of *metals*, and the abſolute want of *tokens*: to the word *ſpecie* ſubſtitute the word *paper*; it will anſwer the ſame end; and will anſwer it much better; it will be twenty times more ſupple and more active; and will vivify the cold and ſtagnant parts of the kingdom. Poliſhed ſociety will not attain its full perfection, until the abundance of tokens ſhall have eſtabliſhed no difference between *buying* and *ſelling*, that is to ſay, until the nation ſhall be as prompt as the action. With her two milliards of aſſignats, how very diſtant is France ſtill from this point?

The wiſhes of enlightened men will not be accompliſhed on this head, until human prejudices ſhall have been ſubdued. How is the maſs of ſociety to be perſuaded that their *idol* deceives them? Accuſtomed to *metals*, they will only be reconciled to paper when it advances the intereſt of opulence and avarice: they do not perceive that to give a new life to an empire, it is neceſſary not only to multiply the token, but to raiſe it alſo to the height of all the *moveable* and *territorial* property. They ſeem to feel for the people, and to dread on their account the good effect it will produce on perſons in affluent circumſtances: but where, unleſs in *aſſignats*, is the token to be found that

 will

will free the ground from its ſterility, and induſtry from its ſtagnation? Where the token that will replace the eclipſed ſpecie; that will create riches by the ſimple movement of circulation; that will decompoſe the terrifying maſs of accumulated merchandize; and, giving a new confidence to the ſtate creditors, that will at once ſatisfy juſtice and public intereſt?

" Allow me motion," ſaid Deſcartes, " and I will create a world." Give me, I ſay, an *abundant token*, and France will be ſaved.

The pyramids of Egypt were built with onions; and oak leaves alone will ſuffice to re-eſtabliſh public affairs, provided there is prudence in the nation and firmneſs in the government. If a mine of gold or ſilver were to be diſcovered in France, France would be loſt; by gold Spain has been undone.

If the token is multiplicable, there is a ſtill ſtronger reaſon why it ought to be diviſible: it is the indigent claſs that has the greateſt need of this token, ſeeing that it poſſeſſes no credit in itſelf, but borrows one from the ſtate. The ſtate anſwers for all thoſe who cannot make the ſmalleſt advance, which it makes for them, communicating to them all its force. Out of nothing, nothing can be made, and the ſlighteſt burthen requires a lever: the token, whatever its value may be, is the leaven thrown into the paſte; it diſappears, but imparts its ſubſtantial quality. So a multitude of men do nothing, and can do nothing, becauſe with an immenſe quantity of *paſte* they have not an atom of *leaven*.

Tyrants have always contrived to derive a great advantage from national credit, but have applied it to their inſatiable cupidity, and made it the inſtrument of much miſchief. If as much had been attempted for the ſplendor of the ſtate, as has been done to accompliſh its overthrow, France, the miſtreſs of the fineſt productions of Europe, and excluſively ſo of ſeveral of them, would in commercial matters have invariably given the law to the ſurrounding nations; ſince the nation that has need of the moſt eſſential productions is always tributary.

As a ſlumbering property ſpecie is nothing; when it is active it is every thing. Wherever any good and uſeful aim is to be accompliſhed, if the *ſpecie* or the *token* be needed, the thing remains to be done: but I have already proved that the ideal token is infinitely preferable to the material token.

Two milliards of aſſignats have a terrific aſpect; but they are to be diffuſed over an immenſe and poor population: they are a vaſt refervoir which is about to feparate into a million of fmall ftreams, and thefe again are to terminate in the arts, in commerce, and more efpecially in agriculture. This capital, which the nation appears to lend, will be again poured into the national treafury, the people returning with the one hand what they fhall have received with the other.

Even although affignats fhould beftow on a ftate merely a momentary ftrength with which it fhould triumph interiorly over its enemies, this firft iffue might be confidered as a victory, feeing that it is important to give to the wheels of the new and fuperb machinery their full fcope: the motion being once impreffed, the machine will move by its own weight, and by the general intereft. Then will the enemies of the conftitution, themfelves hurried on, abandon their romantic ideas; and the ancient idol of defpotifm, ftripped of its laft golden fringes, will have no longer either priefts or adorers. The foil of France, a fine foil open on every fide to cultivation, is the power which will receive the incenfe, and be cherifhed; while the flaves who fought gold at the foot of the throne, will fearch after it in the entrails of the common mother. The national affembly will thus imitate the father who addreffed his children: *dig the garden, my ſons, you will there find a treaſure.* But the garden is not to be broken up without a ploughing inſtrument; and aſſignats are the ſole and great means of cultivation and fecundity.

*** This fragment was compoſed and publiſhed two months before the firſt emiſſion of aſſignats in France, and when it was in contemplation to iſſue them to the amount of two milliards of livres. The meaſure then experienced a ſtrenuous oppoſition; and the author flatters himſelf that by this effort of his the public were reconciled to the expedient.

ADDRESS TO THE CONSTITUENT ASSEMBLY.

GENTLEMEN, *February* 11, 1790.

WHEN in your wiſdom you decreed the liberty of the preſs, you wiſhed to cruſh a deſpotiſm the moſt debaſing and moſt dangerous of all, which hung upon the mind and depreſſed the flight of human genius, and which ſtrove to extinguiſh all public knowledge. You were ſenſible that if it was important for nations to improve continually their internal organization, to enlighten their legiſlators, their adminiſtrators, and directors of every kind; and it was of no leſs moment to erect a tribunal which might be at once the greateſt reſtraint upon the enemies of the country, the firſt chaſtiſement of eſtabliſhed tyrants. This active ſentinel rouſed the people at the very moment it was intended to load them with fetters; he it was that prepared and accompliſhed the revolution."

What is it that really creates the public opinion? The liberty of the preſs. This is the ſource of the great political truths upon which depends the fate of all the nations of the earth, and without which ſervitude and oppreſſion alone would go unpuniſhed.

You have recognized, Gentlemen, that nothing could belong to man, if thought belonged not to him; that to deny him the power of ſpeech was to annihilate the freedom of thought; that there was no medium between the right of ſpeaking and that of writing; and that, the induſtry of man having invented the preſs, it was his organ which acted wherever his thought was entitled to act.

The enemies of the revolution tremble at ſeeing the liberty of the preſs, that organ of the public opinion which diſpenſes glory or ſhame, eſtabliſhed in the two worlds. They would fain interrupt that communication of the ideas which is the beginning of ſocial felicity: it is to the intereſt of the republic that the wicked ſhould be known, and this they fear. By whom would the faults or crimes of governments be now puniſhed, if not by that moral action which, giving to obſcure offences an avenging notoriety, tranſforms a bold denunciation into an act truly civic.

God has willed that there ſhould exiſt on earth a thing ſuperior to legiſlators, to the laws themſelves, a thing to which every kind of power owes the homage of ſubmiſſion and reſpect:— it is the information of the public, and its organ is a free preſs. Alas! that gift of the divinity, that great benefit of the legiſlation, is on the point of being deſtroyed—and by whom? by the judges of the *Châtelet*.

If the preſs be a moral action, why do not our adverſaries oppoſe to it a moral action? Have ever the enemies of the conſtitution been laid under any conſtraint? Are they not permitted to reply to every thing if they can? Has their glaring averſion to public liberty been otherwiſe combated than by the ſtyle of compaſſion? There is no diſtinction between citizen and citizen; conſtitutional toleration extends to all civil and political opinions. You have not allowed fanaticiſm, baniſhed from our altars, to take refuge at the altar of our country. The partizans of the old government have enjoyed an unbounded freedom of the preſs, and have heaped up accuſations and abuſive reproaches upon the friends of the revolution, without the latter having ever deigned to complain.

By what wayward diſpoſition have the judges of the *Châtelet*, in preſence of a mild and tolerating legiſlature which abhors equally the perſecutions of ſtate and of religion, been induced to ſerve none but deſpotic miniſters; and why have they liſtened only to their agents, and manifeſted a diſpoſition to ſtrike the friends of the conſtitution alone? Why have they not left the public, that ſupreme cenſor, to judge of the errors and immorality of authors? Why? It is becauſe, enemies of the rights of man and of nations, they wiſh at preſent to ſtifle all patriotic writers, only that they may cruſh the human race with impunity under the weight of arbitrary power.

Individual liberty being extinguiſhed, the *Châtelet* has ſnatched the moſt odious weapon of tyrannic ſway, the ſureſt to intimidate a whole people, by having the air of puniſhing only a few. It is the public liberty that is menaced, it is the legiſlature itſelf, for the ſentences of the

judges

judges of the *Châtelet* ſhamefully contradict the law; their abſurd ſentences compriſe all the exceſſes of the moſt dreadful ariſtocracy, and, to crown their audacity, the *Châtelet* would fain perſuade us that it reſtrains the preſs only for the intereſt of virtue and of mankind.

To regulate the liberty of the preſs, is to annihilate it: to write is a moral act; it muſt be unlimited, or it muſt not exiſt. Determine then the limits of time and of ſpace, if you would give bounds to thought. Eſtabliſh an inquiſition rather than create reſponſibility. Yes! an inquiſition would be preferable, for one either braves it or is ſilent; but reſponſibility opens an immenſe field for conſtraint, violence, and tyranny. How mince a truth, how ſay that a thing is and is not, how ſoften the hideous colours of vice? There is no term to liberty when the public ſafety is concerned; and the ſlavery of thought becomes more ſhameful than its total abſence. To deprive ideas of their independence, is entirely to eclipſe the human mind; becauſe its flight can only be meaſured by its energy, its virtue, and its grandeur.

If a man is born to have an influence upon ſociety, who will dare to repreſs a prolific idea! an idea which may in an inſtant decompound

our

our calamitous and erroneous notions, and present to us a truth uſeful to mankind! Deny Providence, if you believe not that it has always in ſtore ſome few men of genius who ſuddenly inundate the globe with a new flood of knowledge, deſcending with an accumulating progreſſion from age to age.

The entire liberty of the preſs, or its annihilation! This is our requeſt; for thought being infinite, the inviſible chain of ideas cannot be divided; and the power which tranſmits them, being equally unlimited, can ſuffer no conſtraint.

What would reſponſibility become? The perfidious dagger of deſpotiſm, claiming the appellation of the ſword of juſtice; and ſoon this dagger would aſſaſſinate patriotiſm.

The pretext aſſumed for murdering the conſtitution is to call out a libel! At this vague word one would ſuppoſe it neceſſary to ſhut out truth, to obliterate the art of printing, to efface the ſhifting picture of the human mind, which by turns repreſents different things, and to extinguiſh in man the capacity of diſcerning between good and evil. Then would men be automata, and no longer ſtand in need of laws. But there is no ſuch thing as a libel; it is a phantom which impoſes upon a timorous imagination.

gination. If the compoſition contains ſome truths, it cannot be a libel; and if it be a heap of falſehoods, let it be detected, and it will ſink into contempt. Beſides, are there vivid colours in the univerſe without ſtrong contraſts? Every thing here below muſt endure oppoſition and contention; and virtue in my opinion is only real, when it has maintained an obſtinate conteſt. A thought is not an action, and tribunals can only reſtrain actions: if my fellow citizen adopt my thoughts, it is only from a conviction of their juſtneſs and propriety; for I do not force his choice or adherence. My thoughts are nothing if nobody adopt them; if my thoughts are formed to overturn a great abuſe, that abuſe will not fall till my equals have perceived the danger of it. The exerciſe of my mind is natural, and conſequently lawful; it is this that modifies the univerſe: but unleſs generally adopted, what would it become? I ſpeak to intelligent beings like myſelf, and if their conceptions do not tally with mine, I have been miſtaken; if our notions agree, I no longer act, it is the general body, and that prohibitive law would then wither the nerves of activity and conſcience. You wiſh man to act, and you forbid him to think; annihilate all liberty, annihilate man; there

there is no medium between ſlaves or mere machines, and citizens perfectly free.

Need I repeat here that thought is no more contained in a book than heat is in fire or cold in ice; it is the reader that creates the idea, and if his idea be not in concord with yours, the book is nothing but black upon white. Thus fall to the ground all fooliſh accuſations, all ſenſeleſs aſſertions; thus the negative deſtroys the affirmative; and thus, in the torrent of opinions, whatever is falſe ſinks, and truth alone floats upon the ſurface. There is no libel when an anſwer is not prohibited. Patriotiſm may and ought to have its enthuſiaſts; it is a reaction againſt the overflowing of anti-patriotic cries. Although enthuſiaſm ſhould give birth to a new world, the love of its country would excuſe ſuch extravagances; and ſince the days of Plato, thoſe who dream of the great changes that may be effected by theſe three fundamental points, nature, liberty, and equilibrium, only view in anticipation the revolutions which time will infallibly bring about upon the earth.

I do not mean to ſay that there exiſt no criminal writings; but theſe criminal writings are ſuch as contain treaſon againſt the nation; they alone provoke the public vengeance. When an individual attempts to be ſtronger than

than the whole maſs of the nation, when he contemns the authority of the legiſlator, he is ſubject to the tribunal, which ought to puniſh the crimes of national treaſon; but where exiſts this tribunal, or where ought it to exiſt?

Enlightened Europe, and men of letters in particular, are not recovered from their ſurpriſe at ſeeing the national aſſembly create an extraordinary tribunal, which may combine with the enemies of the repreſentative body to ſubdue and annihilate it. The crime of treaſon againſt the nation appears in the conduct of the judges of the *Châtelet*, and all France accuſes them. The miniſterial rage is abſolute madneſs, and inflames theſe iniquitous judges. Thus among the Romans, the Decemvirs, who aſpired to tyranny, took no care to follow the ſpirit of the republic; and was not their criminal intention fully unmaſked? The judges of the *Châtelet*, in attacking patriotic writers, make a guilty eſſay of the means of diſſolving the repreſentative body of a ſovereign nation; they employ the moſt odious means to bring it down to its former debaſement. But the national aſſembly will not ſuffer the faireſt attribute of ſovereignty to paſs into the hands of the judges of the *Châtelet*: that tribunal would be a principle

ciple of diviſion which might diſſolve the ſtate; and France would exhibit only a fantaſtic government, if the national aſſembly ſhould diveſt itſelf of the power of judging all crimes of national treaſon.

I accuſe the judges of the *Châtelet* of the crime of treaſon againſt the nation, and appeal to the conſtituent power to have them caſhiered. The conſtituent power emanates from the nation; the conſtituent power muſt either be denied or admitted without reſerve; and where can it be, if it reſide not in the repreſentatives of the nation? The conſtituent power is ſole; the other powers are produced by it: it equals, it ſurpaſſes all the other wills; and ought to accompliſh the ſpeedy abrogation of the *Châtelet*, becauſe the national liberty is more in danger at this moment than when the ſoldiers of deſpotiſm ſurrounded the capital, ſince the atrocity of the plot excited an inſurrection, and ſince the ſword may be oppoſed to fire. But in the preſent caſe, it is inconceivable how a national decree could have been given up to the diſcretion of the judges of the *Châtelet*. This guilty tranſaction proves the inſidious dexterity of the enemies of the revolution. But hear what Tacitus addreſſes to all nations who imagine themſelves free when they have made laws, and yet at the ſame time

time abandon the execution of them too blindly to impure hands.

Plus togâ quam enſe tyrannus ſeipſum ſervabit.

When one nation is threatened or attacked by another nation, what does it do? It employs its own forces to repel the aſſault. If the repreſentatives of a nation, aſſembled to give it a political conſtitution, be attacked by private political bodies or by powerful perſons, ought they to intruſt the care of their defence and that of their operations to others than themſelves? Will they proceed to create an extraordinary tribunal, which may combine with the enemies of the repreſentative body of the nation to ſubdue or to overturn it altogether?

Is not all derived from the conſtituent power? It is an incredible miſtake in the aſſembly of the repreſentatives of the nation, not to defend itſelf by its own energy againſt the attacks that may be made upon it, and to take other meaſures of reſiſtance than what the nation takes or would take when it is or ſhould be attacked.

It is inconceivable that the national aſſembly ſhould create a tribunal againſt the criminals who inſult the reſpect which is its due: ought not the repreſentatives of the nation to conduct themſelves as the nation would do in caſe of attack? It would retain its defence in its own hands;

hands; it would charge a select number of its members to inquire into the offence, and to make a report according to which it would judge. To call another power to its aid, is not this unbecoming its sovereignty? And who ought to judge the crimes of national treason, if not the represented nation?

The representatives of the nation have already acted in conformity to this principle upon several occasions; among others in the case of Toulon, of the provost of Marseilles, of the court of vacation of the parliaments at Rennes, of Metz, and of Bordeaux. Why then has the national assembly bestowed on a particular tribunal, out of its own body, the cognizance of offences against its political life and against its decrees? It cannot be doubted but that the national assembly is not aware of the extent of the rights which the nation has conferred upon it; they can be those only which itself would have exercised, if it had not recurred to representation.

As the nation would have chosen a portion of its members to inquire into the offences against its majesty and to report the evidence, that it might pass impartial sentence; so the representatives of the nation ought to charge a part of their number with the business of taking information and of reporting the result to national

tional aſſembly, that it may be able to pronounce penalties ſuitable to the crimes of national treaſon.

It is falſe reaſoning, to ſay that the nation or its repreſentatives cannot have the right of exerciſing the judicial power, and that this would be to act both as judge and as party. Not only ought the nation or its repreſentatives to reſerve to themſelves the cognizance of crimes againſt the national majeſty, but I maintain that the former cannot beſtow this power on any other tribunal without the greateſt danger. Neither the aſſembled nation, nor its repreſentatives, unqueſtionably can exerciſe the ſupreme executive power which is conferred upon the king, nor the judicial power in its details, ſuch as judging between man and man; but when the matter relates to attacks on their political exiſtence or on the conſtitution, the nation or its repreſentatives are the ſole judges, and the executive power cannot, without criminal neglect, diſpenſe with the execution of the ſentences pronounced by the nation or its repreſentatives.

Monteſquieu ſays, that the celebrated Machiavel imputes the loſs of liberty at Florence to the people's not judging the crimes of treaſon committed againſt them in a body as at Rome: there were judges appointed for the purpoſe.

I conclude then, that the national aſſembly ſhould decree, as a conſtitutive article, that the legiſlative body can take cognizance of and judge the crimes of national treaſon, without having the power of transferring the charge to any ſpecial tribunal.

MORTMAINS.

THE eccleſiaſtical bodies have been the moſt eager to aſſume the odious right of ſervitude, and to give it an unbounded extenſion.

Among the ſubjects of the ſame monarch the ſeparation of a road or a river condemns ſome to an eternal opprobrium, and degrades them to the condition of the vileſt animals. There are ſtill Frenchmen, who, when they die without poſterity, cannot tranſmit to the next akin the land their labour has fertilized, who are not allowed to employ their own taſte in the choice of a conſort, and who, when they expatriate themſelves to enjoy elſewhere the rights of humanity, are purſued by their *ſeigneurs*, who, wherever they can find them, ſeize on their property.

The entire abolition of this laſt trace of the

ages

ages of barbarity, of this laſt crime propagated by the nobility even while they were heaping up enjoyments in the midſt of the liberty of the capital, is what we have reaſon to expect from the reigning monarch; and it was neceſſary that the royal authority ſhould be eſtabliſhed in all its ſplendour, to the end that a moſt ſingular contradiction in our manners might be aboliſhed. On one hand, we ſee natives of France the ſlaves of a fief-holder; and on the other, foreign ſlaves who become free the moment they put a foot on French ground.

The people have thus had to ſupport at once the feudal dues, and the royal impoſts: was it poſſible that they could groan under a more decided ſlavery? and if a griping intendant is to replace the poſſeſſor of the fief, will not the rural ſervitude be the ſame?

The mortmains will not feel that benevolent power of kings which can enfranchiſe the ſlaves of the feudal ſyſtem; until ſeveral very burthenſome impoſts ſhall have been taken off: it is then that the liberty which has been reſtored to them will give them the courage entirely to ſhake off the ſhackles of misfortune.

The ſyſtem of mortmain, whatever may have been ſaid to the contrary, is evidently derived from the old military diſcipline: the term itſelf is a ſoleciſm. The mainmortables were no other than *ſoldiers* ſubjected to *captains:* the abrogation of mortmain is therefore a claim, ſince the political conſtitution is entirely changed, and ſince thoſe who have profited by this odious right bring to the ſtate none of the advantages it formerly derived from them.

The poſitive laws of nations ought frequently to be compoſed afreſh after the natural law: the *maratime law*, for inſtance, is ſtill made up of odious uſages, worthy of the ferocity of the ages of barbarity. The laws on which the higheſt encomiums are beſtowed, are, in the view of the philoſopher, no other than ſo many human errors. Whence ariſes it that they have obtained reſpect, when they are founded either on a long abuſe or on an ignorance of what would be better? The progreſs we have made in knowledge muſt and ought to effect ſalutary changes.

OF AN INCOMMODIOUS PRIDE.

AMONG ſovereigns there is no one who, going back a certain number of degrees, cannot count a ſhepherd in the number of his anceſtors; nor is there any ſhepherd who, having recourſe to the ſame reckoning, could not perhaps

haps count a ſovereign or a lord among his, provided ſhepherds were as fond of reckoning the number of their anceſtors as they are that of their ſheep. But although nature ordains that all men ſhall be born equal, civil ſocieties introduce a difference among them, becauſe there is in the firſt place an inequality of ſtrength, ſervices, merit, and fortune; and becauſe, ſecondly, public liberty is in reality compoſed of ſmall ſacrifices made by individual liberty.

We will therefore admit of unequal ranks, and allow ſuch a man to occupy the higheſt ſtation he can in his own imagination. The pride of the great is indeſtructible, and ought accordingly to be tolerated; but let it be directed towards uſeful aims. Nobility, in whatever ornaments it may be clad, can be no other than an accidental quality, ſo long as it is ſeparated from virtue, that is to ſay, from noble and perſonal acts.

Birth alone can give no claim to glory; and when an idolatrous worſhip of titles is ſought by thoſe who poſſeſs them, it ſhould be recollected that it is always in the power of an enlightened nation, to appreciate and correct theſe exaggerated pretenſions by the inſtructions of its philoſophers and comic poets, and to puniſh their authors by diſdain and the influence of

 opinion.

opinion. It besides belongs to education to lessen the effect of these distinctions, which cease to be humiliating when men no longer consent to be humbled.

A firm reaction of thought is well calculated to check the overweening pride of those who are noble, and to ease from the load of their envy those who are not so: when personal qualities are in a manner fixed in a nation, they destroy the prejudices which have bestowed on birth, unaccompanied by merit, a dazzling splendour to which it cannot be entitled.

It therefore depends on an enlightened nation to mortify and subdue that incommodious pride of the nobles, which is to be found at this time in hereditary monarchies alone. But seeing that the Majesty of the crown absorbs all these little grandeurs; and that these nobles, beginning with the first gentleman, are in the fullest extent of the term subjects, it must follow, that all subjects being necessarily at an equal distance from the throne, the inordinate pride of the nobles, a mania revived in latter times, ought to be combated, by holding out to their view a master under whom they cease to be independent. Thus will this illusion, not calculated for the present era, be destroyed, whenever the enlightened part of the nation ſhall ſtep forward, and point the well directed ſhaft of ridicule at that jargon of *armorial bearings* and *quarterings*, which is merely the baſe counterfeit of real grandeur and virtue. The ſpirit of philoſophy has long *decompoſed* theſe puerile abſurdities, which the vanity of courtiers and the indolence of courts have ſo miſtakenly aimed at eſtabliſhing, among enlightened men who are ſuperior to ſuch prejudices.

OF THE LAW NOT MADE AND NOT LESS EXISTING.

THE law is the rule preſcribed to order and to forbid. Notwithſtanding what certain writers have maintained, the true prototype of every law is the natural law, a deviation from which renders either of them vicious, and in the event detrimental. But the natural law is in its application, if I may be allowed ſo to expreſs myſelf, a law *not yet made*, but as it were merely appreciated. Political ſuperſtitions, ſtill more execrable than religious ones, have invented a kind of magical words and circles, beyond the boundaries of which we are threatened with deſtruction: the foot, however, which paſſes them finds a ſure and ſolid ground. The enlightened ſtate of a renovated people can admit of no phantoms; and we are urged on all ſides to approach the law *not made*, but ſtill exiſting.

As it belongs to the whole of the nation to make laws, and as a nation has neither force nor exiſtence unleſs in the aggregate of all its parts, the code it ought to form ſhould be variable, the laws being at the bottom nothing more than ſo many remedies perpetually applicable to the diſeaſes of the political body; they ought therefore to be combined conformably to the moſt matured knowledge of the preſent genius of the nation; and whatever is no longer analogous to this ought to be corrected in the code.

A nation, therefore, can never be bound by its primitive inſtitutions, ſeeing that by ſuch a tie, the very ſuppoſition of which is abſurd, it would forbid itſelf every amelioration and improvement. The government abſolutely depending on the genius of the people, its modifications ought eternally to ſpring out of the national will; and a ſtate can never become a legitimate aſſociation, unleſs when each individual obeys voluntarily and wittingly the laws framed by all.

Thus,

Thus, a nation cannot by a ridiculous contract bind itself to despotism, or to the excessive and unreasonable opulence of a single individual; and such a contract is for a still stronger reason null and void for the succeeding generation: a weak or extravagant nation would otherwise chain its prosperity, would crown tyranny and its coffers, and men would become merely vile subsidiaries.

Nations ought invariably to be considered as in the plenitude of their existence, that is to say, as making a daily and hourly progress from the state of nature to the state of civilization, compounding and recompounding themselves in a new and necessary way, by that moral power which ought unceasingly to act, and which forms the association by uniting the wishes of all.

This is the reason why every nation ought eternally to preserve the right of its independance, which belongs to the aggregated body. When we consider the deplorable errors of antiquity, there is so much to be forgotten, that the greatest service a nation could receive from its good genius, would be to be rendered absolutely forgetful of what is passed.

It is certain that we proceed from idea to idea, from reflexion to reflexion; and the ſcience of government is thus freed from its abſurdities, while each diplomatic viſion, and each chimerical terror it engenders cannot ſtay the progreſs of the political machine. It has already been clearly evinced that man can have no controul over his poſterity, becauſe the rights of man are the rights of each generation; and for a ſtill ſtronger reaſon we can upon no plea impoſe on ourſelves reſtraints and ties that fatigue and haraſs us. Policy can have no other rule than the greateſt ſum of liberty and happineſs; and having a pre-eminence over every thing, it can only be controuled by what prudence and local circumſtances may command it to do. It ought therefore to have conſtantly in its view the moral condition of man; and neither can nor ought to oppoſe any perfective means by which he aims at eſtabliſhing a better order of things. Man, unwittingly even, has a tendency towards the laws which are as yet *not made*, but reſt in the boſom of nature: there the life of the body politic repoſes, and there is harboured the deſtruction of the extravagant and chimerical pride by which the human race has been degraded and baſtardized.

To have a juſt comprehenſion of theſe new truths, it will be ſufficient to examine the origin

origin of laws: now we can diſcover but two kinds of laws, the laws *made* and the laws *not made*.

The law *not made* is a relation which one thing has to another, which is independent of the things themſelves, and which exiſted before them. Prior to the exiſtence of a line, there was a law which, ſuppoſing a line, rendered it productile, and which, ſuppoſing another parallel line, had ſo ordered as that theſe two lines ſhould never touch or meet, even were they to be lengthened out to infinity. Before the Creator formed any one individual, there exiſted a law according to which each individual was to depend on him from whom he was to receive being and ſupport.

Before God had created eſſences, there was a law according to which of two equal eſſences one ſhould be worth as much as the other; the *two* were to be worth the *two*, the man worth the man; conſequently, it was already determined that the individual who ſhould not eſteem every other individual as highly as he ſhould prize himſelf, would contravene this law *not made*; ſuppoſing the *two* intelligent, he ought to prize the *two*, and, failing to do ſo, would ſin againſt the above-mentioned law.

Prior to the exiſtence of a ſociety of intelli-

gent

gent men, there was a law according to which, ſuch a ſociety being ſuppoſed, each individual compoſing it could neither deceive, tyrannize over, nor contemn any other, becauſe truth exiſted before things, becauſe art is poſterior to things, and becauſe deception, fraud, and lying are poſterior to art.

Before men exiſted, there was a law according to which, the ſuppoſed men being to be created equal to each other, they could obey their own conventions alone. In the ſame way alſo, ſuppoſing one man to oblige another, this law not made required that the latter ſhould be grateful to the former, and that ingratitude ſhould be puniſhed, as diametrically oppoſite to the law which exiſted before things, that is to ſay, the law of gratitude. If, on the contrary, it ſhould happen that one man ſhould offend another, the ſame law required that he ſhould be puniſhed in proportion to the injury and miſchief he had done to that other; and this puniſhment had for its object, not only the revenge due to him who received the injury, but alſo the eſtabliſhing of an example to thoſe by whom it ſhould be witneſſed.

This law not made is in itſelf an intrinſic and univerſal juſtice which comprehends all that has been created, but which exiſted before any thing

was

was created. This invariable and eternal law is the only one that can afford us juſt agreements, and can regulate with nicety the duties and relations of each individual to any other individual.

Man was viſibly deſtined to live in ſociety with man. The perſonal paſſions, inherent in all men, leading each individual to break through the bonds of ſociety, men, by way of repreſſing theſe abuſes, found themſelves obliged to make ſuch laws as ſhould give force to the laws *not made*, and ſhould equally bind the whole of the ſociety: theſe laws were denominated the *right of nations*.

But as this univerſal ſociety is compoſed of an infinite number of particular ſocieties, placed in different climates, and the relations of which depend on the different ſituations of nature in which they are found, ſome of them being ſtationed at the ſea ſide, others in foreſts, others on mountains, and others again being ſuſceptible of various commercial intercourſes, legiſlators have beſtowed different laws on theſe different nations; and theſe are what are termed *civil laws*. But as man might alſo often forget himſelf, and might ceaſe to recollect his duties towards himſelf, philoſophers have contrived what are called *moral laws*.

All theſe laws, however, whether written, civil, or traditional, are no other than ſo many means contrived to facilitate to us the intelligence and execution of the laws not made. Theſe may properly be conſidered as the beſt and moſt ſublime laws, becauſe they ſpring out of the *natural right*, the tranſgreſſion of which is the moſt extenſive and moſt cuſtomary cauſe of the phyſical evils that oppreſs the human race. Men collected together in ſociety ought therefore to be governed by the natural laws, by the laws which are not as yet *made*, but which nevertheleſs exiſt; becauſe theſe alone can be productive of the poſitive good order which is moſt advantageous to men. To theſe ſovereign laws, inſtituted by the Supreme Being, all men, and all human powers, ought to bend. They are immutable and irrefragable, ſince man has here below the right to make the moſt he can of his *portion of liberty*: this ſuperiority of his belongs to his intelligence; he has received it from the author of nature, who has determined that it ſhall be ſo, by the laws of equality he has eſtabliſhed in the order in which the univerſe has been formed. Now, what applies to moral alſo applies to political order: all the poſitive laws injurious to ſociety ought to be annulled, however ſtrenuouſly they may be ſupported, be-

cauſe

cause we are here to exercise our reason, extended and perfected by the study of the physical and natural laws.

The laws *not made* are truly deserving of our admiration, and ought to be developed, being in themselves perfectly well calculated to convey to us a knowledge, founded on evidence, of the progress of the natural laws, and forming the rule by which the best government is squared. Since misery, complaints, and intestine commotions are the unequivocal effects of the greater part of our laws, we ought in the laws *not made* to seek the tutelary authority the protection of which secures the natural right of each individual, a right that is never restrained, and indeed cannot be so, since it is extended in proportion to the best possible laws which constitute the order that is most advantageous to all.

It is entirely for want of having recurred to these laws *not made* that writers have formed ideas so different and even contradictory on the natural right of man, misleading the people by an endeavour to reconcile things that can never be brought to meet. By adhering constantly to terms, they have unceasingly confounded the sovereign and the sovereignty; and hence have arisen all the errors by which the human species has

has been oppreſſed. How happens it that the periods which have been termed the ages of ignorance, have been thoſe in which the wiſeſt governments have been eſtabliſhed! It is becauſe the avidity of the rich had not yet learned to profit by the wants of the poor, becauſe the inequality of the citizens was not as yet an obſtacle to the work of reaſon.

The firſt principle of every government, and of every doctrine on the ſcience of governing, ought to be the public weal; and this as well as every other principle muſt be independent, becauſe by each of them diſtinctly, and all of them collectively, every thing is to be regulated. The laws eſtabliſhed by the author of nature are juſt and perfect in the general plan, at the ſame time that they are immutable: we have for ſome time advanced towards them, but more ſtill remains to be done, for they are not yet *made*. Has not man, endowed with intelligence, the prerogative at leaſt to contemplate them, waiting until they ſhall be realized? When men ſhall at length have exhauſted a multiplicity of errors, and all the evils which are the reſult of them, they will feel the neceſſity of renouncing the greater part of the made laws, and of recurring to thoſe that are

not

not made, as the only ones which can conſtantly ſecure the glory and tranquillity of the human race. Nature herſelf holds out to them the invitation; and theſe *unmade* laws will be the imperious ones to which ſhe will force them to recur. Then will mankind be ſenſible of all their beauty and utility, and will liſten to the call of philoſophy, without the help of which all legiſlation is vain. The empire of the laws of humanity has been miſunderſtood, and individual laws have been ſubſtituted in their ſtead: but if the dignity of man reſides in the perfection of the political laws, and if men, equally provided with hands, give action and energy to every thing on this earth, the taſk of political regeneration is moſt aſſuredly theirs. In the auguſt ſanctuary of nature they will ſeek the laws *not yet made*: they will call theſe to their ſuccour, and by no effort of reſiſtance will their publicity be defeated. No, reſplendent with their innate beauty, they will dazzle the view of each enchanted ſpectator, on the day appointed for the termination of the miſeries and degradation of the human race.

FUNERAL ORATION ON THE CLERGY OF FRANCE.

MASTER Clergy, whoſe obſequies we now perform, my deareſt friends, was born in France in the middle of the ſecond century, of indigent Italian parents. To vex him you had only to mention his primitive origin; and he would bluſh and foam with rage. The duty of Maſter Clergy was to teach religion in France by the practice of the virtues which it enjoins; his power was confined to things *ſpiritual*; but, as early as the third century, he entertained the ambition of extending his rights and his power over things *temporal*.

In the fourth, fifth, ſixth, and ſeventh centuries, Maſter Clergy acquired immenſe wealth, increaſed his power, and obtained a great influence in affairs of ſtate. Nothing was eaſier; the people, cruſhed beneath the load of various calamities, ſought a refuge with him, and made rich donations to purchaſe a remiſſion of their ſins. Maſter Clergy made it an article of faith, that valuable preſents to the church opened the gates of paradiſe and ſhut the gates of hell.

In the eighth century, Maſter Clergy manifeſted his diſcontent againſt Charles Martel, who held the ſlothful kings of France under his tutelage:

tutelage: Charles had made free with ſome of his poſſeſſions, and Maſter Clergy, who was not fond of loſing his acquiſitions, was prodigal of anathemas. At that time ſome of the laity had the cure of pariſhes.

In the ninth century, Charlemagne bitterly upbraided Maſter Clergy with his paſſion for worldly goods. What! ſaid he: you have renounced the pomp of the world, and yet you ſeek every day to increaſe your wealth by all ſorts of artifices; you promiſe paradiſe, you threaten hell, you employ the name of God, and that of certain ſaints, to ſtrip the rich and the poor who have the ſimplicity to ſuffer themſelves to be over-reached; you ſee plainly, Maſter Clergy, that you deprive the lawful heirs of their property—if this continue, my ſubjects will ſoon be ruined. My paternal heart is wrung while it thus reproaches you, and I therefore hope you will ſet bounds to your immoderate ambition. Theſe reproaches had the ſame effect upon the mind of Maſter Clergy as the replies which overturned his ſophiſms had upon the Abbé Maury. The ariſtocrates are very ſenſible that they are in the wrong, but they never mend. Maſter Clergy did the ſame: he gave a looſe to his fruitleſs rage; and ſoon afterwards, to revenge the ſtern reprimand of Charlemagne, he revolted againſt the rights of the crown and againſt the perſon of the ſovereign.

Louis the Debonnaire took it into his head to reform the manners of Maſter Clergy, but Maſter Clergy obliged him to wear the robe of penance, and found perſons to execute that inſolent and ridiculous farce; he diſpoſed of the royal ſceptre, and proceeded to this exceſs of audacity, becauſe Charles the Bald had had the weakneſs to acknowledge his juriſdiction.

The voluptuous ignorance of Maſter Clergy in the ninth, tenth, and eleventh centuries, was ſuch that he could not ſign his name, or if he did, it was like the deceaſed Chriſtopher de Beaumont, who was obliged to ſpell his clerical mandates. An author, no doubt a contemporary, pleaſantly attacks this clerical ignorance. *Otius deditus erat (clerus) gulæ quam gloriæ. Otius colligebat libras quam libros; libentius intuebatur Mariam quam Marcum, malebat legere in Salomene quam in Salemone.*

Here is latin, my friends, more eaſy to comprehend than to explain. Notwithſtanding his ignorance, Maſter Clergy knew how to turn the ſtupidity of the people to his own profit; the donations multiplied. There was at this time a theological war to ſupport: Maſter Clergy

Clergy loved theological wars, becaufe he could then perplex at will the fmalleft efforts of human reafon. This theological war gave birth to a fect called *ftercoronifts*.

Mafter Clergy, plump with good cheer, wifhed to tafte of the forbidden fruit. Complaints were made againft his concubinage; but he replied triumphantly that they might feek angels to govern the church.

In the twelfth century, Mafter Clergy had fome difputes with the monks, who having in their turns acquired a ftrong relifh for the fruits of the people's credulity, carried off from the bifhops fome oblations of the living and of the dead. Mafter Clergy feared much left thefe monks, already in poffeffion of the minds of devotees, fhould take it into their head to feize upon his ring and his crofier.

It was in this age that Mafter Clergy was fuddenly captivated with martial glory: he fought, in the crufades, conquefts ftill more temporal than fpiritual. All thofe who flocked to the ftandard of the crofs obtained the full remiffion of their fins, and the fouls of the foldiers in the army beyond fea who had the happinefs to be killed, were inftantly admitted to the joys of paradife. Hiftory fpeaks little of the deeds and achievements of Mafter Clergy in theſe holy wars, but it repreſents him changing modes, and bedecked with precious ſtones: he wore a ſhoulder-belt, and handſome ſpurs; and a cutlaſs, ſtudded with jewels, hung from his gilded girdle. Maſter Clergy loved a little expenſive ſhow, and carried that diſpoſition to ſuch lengths, that it was found neceſſary to reform his ſtables; he was not allowed to keep more than forty or fifty horſes; he was reſtrained from hunting and hawking, eſpecially when on an epiſcopal viſitation to his vicars. His vicars were probably richer than they are now with their *portion congrue*; for their *portion congrue* would hardly have been ſufficient to furniſh Maſter Clergy with a light collation.

In the thirteenth century, Maſter Clergy felt his genius begin to dawn; he ſtudied at the univerſity of Paris. Scholaſtic theology, with its train of diſtinctions and ſubtleties, was then the maſter-piece of ſcience; he waſted his intellects in diſcuſſions equally frivolous and laborious; and he encircled himſelf with fantaſtic ideas which he exchanged for others, eager to beſtow a real body on all theſe impalpable beings. It was in the ſame century that Maſter Clergy eſtabliſhed a tribunal of inquiſition which roaſted heretics alive, as victims pleaſing to the Divinity.

In the fourteenth century, Philip the Fair assembled the states-general of his kingdom; the third estate was called now for the first time, and was much tickled by this honour, for it yet knew not that itself was the nation: this information it was afterwards to receive from philosophy and philosophers. In this assembly, Master Clergy began to shuffle, and afterwards gave very equivocal signs of adhesion. In the same century, he was excluded the parliament, and reduced to his spiritual government alone, which greatly humbled his worldly pride.

In the fifteenth century, Master Clergy was guilty of a heinous crime; he had a great share in the death of the brave Maid of Orleans, that martyr of her country who perished by the most cruel torments. About this time the disputes between the nominalists and the realists engaged the attention of Master Clergy, and, suitably to his rapacious policy, he made that controversy an affair of religion and even of state.

At all times, Master Clergy had a strong attachment to fire and faggot; he more than once regaled himself with the fumes of twenty or thirty thousand men burnt for a theological argument. Excommunication was always with him the prelude to the stake.

In the sixteenth century, a great dissension

having arisen among the inconceivable retailers of indulgences, the disorders of Master Clergy, his scandalous pleasures, and his haughty domination, gave birth to the reforms of Luther and Calvin. These great scourges of the insolence and rapacity of Master Clergy converted into current specie the gold and silver of the churches, burnt the archives, and uncloistered the monks and nuns. But while Master Clergy was fighting theologically, and had totally neglected morality in unintelligible controversies, the good Henry IV. tenderly censured him about his manner of instructing the people. Preach by your good examples, said he; let the people be incited to goodness by your behaviour: I would with all my heart conform to the doctrines you preach, but surely you cannot think that I am ignorant of what you do.

In the seventeenth century, Master Clergy, who had been intolerant during the four preceding ones, and desirous of crowning his intolerance with the royal diadem, thought to strike a great political blow by advising Louis XIV. to revoke the edict of Nantes: but he was egregiously mistaken; he sowed against the monarch, against himself, and against the national splendor, the seeds of indignation, of revenge, and of patriotism. In vain did he endeavour to bewilder

bewilder the minds of men in the diſputes of Janſeniſm; in vain did he raiſe the confeſſors of the king, of the princes and princeſſes, to pre-eminent importance; his coalition with ſatrapiſm was to be of ſhort duration. A century more and this Coloſſus, inſulting to human reaſon, reduced to the rank of the loweſt courtiers, was deſtined to fall, becauſe his enormous opulence was not even apologized for by thoſe virtues which the moſt ordinary policy would have enjoined him.

In the eighteenth century, Maſter Clergy was ſeized with a new ſpecies of ambition; this was an inordinate deſire for the adminiſtration of public affairs. Maſter Clergy wiſhed to rule the ſtate. Mitred adminiſtrators are bad adminiſtrators indeed.

The opulence of Maſter Clergy, his inutility for inſtruction, his degrading occupation in the palaces of our monarchs, the palpable contradiction between his duties and his conduct, all ſhowed that this pompous perſonage was a very ordinary mortal. This is but too true, my deareſt brethren: a moral portrait, without the varniſh of the virtues, is always a wretched performance. Our worthy repreſentatives obliged Clergy the Great to ſwallow a draught, compoſed of maſculine and thundering eloquence,

of

of urgent logic, and of true and chriſtian principles. In vain did the abbés Sieyes, Maury, and d'Eymar endeavour to oppoſe the ſalutary effect; it was requiſite for his glory and his ſalvation that Clergy the Great ſhould die: he is dead. All the family of Clergy the Great is overwhelmed with the deepeſt ſorrow; his good mother the church of Rome is much offended at finding that her croſſed and mitred ſon has made his will in favour of the nation. The nation has only reſumed her own conceſſions: theſe, when purified, will afford ſalaries to uſeful functionaries. A great leproſy is cleared away from the political body: healthier and more robuſt, it will no longer be preyed upon by the *princes* ſtyled *eccleſiaſtics*; and as the regeneration is complete, the altar of the God who was himſelf poor and humble will attract a greater affluence of worſhippers: they will be more diſpoſed to receive the words of the goſpel. Clergy the Great is dead; thoſe who ſhed tears for him are few; and ſoon will they join the numerous and ſound part of the kingdom, which exclaims: *Long has Clergy the Great lived*; *let him reſt in peace.*

P. S. Every kind of ſuperſtition had made its way in our country; the monks, the plurality of benefices, idle profeſſions of every kind, devoured

devoured the ſenſe of the people: theology ſeated on the benches made the ſchools re-echo with noiſy diſputes; furred doctors, and libraries ſtocked with commentaries on the canon law—what precious hours devoted to inutility!

We have pruned the voracious branches of eccleſiaſtical power; they are lopped: prieſts are no longer totally independant of political laws; the clergy is no longer aſſociated with the *orders of the ſtate*, with the right of pre-eminence; its ſuperiority over the temporal power is now the object of deriſion; it no longer interpoſes its authority in all the affairs of ſovereigns. The time is paſt when the ſword of the church was eternally brandiſhed, and its thunders hurled from the lofty ſeat of St. Peter. Its famous quarrels are buried in oblivion; the declamations of the monks have returned to their tranſalpine origin. We look from afar upon Spain and Portugal, ſubject to the inquiſition, as nations ſtupidly ſlumbering under a ſacred yoke. The ſpirit of letters has reſtored to philoſophers all their boldneſs; they have introduced into chriſtian ſocieties an exalted and mild harmony, a temperate ſubordination; and the reſpect for firſt principles has caught from the genius of religion its nobleſt attribute, forbearance,

FEUDAL GOVERNMENT.

WOULD you wiſh to be made acquainted with the outrages of feudal government? The Empreſs of Ruſſia ordered a whole village to be maſſacred for having killed its lord; neither the women nor children were ſpared. This act of cruelty is entirely ſuitable to the perverſe genius of nobility.

Our *French princes* wiſhed literally to form among men a diſtinct order; but the people in their turn become the kings of the earth. We, who were formerly ſubjects of a king, and even of princes, are at preſent ſubjects of our country.

OF THE TITLE OF EMPEROR.

UNFORTUNATELY for them, men are too apt to allow themſelves to be governed by words. The ſupremacy of the empire of Germany was excluſively owing to the title of *emperor*, a title which aided the authority of the ambitious princes, and preſerved that of the weak ones: the idea which the people attached to the word *empire* was the cauſe of their ſubmiſſion

miſſion to the *emperor*. Thus by a ſtrange ignorance of the rights of man, and by the yet ſtranger acceptation of this term, did the houſe of Auſtria, which, but for Richelieu perhaps, would have poſſeſſed no aſcendancy whatever, aggrandize itſelf, and eſtabliſh a controul over all Europe.

From that time the emperors fancied themſelves the legitimate ſucceſſors to *the patrimony of the Ceſars*; and, independently of theſe pretenſions, they arrogated to themſelves rights degrading to man and to nations: impoſed upon by a term, the latter acknowledged an uſurped ſupremacy.

The grandees held fiefs, the titles of which they received from the emperors; ſeveral cities agreed that they were their ſlaves; ſovereigns conſented to appoint them the ſole heirs of their domains and ſubjects; and the popes alone refuſed, after having ſanctioned this abuſive authority over the univerſe, to ſubmit to it: being ſhortly after zealous to preſerve it for themſelves, over Italy at leaſt, the pretenſions which enſued on either ſide occaſioned for more than ſix hundred years that bloody conteſt between the papal ſupremacy and the empire, in which the princes of Europe declared for the one party or the other, juſt as their prejudices

happened

happened to ſway them. Thus did the exaltation of a ſingle word, and the miſinterpretation of a title, deſolate the human race.

When the popes rewarded the ſervices of the predeceſſors of Charlemagne with the empty title of Roman patricians, Leo ventured to declare Charles *emperor!* In doing ſo he diſplayed a policy at leaſt equal to his gratitude: this flattery to a powerful prince enabled him to ſhake off all dependance on the emperors of the eaſt, and ſecured him a protector againſt his enemies. Indeed, the new title ſo conferred did not appear to him to be more injurious either to his rights or authority than that of *Patrician*, as he entertained a full conviction that Charles would never reſide at Rome. On their ſide, the people, dazzled by the warlike qualities of Charles, jealous of the credit of the biſhops, conſidering themſelves as degraded by the magiſtracy of private men who governed them under the diſhonoured title of ſenators, and carried away by the attraction of novelty, received the new emperor with the tranſports and acclamations peculiar to Italian enthuſiaſm.

Charles was proclaimed. The *biſhop* of Rome fancied that he merely beſtowed a title, that he ſimply manifeſted his gratitude by the ſhadow of an uſeleſsly apparent grandeur; and the

the pope did not know what he beſtowed: he, nevertheleſs, in reality inveſted Charles with the moſt dangerous authority with which a prince could poſſibly be armed; with a power, the conditions of which had not been regulated, nor its extent bounded by any convention or any contract between the ſovereign and the people. Such a title could not fail to ſooth and augment the vanity of the prince, becauſe it conveyed the expreſſion of the moſt noble of all ſovereign dignities, and, as it was indeterminate, moſt effectually favoured his ambition. It was beſides extremely well calculated to awe nations, exacting from them a higher reſpect and a more effectual ſubmiſſion, becauſe they could but imperfectly appreciate its rights, at the ſame time that they were diſpoſed to make ſtill greater ſacrifices, becauſe they eſtimated theſe ſtill more by the title of the prince than by the extent of their means. But the *biſhop*, the people, and even Charles himſelf, were very far from conceiving a juſt idea either of the authority which this fatal title was about to place in the hands of the ſucceſſors of the latter, or of the wars, devaſtations, crimes, and horrors of every deſcription of which it was to be the ſource. Unleſs for this deteſtable flattery of *Leo*, no one of the weak, daſtardly,

and

and perverſe ſucceſſors of Charles, would ever have thought of aſſuming the name of *emperor*, far from Rome, where no one of them ever reſided! Never, at the extinction of this guilty race, would it have entered into the ideas of a teutonic count or duke, who commanded at moſt a few thouſands of vaſſals in the foreſts of Franconia, or in the barren and rocky waſtes of Bavaria or Suabia, to beſtow on himſelf the title of the vanquiſher of the earth, and to perſuade himſelf that this title eſtabliſhed his right over the ſtates which had once compoſed the dominion of Rome in the weſt, and particularly over Germany and all Italy! But this *title* being once received and accredited, the nobleman who was decorated with it did not conceive a leſs idea of the high deſtiny of himſelf and his houſe, becauſe, as was often the caſe, his deſcent and origin were mean and contemptible; while each of the titulary princes ſtrove with all his might to convert the authority it gave to the eſtabliſhment or aggrandizement of the houſe of which he was the head. What ſerved to inflame this paſſion ſtill more in the greater part of them, was to ſee a prieſt, a reſident at Rome, under ſhelter of *another title*, the import of which was not preciſely underſtood, contrive in an inſidious and indirect way to usurp a power he pretended to hold exclusively over Italy: this was another of the causes which rendered the empire and the emperors so disastrous to Italy.

The indiscreet admiration we have bestowed on the *throne* of *Rome* and that of Italy has contributed more effectually to their grandeur than even their successes. In the history of the unfortunate race of mortals we every where see the fatal example of the ascendancy of words over nations, and the peril which attends the adventitious usage of them.

Germany is an assemblage of states embarrassed with privileges, customs, laws, monies, prejudices, pretensions, ridiculous usages, barriers, and governments which unceasingly thwart each other. So many, and such little and needy sovereigns, every where in opposition, every where jealous, and every where affecting the importance of a natural enmity, announce that such a chaotic mass cannot long hold either its shape or its consistency.

DANGEROUS CALCULATIONS.

POLITICAL arithmetic originated in England. In the rectifying of errors it is absolutely necessary; but it is at the same time useful to tyranny, because it teaches how far a nation may be loaded with taxes, and bear its burthens tranquilly and patiently.

In the hands of a statesman political arithmetic is admirable; but if you intrust it to those nice calculators who scarcely leave to men what is physically necessary to their existence, it becomes a dangerous weapon. If it is in the possession of a mere financier, tremble; he will augment the population, to increase the supplies.

If political calculations could be extended to the physical accidents and moral revolutions which change the fortune of the citizens, they would then contribute to the happiness of nations: but they are faulty and objectionable on this account, that they consider alone the money they can squeeze and extract. The result of M. Necker's work is terrible, when we reflect both what the nation paid under the ancient regimen, and what the spirit of financing still endeavoured to add to so enormous a charge: the nation proceeded under this annual load; and a bad policy calculated on how many millions more it would be able to bear without sinking under the accumulated weight.

If execution be the touchstone of the finest

theories,

theories, political arithmetic has not wrought in France all the good that was expected from it, its calculations having altogether tended to invent new taxes on industry. Could any thing be more deplorable or more unjust?

Thus, in the closet of the man who is not sincerely attached to his country, and still less so to the human race, does every thing become a poison.

We find in history that republican governments have oftentimes treated the citizens with the highest severity. An attachment to political justice does not therefore always belong to the freer governments; and a simple society may become as tyrannical as the proudest despot. The English aspire at liberty, but it is for themselves alone, as is evidenced by the almost insupportable yoke they have imposed on the inhabitants of India.

A tyrant has occasionally his moments of humanity: in the hands of an individual possessing an unlimited power, a pure despotism may be less terrible than the decisions of republican societies, some of which have been known to follow up their principles with inflexibility, and to be in all cases devoid of pity.

A tyrant may open his eyes on the follies and enormity of his enemies: but an oppressive republic neither blushes nor trembles. The most dangerous of all tyrannies resides in the breasts of those administrators who fancy they add to their own liberty when they reduce others to a state of slavery.

In the regions favoured by liberty, foreigners are oftentimes hardly dealt by: Switzerland abounds in exclusive privileges; the cruel citizen there persuades himself that the air and the sun's rays being his property, he can deprive him of them who sojourns on his territory.

When Rome had not yet completed her plan of conquest, the Romans studied to conciliate the affections of the conquered nations: they allowed the provinces to make choice of the government they should deem to be best calculated for their internal policy; and the subsidies they demanded from them were on the condition of effranchisement: with respect to their laws, they were their own masters. But when the work of subjugation was completed, Rome, which had before enchanted the nations by her beneficent sway, did not neglect to terrify them: she sent her pretors and her presidents into the provinces. Paulus Emilius received an order from the senate to deliver up Epirus to pillage, and this order was executed throughout the whole

whole province: in one day an hundred and fifty thoufand flaves were made, and feventy cities and towns facked. Could any tyrant have given a more cruel order?

To come to lefs confequential objects, we will take a view of the fmall republics, and fee there the infupportable pride of a little inhabitant, who with the quality of *bourgeois* fancies himfelf fuperior to the reft of the world, and who in the little village where he exercifes his authority perfecutes the ftranger with all his might: his quality of *bourgeois* is his fole title and inheritance: and to fuch a degree does it infatuate him, that his infolence and audacity exceed every thing.

OF PRECISE LAWS.

IN England there was a law which forbad *bigamy*, or the having of two wives. A man was accufed of having five; and as this cafe had not been fpecified, the culprit was acquitted, upon a decifion that the law ought to be interpreted literally, becaufe, according to the Englifh, it fhould never be equivocal. It was afterwards amended, and declared exprefsly, that he who ſhould take more than one wife ſhould be conſidered as guilty of *bigamy*, and puniſhed accordingly.

About the ſame time, and in the ſame country, a man cut off his adverſary's noſe: he was tried for this offence, and the charge of having mutilated a member was laid in the indictment. The counſel for the accuſed maintained, in his defence, that the noſe was not a member; and upon this an act of parliament was framed, declaring that for the future it ſhould be conſidered as ſuch.

Preciſe laws afford no room for *ſubtleties*, while thoſe that are equivocal beget proceſſes to infinity: upon theſe the ſubaltern miniſters of juſtice live, as worms are nouriſhed by putrefied bodies.

In France, ſucceſſions and contracts have been the moſt cuſtomary aliments of chicanery. Lawyers and proctors deteſt whatever is clear: and notaries, by their enigmatical expreſſions, ſeem in a manner to have nothing elſe in view beſides veiling their ignorance and puzzling every thing. If the laws were to be literally expreſſed, they would be as literally interpreted; and the fortuitous intervention of a few abſurd caſes would not prevent their majeſtic diſplay.

The

The moſt neceſſary reform in French juriſprudence that I know of, would therefore be to ſilence the advocates, the moſt determined wranglers in exiſtence. They ought merely to narrate, to prove, and to conclude by a ſhort recapitulation ; or rather, the inſtruction on each proceſs ought to be made out in writing, an expedient that would put an end to the unneceſſary and diſguſting prattle of the bar. The pleaders would be more aſhamed to write than to ſpeak prolixly ; and their *obſtreporous bawling* would ceaſe to diſhonour daily the ſanctuary of the laws.

Lycurgus and Solon forbad the uſe of that verboſe eloquence which they conſidered as having no other tendency than that of leading men aſtray from the path of truth. Some of theſe *ſpeech-makers* have a knack of ſeizing on the minds of weak men, and of communicating their borrowed paſſions to their hearers, juſt as a madman communicates his diſtortions and grimaces to thoſe who look upon him.

In proportion as patriotic eloquence is admirable in its great movements, when, by the mouth of public orators, it thunders in ſupport of the national cauſe, as it once thundered at Athens and at Rome ;—in proportion as it is venerable when it ſpeaks to the people on their great intereſts, which it determines by an inſtinct more ſure than reaſoning, ſo is it ridiculous when it waſtes itſelf in obſcure controverſies, and when, a ſlave to the little venal paſſions, it tends to no other effect than to weaken the wiſeſt laws. It then begets a long courſe of *pleadings*, and the multitude of forms through which the pleader is obliged to paſs before he can reach the end of a conteſt.

The ſubtlety of legal commentators throws a thick veil over the beſt right: and as whatever prolongs the trial is uſeful to the rich client and injurious to the poor one, thoſe of the former claſs keep in pay the multitude of *intrepid, babbling* advocates, who would weary the patience of the judges, and exhauſt their faculties, if ſilence were not to be impoſed on them. They would drive Themis from her temple, and in deſpite of all juſtice would remain maſters of the field of battle.

It is really diſtreſſing to ſee theſe advocates, perfectly indifferent to the cauſe chance throws in their way, follow it up with the moſt tenacious obſtinacy: if there were as many tribunals as the myſterious ladder of Jacob had ſteps, every cauſe would have its appeal, and the diſputes would be eternal.

I have introduced the above images into this ſerious

ſerious diſcuſſion, the better to deſcribe the legal abuſes which certainly call aloud for reform, and which are haraſſing in the extreme both to the judges and the public.

Let me aſk who can digeſt the multiplicity of local cuſtoms in France? and how can a way be ſeen through the prodigious number of foreign edicts; the obſcurity of the code, the digeſt, and the new laws; the acceſſion of the canonical ones; the various ordonnances, ſtatutes, and declarations; the collection of reſolutions and awards of tribunals; and the commentaries and annotations of the legal body? The patience, the reaſoning, and the views of the philoſopher are terrified at their recollection.

In the obſcure juriſprudence of decrees chicanery ſucks the blood of the people. Ah! what bold ſpirit will ſtep forward and ſimplify the laws? A king of China had a diamond mine cloſed, to the end that the attention of his ſubjects might not be diverted from agriculture: but to what monarch will it belong to diſpel the frightful chaos in which juſtice ſo often ſtrays? The Augean ſtable once found a Hercules to cleanſe it: it cannot be that we are condemned everlaſtingly to grovel in filth.

WISE LAW AMONG THE HEBREWS.

IF political equality is the impoſſible thing; if Lycurgus himſelf ſaw during his life-time the derangement of his ſyſtem; if democracies have ſeen their principle of equality diſappear; and if the remedy of an equal diviſion of lands is a greater evil than inequality, the government ought nevertheleſs to recollect that an individual can owe nothing to the ſtate, provided the ſtate owes him nothing; that the baſis of every political body reſides in a juſt temperament; that it has been formed to concur towards the general happineſs by eſtabliſhing that of each member; and that the law ought to reſtrain as much as poſſible the cupidity which heaps up exceſſive wealth, afterwards to adopt ſuch expedients as may tend to render properties leſs unequal.

Among the Hebrews there was a law eminently wiſe: land could not be alienated by ſale for a longer period than forty-nine years. The purchaſer's enjoyment was for a ſufficiently long term; and the ſeller was not irretrievably deprived of his property.

If the ſtate were not occaſionally to reſtrain the covetouſneſs natural to certain men who derive enormous profits from the public revenues, all

all the riches would soon be confined to a particular claſs. To deſtroy this monſtrous diſproportion, and the inconveniences that reſult from it, there are ſyſtems that make a ſweep of riches, taking the treaſure out of certain coffers that are too full to pour it in elſewhere. Theſe commotions, notwithſtanding they do not take place in a well ordered government, are ſtill not without their utility, when they wage a ſpecies of war on fortunes illegitimately acquired, and founded on malverſations authorized in times of trouble.

Wealth acquired by the misfortunes of the ſtate periſhes of itſelf as it were in an inſtant: a gnawing worm, which labours unceaſingly to devour the root, is at the foot of the tree. Where is now the race of each of the Midaſſes in whoſe hands every thing was converted to gold? I have witneſſed the ruin of thirty houſes ſcandalouſly enriched, either in the ſubaltern departments of the miniſtry, or in the odious revenue appointments: I have ſeen the children of theſe criminal fathers diſſipate the property on which the public malediction has fallen. A ſimilar fate will befall the opulence of the jobbers, contractors, and monopoliſts of our days: their ill gotten wealth will be ſcattered abroad, and their names consigned to oblivion and contempt.

The list of all the rich financiers who have inundated France since the death of Henry the Great would be curious! Where are they, and where their posterity? Is it not surprising that not the smallest trace of them and theirs is to be found? Certainly an exterminating angel must have been charged to destroy these sons of fortune, these ephemeridal giants who threatened to swallow up every thing: how can otherwise such a phenomenon be explained? What a consolation to groaning virtue, and what a lesson to the robbers who subsist on rapine alone! they are destroyed the first by their own destructive systems.

However, waving all this, there are revolutions which, attacking in a manner the proprietors of specie only, are neither so injurious nor destructive as if they were to bear on the industrious classes, the cultivators more especially.

HISTORICAL APPROXIMATION.

IT is impossible not to call to our recollection the Gracchi, who refused to employ the prodigious advantages nature and renown had bestowed

ſtowed on them in any other way than for the good of their fellow citizens: the elder Gracchus fell; and as in this great man all the ſtrength of the people reſided, the people fell with him.

The younger of the Gracchi periſhed at the head of the ſame party, for the ſame cauſe, and under ſimilar circumſtances.

Nearly ſeventeen centuries after, hiſtory afforded a ſimilar event in Holland. In the midſt of his ſervices and his toils, De Witt had no other objects than the glory, the happineſs, and more eſpecially the liberty of his country: it was attacked, and he defended it with wiſdom and intrepidity. The party againſt which he had to combat eſteemed him too much not to dread him: it was therefore judged expedient to get rid of him by aſſaſſination. He had a brother equally beloved and eſtimable, but not in the enjoyment of ſo high a reputation. The elder having ſurvived his wounds, the party which attacked the grand penſionary changed its means: it attacked his virtue, and publiſhed a number of grievances, all tending to render him odious. Theſe perſecutions were ſo long protracted, ſo craftily managed, and ſo cruel and vindictive in their means, that De Witt formed the reſolution to give up his poſt of grand penfioner of Holland: he fent in his refignation to the affembly of the ftates-general, and it was accepted. This refignation ferved to kindle up afrefh the bitter animofity of his enemies: he became the abhorrence of the very people whofe idol he had been; they were deceived, and in the fequel they murdered both the brothers.

REVOLT.

CAN we queftion the lawfulnefs of the Roman infurrection, which expelled Tarquin and abolifhed royalty? Before that event, Athens and Sparta had fubftituted a new government in the place of thofe kings who fo wantonly abufed their powers. In our own times, Holland, Switzerland, America, and at length France, have renewed that great fpectacle. Ah! if the Danes had put the cruel *Chriftian* to death, if the Heffians had depofed their laft *Landgrave*, the Moguls *Aurengzeb*, the Maroquins *Muley-Imael*; if the princes, feconded by Philip the Fair, had repreffed the infolent ambition of *Boniface* VIII. would thefe deteftable fovereigns have been pitied in their merited fall?

The firft who afcended a throne was a fortunate foldier:

*ſoldier**: yes, and unfortunately, becauſe men, for want of equality among them, could not chooſe a philoſopher or a virtuous magiſtrate. At preſent, eloquence, profound ſenſe, and genius, would pave the way to the throne: no one however is poſſeſſed of every accompliſhment; and the man the moſt favoured by nature, is brought by innumerable points within the limits of moral equality.

Thomas Paine ſhows the great futility of the *monarchical* ſyſtem, and demonſtrates a decided ſuperiority in the ſyſtem termed *republican*. By *republicaniſm* he does not mean what this word imports in Holland and in ſome of the Italian ſtates; he underſtands merely a government by repreſentation, a government founded upon the invariable principles of the *declaration of rights*.

The monarchical government moſt of all ſhocks humanity, inaſmuch as it degrades the honour and dignity of mankind by the diſguſt we experience in beholding them governed by children and commanded by brutes. It is impoſſible to diſguiſe the ills which monarchy has ſpread on the earth, penury, exactions, wars,

* A line from a tragedy of Voltaire. "Le premier que fut roi, fut un ſoldat heureux."

and murders. All hell, he adds, is to be ſound in a monarchy.

The whole of hiſtory ſhows that the monarchical form of government is always the moſt akin to extreme corruption, and that in it the individual will, with certain effect and in a concealed and inſolent manner, annuls the general will:—this government becomes tyrannical.

When that falſe and monſtrous idea was eſtabliſhed that *kingdoms* were *private eſtates*, the property of one man, a wide door was opened to every abſurdity and to every crime.

Ariſtotle commends monarchy; but he founds the excellence of that government upon the ſuppoſition that a man, firm, prudent, and intelligent, holds the reins and acts according to laws wiſely eſtabliſhed. He depicts the ſovereign elevated above others as much by his knowledge and his virtues as by his power; perſuaded as he is that himſelf like the law exiſts only for the good of the people, the word of the prince may be more depended upon than the oath of other men: then the uniformity of plans, the ſecrecy of enterpriſes, and the celerity of their execution would inſpire confidence and reſpect within the realm and fear abroad. But this ideal perfection which leads us back to unity, that fertilizing principle in nature, has appeared only at vaſt intervals in the annals of the world.

Let us confeſs that liberty can ſcarcely be found except in the *democratic forms*, becauſe theſe alone give to each citizen an inclination to obey; they render him maſter of himſelf, equal to others, and valuable to the ſtate of which he forms a part.

But theſe forms are extremely difficult to eſtabliſh. A nation of cultivators would be the beſt of all nations, as it is already framed for popular government.

Men are equal when they depend only upon the laws, and are all equally charged with the glorious employment of contributing to the repoſe and the felicity of their country. When the laws ſecure the independence of each individual, all the citizens may be free one as another; for the true character of a free government is that the individuals are not ſlaves to men, but only ſubject to the laws.

From the commencement of the French monarchy to the year 1254, the people were nothing at all; long after they had very ſmall influence: but at laſt that gothic edifice is levelled with the duſt, that inſolent barbariſm, that moral and political diſorder.

Politics had always been calculated upon results closely connected with the force and necessity of the times; and this had deceived the most intelligent. But sooner or later the laws awaken, according to the expression of the cardinal de Retz, the people recognize them, and deliverers and avengers arise.

Whatever language may be held, the republics of antiquity have equalled the monarchies in duration, because the entire administration of affairs becomes corrupt among the people, and because the disposition of the multitude, in general virtuous, does not produce villains, nor reward those known to be such, as the monarch does, who has constantly occasion for agents sworn to a blind obedience.

Nothing can equal the resources of republican genius; labours and sacrifices attach it the more to its country. In the genius of the republican there always remains something fixed, I mean the love of freedom; and whatever may be the asperity of internal divisions, the affection of the citizen is never entirely extinguished.

Let us sum up our discourse:—This unreasonable power has since the beginning of the world been the curse and scourge of society and of the human race. A lawful monarch becomes an usurper when he seizes what does not belong

belong to him: how idle a fancy to believe himſelf proprietor of a throne as if it were a farm! what height of folly to believe in the pretended right of poſſeſſing a nation!

Never can a monarchy confer greatneſs on a people; there offices are eſteemed only according to their degree of emolument; men are valued according to their influence, their rank, their income; weakneſs is preferred to capacity; and the baſe mind is preferred to the generous heart: he who breathes noble and patriotic ſentiments receives the appellation of enthuſiaſt; and the moſt devoted ſubmiſſion is the only way to advancement. Weakneſs, ignorance, and abaſement, deſcend by degrees from the firſt to the laſt claſſes of the ſociety; and the great mutually forgive each other their injuſtice, interweave it in every direction, and reduce it to a ſyſtem.

The monarchical government favours hereditary ariſtocracy, which, in the opinion of the greateſt philoſophers, is the fitteſt of all things to ſtifle probity, talents, and patriotiſm.

Every nation, I admit, cannot ſoar at firſt to democracy; it requires either the exploſion of the greateſt courage, or the effect of time, to ſum up the concourſe of particular wills into a predominant will adapted to the public felicity.

 When

When a nation is profoundly and truly enlightened, it will incline to the democratic form of government, becaufe it will no longer take for leaders creatures at once ftupid and wicked, becaufe it will be careful to be directed by great men who may enlighten it, and becaufe fuperior qualities will ever have over it a natural afcendant. What conftitutes the liberty of fuch a government, is that a plurality of fuffrages can never be procured in it without a more than ordinary capacity.

Thus knowledge introduces democracy, which elevates the people to the higheft pitch of which they are capable: its influence upon great objects, and the habit of difcuffing them, fharpen the intellect and enlarge the mind to a degree unknown under every other form of government. What an immenfe difference between a peafant of Schwitz or of Appenzell, and a Ruffian or a Polifh flave!

That democratic leaders fhould be a prey to the unruly paffions of the populace, is indeed an inconvenience; but, in every view, is it not better that many thoufands fhould avenge themfelves upon one, than that one fhould amufe himfelf with perfecuting thoufands?

CITIZEN-SOLDIER.

MAY theſe two words be never ſeparated. Search hiſtory, and you will find that in all antiquity there was never any difference made between the condition of a citizen and that of a ſoldier: each was obliged to fight for his houſehold gods. It was long before ſoldiers were enliſted; nor did the Romans enrolled in the army ceaſe to be Roman citizens. Deſpotiſm began when the citizens believed that commerce and agriculture did not allow them ſufficient leiſure for the exerciſe of arms. Until the time of Louis XIV. moderate armies only had appeared in the field; when that monarch was enabled to keep on foot battalions formidable by their numbers, the national liberty received the greateſt check. Men began to think that armies belonged to the monarch, and that, with numerous forces, a war is ſooner finiſhed. This was a double error: the war of the ſucceſſion of Spain laſted more than twelve years; the war of 1756, which it was ſuppoſed at the commencement could not laſt above two campaigns, was protracted till the year 1763. After the concluſion of peace, war ſtill ſubſiſted under another form, becauſe there yet remained on foot numerous bodies of troops. These have been the true pillars of despotism, but at the same time they shook its lofty fabric as soon as they adopted the first patriotic ideas.

What is the wish of a crowned despot? To employ the army against its country, to behold army butcher army, and citizens murder citizens. It is in secluding the soldier from the citizen that he finds his principal force, and he thus destroys all that adopts the generous virtues of civism.

There have never been greater traitors to their country than those on whom it has conferred the highest honours and the most distinguished posts: the crowned potentate has always been disposed to make himself be considered as superior to human nature, and to give himself out for a being approaching nearer to the divinity than other men. He will take every method to pay his retainers; he will inspire them with ferocious ideas; he will entice them to show an open contempt for their country, the sovereignty of the nation, and the rights of the citizens; and to these eternal truths to oppose those words of a slave, *I serve the king*. It was thus the fanatics committed the murderous deeds on the night of St. Bartholomew, and, at every blow, exclaimed, *we serve God.*

But

But the citizen-ſoldier will deſpiſe the wheedling language of tyranny, he will always have preſent to his mind the fraternal law. As he will be taken from the middle claſs, he will be humane and juſt, for it is in that claſs that we ſhall find moſt probity and virtue. In this happy ſtate of mediocrity, man, content with *his lot*, neither feels nor makes others feel the contemptuous pride inſpired by rank, or the thirſt of gold created by the aſpect of the throne. This reſpectable order of citizen-ſoldiers loves the laws at the ſame time that it is ſuſceptible of the greateſt virtues.

THE SWISS WHO SELL THEMSELVES.

WHAT name ſhall we give to theſe people who make it a particular profeſſion to butcher men? Theſe mercenaries deſcend from their mountains to hire out their arms, to ſtain them with blood in foreign quarrels with which they are unconcerned, and to plunge them into the bowels of their fellow creatures. The iſſue of the war is indifferent to them, they are only carrying on trade—what a trade! The Swiſs cantons may plead in vain that they want money, and that they procure it by devaſtation and the carnage of mankind. No nation on the globe has committed ſuch an inſult upon humanity; for to leave one's country to murder and to ſell one's blood to another, this ſordid and cruel practice is ſo utterly diſgraceful that no epithet is ſufficiently harſh to characterize it.

They pretend to have freedom at home, an aſſertion which merits inveſtigation; but ſurely they are the greateſt enemies of the freedom of other people. The Swiſs during the league always acted on the ſide of deſpotiſm: the greateſt cruelties were perpetrated by them. That military body is without any ſort of country, and conſequently dear to every deſpot who retains it in his pay. I cannot help feeling a ſentiment of horror and contempt at that cohort of ſatellites, which would blindly obey every crowned head, and would execute, if he ſhould command it, a maſſacre like that of Theſſalonica, the moſt atrocious recorded in hiſtory.

In true monarchies, the king is refuſed the right of enacting laws, but is charged with the execution of them; he poſſeſſes force ſufficient to cruſh the violators of the laws, but not enough to oppreſs the nation. It is plain he ought not to have a body of troops of any kind

at

at his diſpoſal, becauſe he might abuſe that truſt; but he ſhould enjoy the privilege of directing a proper force, to ſubdue the refractory. In the due meaſure of this force lies the great ſecret of legiſlation; when that balance is found, the conſtitution is good.

But if what ſurrounds the king inſpires terror, if he encircles himſelf with a hired phalanx, with a ſort of janiſſaries, the conſtitution is vicious. He will labour with this phalanx, however ſlender it may be, to attract other mercenaries, and to augment his revenue or his prerogatives rather than the glory of the empire; he is a ſatrap, and no longer a king.

The government is bad when the king has the baneful power of compoſing his guard of foreigners or of paſſive ſlaves, who will ſerve as inſtruments of his rage or caprice; all the cauſes of deſtruction then ſurround at once the people and the throne. The government, corrupted by the preſence of theſe ſatellites, cannot naturally ſupport itſelf without the moſt violent and moſt ſhameful means.

Foreign troops in the hands of the king! Why? Alas! have not nations at all times perceived the dreadful conſequences of that horrid combination? Oh, Samuel! how wiſely thou judgedſt in holding out to a nation mad enough

to

to aſk for a *king*, the moſt hideous picture of the innumerable calamities which accompany royalty.

It would have been impoſſible for all the banditti and all the highway robbers on earth, to kill as many men in a thouſand years as Louis XIV. deſtroyed in fifty; and without foreign ſoldiers, perhaps he would not have been able to make the nation bow down its head beneath his ponderous ſceptre.

DIALOGUE BETWEEN A AND B.

A. IN what age did the clergy begin to form a body apart from the ſtate?

B. In the reign of Charlemagne.

A. Charlemagne then loved the church?

B. As much as he did his concubines.

A. He is ſaid nevertheleſs to have made excellent laws.

B. Very excellent!

A. What benefit do we enjoy from them?

B. He introduced the Gregorian mode of ſinging into our churches; he founded many biſhoprics and monaſteries; and he brought to his court with much pomp the miniſters of the humble religion which we profeſs.

A. Was

A. Was that prince a ſaint or a fool?

B. Neither. He was ambitious, amorous, and fond of ſhow; he made a diſtinct body of the ſons of the church, who in the pompous aſſemblies of the ſtates-general, trampled the third eſtate under foot. He was a high-ſpirited prince and a good chriſtian, who demonſtrated to the regions which he conquered, that thoſe who were commanded to travel on foot with a ſingle coat and without ſhoes, ſtaff, or purſe, might, without infringement of the divine precepts, travel in a carriage, keep miſtreſſes and ſlaves, and clothe themſelves with the ſpoils of Aſia. Since his time the clergy were diſtinguiſhed from the two orders of the kingdom by the privilege of paying no tribute except under the name of a benevolence or voluntary donation, of reſiſting the ſovereign, and even of depoſing him, when he would not comply with the views of the church. It is true, to the great ſcandal of God and of the angels, the power of that ſacred body begins to decline.

A. What could occaſion this revolution?

B. Philoſophy: and accordingly they thunder againſt it in the towns and in the villages. But our lords the clergy have a greater adverſary to repel, and are deſtitute of ſtrength; the league has totally exhauſted them.

A. What

A. What is this terrible adverſary?

B. Pleaſantry. The proud ſtate with which they formerly intimidated both king and people is turned into ridicule; and the title which they claim of the *divine organ*, affords excellent ſubject of raillery: they bluſh themſelves at being what they are, and if they could lay aſide the crozier and the mitre, and retain the revenues which they get by theſe hieroglyphics, we ſhould ſee them with a ſword by their ſide, eating fleſh-meat on Friday, and keeping publicly an opera girl. What vexes them is, that every day well-digeſted plans are offered for ſtripping them of their riches, which however they employ to very uſeful purpoſes; for without them how many ſhopkeepers would not have an honourable opportunity of becoming bankrupts; how many tender chickens would not be acquainted with the prolific virtue of the holy Roman church; how many farmers would be compelled to grow rich by the proper cultivation of the ground?

A. Why deprive them of the poſſeſſions beſtowed on them by the munificence of our anceſtors?

B. It is to imitate Catherine II. empreſs of all the Ruſſias.

A. What has ſhe done ſo remarkable?

B. But

B. But a ſmall matter: ſhe ſeized the property of the eccleſiaſtics in 1768; and now penſions, perhaps too liberally, the archbiſhops, biſhops, monks, and prieſts.

A. Churchmen are then very rich in France?

B. They poſſeſs a full third of all the revenues of the kingdom.

A. Whence have they obtained ſuch riches?

B. From the weakneſs of our kings, from the ſuperſtition of the people, and from their own pious induſtry.

A. What do you mean by pious induſtry?

B. I mean; 1, the cruſades; 2, diſpenſations; 3, indulgences; 4, teſtaments; 5, the inquiſition; 6, confeſſion; 7, purgatory; 8, the Roman chancery; 9, maſs; 10, baptiſms; 11, marriages; 12, interments; 13, the civil wars; 14, miſſions.

A. What mean you by the cruſades?

B. That famous expedition of the French, Germans, Italians, and Engliſh into Aſia, in which, with a view of wreſting Paleſtine from the hands of the Muſſulmen, they pillaged, robbed, ſacked, and raviſhed wherever they paſſed. The two firſt cruſades coſt Europe ſixteen hundred thouſand men.

A. But

A. But how were the cruſades made ſubſervient to the induſtry of eccleſiaſtics?

B. In this way: the barons, in equipping themſelves for the expedition, ſold their eſtates at a low price; the biſhops and monks who had money, purchaſed them, without paying the fines of alienation; the monks made their purchaſes with *oremuſes*, and good paſſports to heaven.

A. Tell me what is a diſpenſation?

B. It is a certain permiſſion granted by the pope or the biſhops to do what is forbidden by the laws of which the popes and the biſhops are the authors.

A. And what is an indulgence?

B. It is a kind of currency eſtabliſhed to attract money; it is an abſolution of the ſins committed againſt the holy church, and this abſolution frees you, even beyond the grave, from the ſtripes, the faggots, the caldrons, and the red-hot coals of hell.

A. And how have teſtaments become, in ſacerdotal hands, a pious kind of induſtry?

B. Nothing was eaſier: an old debauchee, whom death hems in on all ſides, calls a prieſt; he recounts his wild ſallies, and, appalled at the imaginary horrors of hell, aſks, with a voice interrupted by ſobs, if he may hope for mercy.

Perhaps

Perhaps you may, perhaps not, replies the prieſt; divine juſtice muſt be ſatisfied, it muſt be appeaſed by ſacrifices; no ſacrifice is more agreeable in its eyes than a real and complete diſengagement from the good things of this world. This abnegation cannot be entire and meritorious unleſs it be performed according to the canonical laws; theſe laws require that chriſtians ſhould divide their effects among the poor: now, the poor are the children of the church; it is therefore to the church that you ought to give your riches, that the diſtribution may be made in the beſt poſſible manner. The Jeſuits were dexterous in recommending this expiatory ſatiſfaction to their penitent hearers: they obtained ſeven thouſand three hundred and fifty legacies in Flanders, twelve thouſand throughout Germany, more than twenty thouſand in Spain and the Indies, ſix thouſand two hundred and thirty in Italy, and a great many in England, not to mention the gun-powder plot. Seeing in France that they could not prevail on Henry IV. to make a bequeſt in their favour, they contrived to aſſaſſinate him: the Jacobins had ſet them the example.

A. What is the inquiſition?

B. It is a holy and pious tribunal eſtabliſhed by the repreſentatives of God on earth, to curry-

comb

comb and burn thoſe who believe not that the goſpel commands to curry-comb and burn. The criminals at this tribunal forfeit their effects, which are ſhared between the holy father the pope, the reverend fathers the Jacobins, and the beneficent officers of that ſacred court. When the accuſed is rich, he generally eſcapes the roaſting. The kings of the ſouth employ it to keep their grandees in ſervitude. In France, this tribunal is held in abhorrence; and, from a ſpirit of humanity, *letters de cachet* have been ſubſtituted. Formerly the biſhops had blank ones in their pocket; at preſent, to obtain theſe letters, they muſt preſent memoirs, which are either not read, or, if read, not approved.

A. I ſhould think that confeſſion can ſcarcely be beneficial to the clergy; it concerns only the ſins which all the world knows.

B. Let me take the liberty to ſay:—1. Confeſſion is very uſeful in religious wars: 2. A penitent credits blindly what a holy director announces to him from heaven: he may indeed be enlightened, in which caſe he ſmiles at the confeſſor and returns to the war no more; but if he is not, which is the caſe with at leaſt three fourths of the catholics, he obeys, and thereby the church gains its object: 3. Confeſſion gives the prieſts of the Moſt High a perfect know-

ledge

ledge of affairs and characters; it is by this mean that our worſhipful prelates learn what paſſes among their rectors and in families: 4. Confeſſion is wonderfully ſervicible in law-ſuits: 5. By confeſſion our benign apoſtles become acquainted with all temperaments, and can with certainty fix on the object of their beloved miſſion: 6. Confeſſion contributes to the augmentation of church caſualties; it is enjoined by way of penance to ſay maſſes at the rate of fifteen ſous, to build a chapel, to found a charity,—and all this contributes to the prieſt's intereſt. The church is poor, and muſt be relieved from its embarraſſments.

A. I have always heard it ſaid that purgatory is the place where the ſouls of thoſe who die under a venial ſin wait a full juſtification to enter into celeſtial glory: I ſee no connection this has with prieſtly rapacity.

B. But you ſhall ſee; and ſo liſten to me.—When Saint Odilon, abbot of Clung, diſcovered purgatory, he fancied that, to ſecure a decent ſubſiſtence for his monks, it was requiſite to engage the people to embrace this diſcovery. The Roman Court, which foreſaw the advantages that would accrue from this Benedictine dream, declared poſitively that Saint Odilon was a man gifted with a ſtrong diſcernment, and had found out a place unknown for more than ſixty thouſand years. This court afterwards perſuaded the people that it would be neither prudent nor decent in them to allow their fathers, mothers, brothers, ſiſters, friends, &c. to be burned for a peccadillo; that the prayers which were eſtabliſhed would ſhorten the duration of the chaſtiſement; and that, by paying handſomely, a thouſand ſouls at once might be liberated from that abode of darkneſs and horror. Twenty troops of monks inculcated ſo deeply this ridiculous jargon into the minds of the catholics, that the holy and poor church of Jeſus was entirely deluged with effects moveable and immoveable, till Luther determined, out of ſpite, to ſhut up purgatory, into which none now enter except German and Italian bigots.

A. Does the Roman Chancery reſemble that of France?

B. No. At Paris ſums are paid, it is true, which ought not to be paid; but this is only to liquidate the debts of the chancellors. At Rome there are certain rates fixed for all the ſins committed or to be committed: ſo much for having gone to bed to one's ſiſter, one's aunt,

aunt, or one's brother; ſo much for having murdered one's king, one's father, one's friend; ſo much for having blaſphemed God, heaven, earth, and hell. When you wiſh to recommit a ſin, you muſt there pay double.

A. Do the prieſts draw a great profit from the maſſes?

B. In Portugal, on All Souls Day, an hundred thouſand piaſters are received for maſſes: at Paris, among the Genovefains, the Cordeliers, the Capucins, and at St. Martin in the fields, a regiſter is kept of the maſſes paid, and when there is a ſurplus, the ſacriſtans who receive them at twelve ſous, ſend them into the provinces at eight. I maintain that in this city there are ſold, taking one year with another, a million of maſſes.

A. Money is alſo paid, is it not, for baptiſm and interment?

B. Undoubtedly: ſome of the funeral ſervices coſt 15 and 18 hundred livres. Beſides every thing is well regulated in this article; an exact price fixed for the bell-tolling, for the lights, the hangings, the number of prieſts and of chandeliers, and the quality of the ornaments—this price, I ſay, protects chriſtians from all impoſition.

 A. Of

A. Of what ſervice is marriage to the prieſts? It is a matter entirely ſecular.

B. You are ignorant then that the nuptial benediction is taxed, and that this taxation renders marriage a mixed buſineſs—nothing can be more juſt; for this being a carnal act, and conſequently little ſuited to beings ſpiritualized by religion, it is very proper to mulct the parties, and make them feel all the vileneſs of their mutual intercourſe. The ſacred celibacy which leaves to the prieſts the advantage of a ſecret concubinage is of ſo high importance that marriage cannot be loaded with obligations too burdenſome: it is well that the church does not reckon this union a crime. Beſides, the caſuiſts, Sanchez excepted, have bound it by ſo many ſhackles, that it is very difficult not to ſin in the married ſtate: every thing, even to dreſs, is preſcribed in the new canons.

A. Civil wars ſurely cannot be uſeful to the church?

B. Very well, indeed! You are then ignorant that the clergy have excited almoſt all of theſe in Europe? It is by theſe wars that prieſts have acquired an abſolute dominion over conſciences; and if ſometimes their hopes have been diſappointed, as was the caſe in the north of of Europe, they have elsewhere been gainers by them. If they do not stir up these wars, they come between the parties, and *shuffle the cards* with more address than does the Sieur Comus, the conjuror. Consult history, and it will instruct you better than polemical writings. There is no theological dispute of any note, but has overturned thrones, ruined empires, and deluged whole regions with blood.

A. Missions, far from being lucrative to the church, have on the contrary deprived it, and that frequently in the cruelest way, of its best subjects.

B. The subjects sacrificed were the devoted sentinels of the priestly army: while the pagans were murdering them, they were canonized at Rome, and this brought money. But all the missions have not been similar to those to Japan. Those to China produced 187,200,000 livres for the Jesuits; 1,120,000 livres for the Dominicans; and 1,400,500 livres for the secular priests: at Paraguay they afforded for the Jesuits alone 4,878,912,000 livres; at Mexico, more than six billions for the whole clergy, &c.

FINAL CAUSES.

ETERNAL order has willed that animals ſhould devour each other; one half of whatever is endued with life is perpetually at war with the other half; and one part of the living ſubſtance conſtantly feeds upon the other part. We muſt confine ourſelves to facts when we would form juſt notions of this eternal order; obſerve the voracity of the eagle, the terrible force of his beak and his keen glances, which deſcry the remoteſt objects; this aerial bird ſhoots upon its prey with the ſwiftneſs of lightning. Examine the net-work which the ſpider forms to entrap the inſects; what nicety! what addreſs! But the law which ordains the deſtruction of one animal for the good of another contributes undoubtedly to the increaſe of life, and the world advances and improves by this immutable order. It loſes none of the living ſubſtance; and, by a wonderful œconomy of nature, its deſtruction ſerves for its reproduction. Thus the fire of life, extinguiſhed in one claſs of animals, rekindles immediately in another, grows purer, and burns with increaſed vigour. Life is an impetuous torrent which requires only to be diffuſed. A cod ſpawns a million of eggs; and all fiſhes are prolific. The deſire of multiplying is inherent in every ſpecies, and ſeveral of them need coercive forces to reſtrain their progreſs and maintain their juſt proportion with the other ſpecies. In the animal ſyſtem therefore the reproduction of the carnivorous tribes is not injurious to the other ſpecies, but is on the contrary both uſeful and neceſſary to them. The birds of the air eat the inſects and worms which gnaw the trees to the very ſap, and ſtrip the earth of all its riches; this ſuperabundance of life would occaſion the horrors of famine, if certain ſpecies had not been placed by the eternal order to oppoſe theſe exceſſes.

Is it credible, after this prodigious multiplication, that men in the moſt civilized countries have ſtill ſuch difficulty in providing their ſubſiſtence? Is not this owing to the ſcourge of a political error which deſtroys fecundity, and defeats the force of propagation?

We muſt not, therefore, imagine that agriculture contributes every where to the increaſe of life; there are countries in which it is at leaſt doubtful if cultivation does not diminiſh its quantity. By clearing away the foreſts, many advantages undoubtedly have been loſt, ſince animals of the greateſt utility in ſupplying food were extirpated.

It was neceſſary that nature either ſhould cut off the ſtream of life and ſtop it in the univerſe, or, to prevent a ſingle ſpecies from getting head, and cauſing a general mortality in the whole animal ſyſtem, ſhould ſet the different ſpecies at war with each other: ſhe could admit no medium between the total extinction of life, or a counterpoiſe given to it, by directing that one part of the living ſubſtance ſhould feed upon the other. Such are the eternal barriers which nature oppoſes to that exceſſive increaſe which would entirely deſtroy the balance; for it is of advantage to all the ſpecies, that there are inſurmountable obſtacles which confine each of them to its due progreſs.

In a dearth of the feathered tribes that feed upon inſects, do you not perceive that the coldneſs of the ſeaſon completes the deſtruction of the flies which pullulate in the air, and prevents a frightful redundance, which would engender peſtilence or contagious diſeaſes, if theſe inſects were to continue to multiply only a few weeks longer.

If one part of the living ſubſtance is at war with

with the other, it is because supreme wisdom has so ordered it. We do not perceive that this law of nature has occasioned hitherto the extinction of a single species: on the contrary, it has preserved each of them in a state of vigour and of immortal youth; and without such a salutary appointment, life would long ere now, by breaking down the equilibrium between the different species of beings, have been totally effaced.

Is not the universal harmony of the living species manifested in those respective enemies which maintain the balance and are provided with all the weapons and all the faculties necessary for that end? Behold the insects and reptiles which, covering the surface of the earth, are opposed by an army of birds, active, vigilant, and voracious. The hares, the rabbits, the rats, and the field and house mice, which multiply so prodigiously, are preyed on by quadrupeds equally nimble in their motions, and endued with more force and a quicker sight. The enormous weight of horned cattle and the swiftness of deer lessen not the empire which man holds over the brutes.

Lastly, carnivorous animals, notwithstanding their formidable weapons of defence, experience

in

in the human race innumerable powers which every where check their progreſs, or drive them to the deſerts in which to exerciſe their ferocity.

And man, alas! who rules over other creatures, how often does he not direct his force againſt himſelf! how often is man with reſpect to man what carnivorous beaſts are to other animals! And this is the fault of that intelligent being called man, of him who puniſhes himſelf by this dreadful error.

Hobbes has aſſerted that men are born in a ſtate of warfare with each other. This opinion is falſe when applied to the individuals of the human race; the organs of man are not adapted for deſtroying or tearing. His faculties, his wants, and his deſires, all announce that he is formed to live in ſociety, and that the more men are mutually connected by affection and benevolence, the nearer they approach to the ſtate of felicity.

This opinion of Hobbes is alſo falſe with regard to civilized nations, conſidered in relation to each other, ſince they can obtain, from the inexhauſtible cultivation of the arts and ſciences, the means of preventing the cruel neceſſity of making war; and the human race is very diſ-

tant

tant from that term of population, when a redundance of numbers ſhall become pernicious. The agricultural life, the attention to the phænomena of vegetation, and uſeful experiments, will ſhortly juſtify, and for ages, the infinite wiſdom and goodneſs of the Supreme Being. The firſt ſtep towards truth is to ſacrifice pride, and to acknowledge the dependance of all beings on thoſe general laws which nature has eſtabliſhed for the reproduction and preſervation of that immenſe quantity of living matter which circulates in the world. Imaginary irregularities will thus diſappear; for in the profound ſtudy of nature we ſhall have learned to recognize a *providence* and *final cauſes*, that is to ſay, the proſperity of the univerſe, and the limit to which it tends, *perfectibility*.

Without a certain degree of light caſt upon the operations of nature, the phantoms of our imagination would diſplace important truths; our mind, alarmed by appearances, would loſe thoſe ſentiments of confidence, thoſe ſublime and cheering ſentiments which diſcover to us a *ſole being* animating and governing all the maſs of the world, and which imprint on this *neceſſary being*, beſides his infinite power, the attributes, ſupremely amiable, of wiſdom and

goodneſs:

goodneſs: it is by this happy contemplation that the ſoul riſes to the great whole, and diſencumbers itſelf from thoſe vile and earthly errors which load human reaſon in the ſchools.

HOW DARES COMMERCE TO DISPUTE THE PRE-EMINENCE WITH AGRICULTURE.

THE cultivator! To him is eſpecially committed the depoſit of public liberty. The men who are ſpread over the plains, theſe are the true true defenders of a free conſtitution! I reckon more on the cultivator than on the trader. The huſbandman poſſeſſes confidence, and is diſpoſed to be communicative; he is not ſatisfied with the ſucceſs of an undertaking or of a ſimple experiment, unleſs he cauſes his neighbour to repeat it: he feels that people acquire only in common, and enjoy only in participation; he is not envious of another's field, becauſe proſperity ought to be the ſame in all fields equally cultivated; the fertility of one field becoming the pledge of the fertility of that which is adjacent. The trader on the contrary ſtands aloof, becauſe he dreads a rival;

 his

his gain ſometimes depends upon the ſecret of a particular enterpriſe, and oftener upon an obſcure market, or a mercantile ſtratagem which he conceals from others. Every merchant's warehouſe becomes a diſtinct republic; and the harmony of the whole affects not the proprietor, whoſe proſperity is only completed by the ruin of all his competitors.

The cultivator has a gentler, milder, and humaner ſoul. As he produces by the aid of nature, he deſires not immoderate gains; he cannot pant after thoſe which are arbitrary, and ſtill leſs after thoſe that are unlimited; he deals not in the lottery; he creates with the ſun, with the ſeaſons, with an experimental and daily induſtry. The merchant, whoſe object is to acquire exorbitant profits, tries and forces all kinds of enterprizes; bent on incidental gains, he deſpiſes them if they are moderate; he is not ſatisfied with a competence, but aſpires to a fortune. Mercantile cunning invariably makes impreſſions which in time contract the moſt enlarged mind and moſt extenſive capacity. The huſbandman, whoſe aim is to labour and gain with the peaceful courſe of nature alone, nouriſhes not thoſe preying conceptions which waſte the keen merchant and place him perpetually

petually between a lofty criminal fortune and a bankruptcy; running all the hazardous chances, he is never acquainted with the repofe enjoyed by the cultivator, who is moderate in his wifhes, and, like the child on its mother's bofom, fleeps in the lap of the earth.

Have we witneffed humane and patriotic ideas in commercial bodies? No. All their views are exclufive. Hear the manufacturers; every thing muft be facrificed to their avarice: hear the merchants; war muft be commenced on account of their commodities: hear the *white colonifts*; humanity muft be facrificed, that they may fell their fugar and coffee at a higher price. The fordid idea of adding to their daily gain, of augmenting their yearly income, renders them ftrangers to found political notions. They would have feparate laws for themfelves to favour continually their avarice, and would impofe coercive regulations on others, calculated for their own intereft.

There is no cultivator at this day who, in the hope of leading a happier life under a fky more fuited to the freedom and expanfion of genius, would quit France to retire into Germany, Holland, Spain, or Ruffia. The princes, the priefts, and financiers have emigrated: nothing

thing proves better the excellence of our conſtitution. The Engliſh, the Poles, the Swiſs, and the Swedes are not ſo free.

The nobles, notwithſtanding their ſubtlety of genius for intrigue, reſemble ſavages; they admit with extreme difficulty new ideas, however analogous they may be to thoſe which they already poſſeſs: their brain is quite impenetrable to notions out of their ordinary conception; they are and will be, in that reſpect, much below the peaſant.

Behold then the word *great* happily aboliſhed! The cultivators will feel that they ought to be governed ſolely by the laws, and not by thoſe who diſpenſe them. By the appellation of *great*, was always underſtood in France a man whoſe authority among his fellow citizens enabled him to do much injury; if he enjoyed in addition a lucrative poſt, he was completely *great*. An intendant was a *great* man in country places. Where are the intendants? Do you flatter yourſelf to re-eſtabliſh them in the provinces? Though all the towns ſhould yield, ſtill would the cottages reſiſt. The cultivators! theſe are the firmeſt ſupports of the revolution.

A government was to be eſtabliſhed which ſhould

ſhould admit men of office and not grandees. It was neceſſary to grant to all the cultivators the right of atending the primary aſſemblies, of filling the magiſtracy, of keeping arms in their houſes, and of augmenting their ſtrength by public exerciſes; for it is but equitable that the people employed in tillage ſhould be under the immediate protection of the government, that they ſhould be as much favoured as the rich in the proſecution of inſults received, and that no law ſhould raiſe bars to their fortune: if the fruits of their labour be not raviſhed from their hands, they will love the conſtitution.

Polity and laws in a ſociety are good in proportion as they conform to the intention of Providence, which certainly has not connected happineſs with the encroachments of ambition and pride.

To equality nature has linked the preſervation of our ſocial qualities; equality muſt produce every good, becauſe it unites men, elevates their ſoul, and prepares them for the mutual ſentiments of benevolence and friendſhip. We may hence conclude that inequality engenders every miſchief, ſince it degrades them, ſows among them diviſion and ſtrife, and takes away *political virtue*, and the ardent love of the community.

Providence

Providence has not permitted that the import of equality ſhould be overſtrained; but the ſtronger it is, the more will it contribute to felicity: never can it degenerate or become a vice, becauſe it can never be unjuſt, and, removing us equally from tyranny and ſervitude, it unites men and gives them the ſame intereſt.

The import of equality is, therefore, no other than the import of our own dignity; by ſuffering it to weaken, men have grown ſlaves, and by its renovation alone will they become free.

If it was expedient for us to form new laws, it was on that account alſo expedient to renounce in the firſt inſtance our independance. But it was otherwiſe with our equality, for this is undeniably the ſource of true bleſſings, and cannot be loſt without riſking the greateſt calamities.

A tyrannical government may be recognized by theſe features:—when it forbids the progreſs of knowledge, the free communication of ſuch ideas as are calculated to enlighten men, and the aſſemblies which are to unite them; when it beſets them with ſpies, and marks every word that is uttered.—Such a monſtrous government muſt unavoidably fall, ſince the hatred and contempt which it inſpires will ſooner or later avenge the majeſty of an inſulted nation. Authority will under ſuch circumſtances return to the ſource from whence it flowed.

But to confer the ſupreme magiſterial appointments on perſonal qualities, without regard to fortune; to prevent the magiſtrates from enriching themſelves by their employments: to oblige them to give an account to the public of their adminiſtration:—theſe are the principal points of every free government. And the huſbandmen then feel that they are again become citizens, and have at laſt a country.

HISTORICAL PASSAGE WHICH DISPLEASED MARIA-THERESA.

THE houſe of Auſtria, it is well known, derives its origin from Haſburg, who, before his being elected emperor in 1273, had been, ſays Voltaire, the champion of the Abbé of Saint Gall againſt the biſhop of Bâle, in a trivial conteſt about a few caſks of wine. His fortune was then ſo diſproportioned to his courage that he he was at one time *High Steward* to Octocarius, king of Bohemia, who being afterwards urged to pay homage to him, replied *that he owed him nothing, ſince he had paid him his wages.* But what is known but to very few, this hiſtorical paſſage piqued Maria-Thereſa ſo much that ſhe made her ſon promiſe, during his travels in France, not to viſit Voltaire. The vanity of the poet was not a little hurt at this.

THE THIRTY-FIRST OF DECEMBER 1789.

ADIEU, memorable year, the moſt illuſtrious of this century! The diſtinguiſhed and unique year in which the French have recovered to Gaul that liberty which deſpotiſm held in chains! Adieu, immortal year which has fixed a limit to the debaſement of the people, by revealing to them the claims of which the originals were loſt! Adieu, moſt glorious year diſtinguiſhed by the courageous activity of the Pariſians, by the death of the moſt lofty and moſt magnificent *clergy*, and by the deceaſe of the moſt potent and moſt elevated *nobility*, who expired in convulſions.

Wonderful year! patriotiſm has emerged in complete armour from your generous loins; it has in a moment placed in their due ſtation a crowd of enlightened citizens, who have produced talents unknown, and have given to attentive and aſtoniſhed Europe important leſſons of which ſhe will undoubtedly profit *.

Incomparable year! you have ſeen the termination of the government of dreadful memory which had ſo cloſe an intercourſe with the *Baſtille*, its favourite miſtreſs, and the moſt pregnant and moſt enormous female ever beheld, who periſhed by a ſudden and violent attack. On the ſame day you witneſſed my brave countrymen ſave the national aſſembly which

* The court of Spain lately iſſued an order prohibiting the pariſh of Varcarlos, ſituated a quarter of a league from the frontiers of France, to celebrate the feſtival which that pariſh gave every year on the 25th of July, and at which a great number of French attended to make merry with their brethren and neighbours the Spaniards. A penalty of 20 livres was to be inflicted on every houſe in caſe of diſobedience. The inhabitants of Varcarlos aſked the reaſon of the prohibition. The anſwer was that it was intended to prevent the intercourſe of thoſe Frenchmen who would no longer adore their prieſts, and who took it into their heads to make laws for themſelves.

" Well! we know how it ſtands," replied an old man; " but if we do not hold this feſtival, we ſhall ſoon celebrate an- " other at which all Spain will dance, and the court of Madrid " muſt pay the fidlers."

was

was to be ſacrificed, and intimidate the ſword which the prince *De Lambeſc* had already made to gleam, that perfidious ſword placed in the hand of foreign troops, and which, whatever be alleged, was aimed to kill us in order to rid itſelf of the trouble of paying us.

What unexpected events does this year comprehend! In the ſpace of a few months, the misfortunes and blunders of many ages have been repaired. Man has recovered his firſt dignity; and the ſyſtem of feudality and oppreſſion which inſulted reaſon and humanity, is annulled*.

I hear the country-people bleſs the year of the revolution. I preſent to you my incenſe, auguſt year! you have changed my Paris †; it is now quite different, and will be the abode of happineſs and freedom. I already breathe in it the air of the Swiſs mountains. I am a ſoldier, not as a dog of war, ſet on by a choleric, weak, or whimſical deſpot, but as a citizen who will

* *Nicolas Lefevre*, preceptor of the prince of Condé, under Henry IV. ſaid to his pupil that *the court is always the enemy of the nation.* He was perhaps the only man then in France who knew that truth: we have ſince had deplorable proofs of the aſſertion.

† Alluding to the *Tableau de Paris* of the author. *Tranſlator*

joyfully

joyfully ſurrender his life in the true cauſe of his country.

For theſe thirty years have I had the preſentiment that I ſhould not die without being witneſs to a great political event: I fed my ſoul and my writings with the rapturous proſpect. This is the year for my pen; I offer you my warmeſt thanks, beneficent year! If my portrait needs to be drawn anew, it will one day at leaſt be ſaid, that in this year the Pariſians diſplayed to heaven and to the throne an hundred thouſand armed men within twenty-four hours! They did not ſuffer their city to be deſtroyed; and they made a general movement which has been communicated to France and to the reſt of Europe.

Great year! you will be the year of regeneration; you will bear that name: you fly away to ſink into the ocean of time. Adieu, ſince it is impoſſible for our wiſhes to prolong your ſtay! but at leaſt tell my dear eldeſt daughter *the year two thouſand four hundred and forty*, that we run to meet her with all our ſtrength, and haſten to embrace her. Without flattery, you much reſemble her; dear fleeting year; I had even a momentary perſuaſion, that it was needed only to change the date of your birth.

But

But your younger ſiſter (be not jealous of her) will have more beauty and wit than yourſelf; becauſe patriotiſm is a virtue which ſtrengthens by exerciſe; becauſe we muſt ſtill meditate on the public felicity to rear an immoveable edifice; and becauſe the grand effort of the human mind is not to frame good laws, but to put them into execution.

Adieu, unparalleled year in our hiſtory! I who was free long before the days of your liberty, can I neglect to be faithful to your memory? No. Every day will I pour forth my gratitude to the Supreme Being for having ſhown me the dawn of the ſun of freedom: he ſhines upon my country, armed with all his rays. Monteſquieu, Mably, Helvetius, Thomas, Voltaire, Rouſſeau, and Turgot, ſleep in the tomb; they have not viewed the days of glory which their genius had prepared. Oh! with what acclamations would they have ſaluted the regenerated French nation! To their voice, alas! and not to mine, it belonged to chant your patriotic virtues! They have outrun my tardy expectation, they have ſurpaſſed my deareſt hopes. But I will write at leaſt what I have ſeen; that ſuch events may never decay in the memory of men; that they may learn at all

times

times and in all places, that they need only their hands and their heads to deſtroy every ſort of tyranny; that they have only to wiſh it; and that God loves equally all his creatures formed of the ſame clay, and protects equally every generous inſurrection, becauſe the book of laws deſcends from his eternal throne. Adieu, tumultuous, but moſt dear and moſt reſpectable year!

THE END.

www.ingramcontent.com/pod-product-compliance
Lightning Source LLC
Chambersburg PA
CBHW021842290326
41932CB00064B/347

* 9 7 8 3 3 3 7 0 7 1 3 1 8 *